To Henry –

all my love

Dad

KEEPING FAITH

KEEPING FAITH

A Father-Son Story About
Love and the United States
Marine Corps

FRANK SCHAEFFER
and
Cpl. JOHN SCHAEFFER (USMC)

CARROLL & GRAF PUBLISHERS
NEW YORK

KEEPING FAITH

A FATHER–SON STORY ABOUT LOVE AND
THE UNITED STATES MARINE CORPS

Carroll & Graf Publishers
An Imprint of Avalon Publishing Group Inc.
161 William Street, 16th Floor
New York, NY 10038

First Carroll & Graf edition 2002
Fifth printing, January 2003

Interior design by Simon M. Sullivan

Library of Congress Cataloging-in-Publication Data is available.

ISBN: 0-7867-1097-7

Printed in the United States of America
Distributed by Publishers Group West

For my son John

For my father

Acknowledgments

We thank our editor Will Balliett for his friendship, guidance, and support. His precise editorial insight made this a better book. We are grateful to Jennifer Lyons for her work as our agent and for her helpful notes. She has supported us at every stage of this project and is a good friend. Our generous friend Frank Gruber took a week off to read the manuscript and make detailed notes which were very helpful indeed. Holly Meade and Heather Currier encouraged us to write this story. Thank you to Pam (Walsh) Kreil for your help on "Walsh facts." We thank John C. Stevens III for his advice. We are grateful to Genie Schaeffer as our first, last, and best reader. Joni Annas Vetne did early copy editing. Rodman Miller was a good friend to us and this project. Charlotte Gordon was kind enough to read through the text and make helpful comments, as was Jessica (Schaeffer) Strömback. Thanks to James Hughes, "The Boys," and to Mollie Meikle for anchoring John in sanity, in life, and in this project. A special thank you to Jessica and Francis for your love and understanding as sister, brother, and daughter and son.

Certain names and dates have been changed to protect people's privacy in both the text and letters. Two minor items, local "news events"—the matter of the power tower and the casino—were included. Though these two events unfolded over a slightly different time frame (than indicated by the dates on our letters), our involvement with them was as reported herein.

This project began early in 1999 as we collected letters and made notes. Work started in earnest early in 2000 and was completed, with the exception of the postscript, by late August 2001. We traded sections by e-mail, as well as working together face-to-face.

—Frank Schaeffer,
John Schaeffer

KEEPING FAITH

1

When John was newly born, his damp hair smelling sweet, the nurse placed his long body in my arms and then, bless her, forgot us while Genie slept. I held him until the sun set, and the stuffy room grew dark.

John, age five: running in from the garden on a bright spring day.

"Look, Dad! I caught a snake! He's on my thumb. Look, Dad!"

A four-foot garter snake was hanging in a writhing black and yellow coil from John's five-year-old pink little thumb. John's eyes were wide with pain and delight.

"*See, Dad!*"

"John! The snake is *biting* you!"

Grinning: "That's how I caught him!"

John, age eleven, in full battle regalia, charging over the sand dunes on Plum Island, ambushing a pack of friends: "They didn't think I'd attack through the poison ivy!"

Dad read books to me out loud that I could have almost recited back to him word for word, sitting hour after hour in our dusty living room. It was good to watch Dad's eyes move on the page and twinkle when he got to the same spot in the story I knew was going to make both of us laugh.

When I was ten Dad fired a rocket at me. It blew a hole in my shirt and burned a patch of skin about the size of a quarter. Mom was furious and of course I stuck up for Dad. Fireworks are illegal in Massachusetts, but "Live Free or Die" New Hampshire is just three miles up the road and they sold them out of the shacks and tattoo parlors that lined the streets of Seabrook.

Dad came back from Seabrook with a cluster of cheap Chinese fireworks, and Francis (my older brother), Dad, and I put ski goggles on and went into the yard to play war. We fired the fireworks out of empty bottles at each other, thinking we'd be safe given the bottles' inaccuracy. We'd aim in each other's general direction and hope for the best. This worked out well until Dad winged me as I crouched under the swing set. It was a great time.

Dad has been an artist, a candle maker, worked in discos running light shows, a movie director, a novelist. Dad has studied more than any man I have ever met. Our house is floor-to-ceiling books: novels, history, and tons of art history and theology volumes all read by Dad—many full of his dyslexic misspelled notes. I could do more math than my father by the time I was eleven but never will read all he has or remember half of what he knows. He also does most of the cooking in our house and is a great chef.

Dinner was Dad's forum and about more than his terrific food.

Dad: "The Renaissance was built on the artistic and cultural foundations laid for it by the Byzantines."

Me, age ten: "Yes, Dad."

Dad: "The only 'rebirth' was that the Medici discovered the classical learning that had always been alive and well in Constantinople!"

Me: "Yes, Dad."

Dad is the only person I've ever met who gets pissed off at something that happened a thousand years ago, say the sack of Constantinople in 1204.

———————————

John was my youngest and I doted on him from the moment of his birth to his last high school poetry reading. Captain of every team, sweet as a lake of warm honey, he made the meaning of life clear.

———————————

I love my father with fierce devotion. We would do the most useless things together just because we were together. We went fishing when we knew the fish would not bite. We sneaked into movies we knew were going to be terrible, because we would have fun making jokes about them later. We'd watch some crummy movie a second time because there was one line of dialogue we liked and couldn't quite remember.

While John grew up we were close as peas in a pod, father and son, but also like a big brother and little brother. The first child, my smart, talented, and forgiving daughter Jessica; my middle child and first son, bright, loyal, and wonderful Francis are dear to me. It is not that I love John more than the others, but he was easier. Part of it was that I became a father to Jessica when I was only eighteen, and Francis was born three years later. Part of it was that after having a little more experience I was more relaxed with John. I was twenty-eight when John was born, and almost a grown-up, almost the age you are supposed to be these days when you have a child. This made John's childhood a rather lighthearted affair for me, at least until he went to high school.

I attended two private high schools, St. John's Prep, in Danvers, Massachusetts, then the Waring School in Beverly. I changed schools when my parents woke to the fact that I was failing every class I was taking at St. John's. It was April and I hadn't done an assignment since January.

St. John's Prep had a chapel with a life-size, suspended, crucified Jesus with no cross, as if he'd been nailed to something invisible and was floating in outer space. We sent John there, surreal spaceship–Jesus notwithstanding. John was a track star. I was so proud of him.

Some coach must have been covering up for John because the first time Genie and I heard about his lack of schoolwork was a late-night call coming from an irate teacher asking why John had done no homework for more than ten weeks. John had always hated school, but before high school he cruised along, his quick wit keeping him a step ahead of his teachers' and my wrath.

John wrote a poem in junior high about his first day in first grade; it pretty well summed up all of John's feelings—and maybe a lot of other boys' feelings—about school.

> they made me go to school in cinder blocks and concrete
> I could not run anymore
> my feet they bound in Velcro shoes
> and they forced me to sit and play with toys
> the other children were excited
> happy to be growing up at last
> I could not see outside unless I went up on tiptoe at the window

John and I almost came to blows over his failure to work at St. John's. Right after that teacher called we stood toe-to-toe in his trophy-cluttered little bedroom. It was the fact that my son had lied that so infuriated me. For three months he'd answered "fine" when I asked how school was going. John was towering over me, practically daring me to take a swing at him. He stood unflinching, fixing me with a defiant stare as I yelled. That night I set some sort of record, even for me, a perennial "screamer." I bellowed at John for over three hours.

I didn't care about his missed work. Crap! I'd hated school—ran away from a British boarding school at fifteen, just his age. It was the fact that John shut me out that made me livid. After I stopped yelling, we sat on the edge of his narrow bed in the dark. When I put an arm on John's rigid shoulder, he did not respond for a long time.

———————

Dad and Mom sent me to St. John's because of the sports program. (Dad denies this.) I was playing a lot of sports in town and at my middle school, so they thought this was a good idea. The typical St. John's parents wanted their sons to either get full sports scholarships or to go to very exclusive colleges. It was a school of "jocks and nerds." There wasn't much middle ground. I hated it.

The Waring School in Beverly was also a place for the children of ambitious, mostly wealthy parents. But it was not a sports school. All the ambition was centered on academic work and getting into top colleges. Dad begged them to take me after I begged him to get me out of St. John's. I did my begging after his yelling stopped, after we finally made up.

My brother and sister had attended the Waring School and loved it. My school work at St. John's had been a mess, but I wrote poems and that counted for a lot in a school where the cafeteria is called the "Victor Hugo Room." I did okay there. The headmaster, Peter Smick, was very kind to me, and I had one great teacher, Charlotte Gordon, who encouraged me to write more poems, including this one about Dad.

my father
short and powerful
with a limp where
polio ate
his leg.
endlessly
encouraging though
somewhat discouraged.
he has been
a light effects
man in a disco,
painter, film director,
activist, speaker
and a writer.
my father
self educated; didn't learn
to read until
he was twelve
and yet
a writer.

In contrast to my sister and brother I never had any particular aspirations to study beyond the point that would let me get through the test at hand, if that. I was more interested in the books I was reading outside class. Sometimes I'd read all night until it was time to get up for school. Then I'd be too tired to go. When it came to reading, Dad was my accomplice.

As long as I was reading he'd let me stay home "sick," at least from time to time.

———————

While still at St. John's, John joined the cross-country track team almost as a lark. After one or two practices he went from the anonymous pack of about fifty to one of the chosen seven freshman team members. I asked John why he always came in seventh out of his team in both the practices and the meets, why he didn't finish stronger, didn't sprint at the end when I knew he had the speed and stamina to blow the runner in front of him off the map. (He was also on the track team as a sprinter and competed well in both state and national events.) About a month into the cross-country season, John finally got sick of my badgering him and explained why he was holding back.

"Dad," said John as we drove home from St. John's one evening, "the reason I don't sprint past Forbes is because he's my teammate."

"So?" I asked, "I see the coaches screaming at you to pass him. You've got to compete against each other or you'll never beat the other teams."

"Yeah, they yell at me but I'm not going to beat Forbes in practices."

"But why? I see everyone in the pack trying to beat you."

"Look, Dad, I'm on the team so what does it matter where I finish in practices?"

"It matters because you need to do your best."

"I will in competition."

"But why do you hold back? I *know* you're holding back!"

"It's a three-mile course, Dad."

"John!"

"Dad, if I knock him into seventh place he'll get cut if somebody in the pack can beat him. I won't get cut because no one in the pack can catch me and they know it. By pacing him I help him, you know, push him and keep him on the team so he won't get left behind."

———————

On weekends I drove around Salisbury and Newburyport for hours looking out the window for something to do, stopping at the same Dunkin Donuts at every pass to get another cup of coffee. I'd smoke a few cigarettes in the parking lot with the same townies who had been there last time I came through a half hour before. I sat on the boardwalk that ran along the Merrimac river, with "The Boys," my old friends from eighth grade, if any happened to be around. Occasionally we'd make half-mile forays downtown to see if anything was "happening yet."

When I ran the cross-country course near our school, through a maple wood in November, it was as if the trees were on fire around me. I ran surrounded by burning trees. Cross-country was a sport I tried because I didn't want to play soccer anymore; ten years was enough. My father came to all my races both at home and away. He was the only parent who never missed a meet.

As a spectator sport, cross-country is about the most boring thing that anyone could ever stand to watch without going into a coma. A pack of runners take off from the starting line and disappear into the trees. They run an obscure course, often through hilly woods on a nearly invisible "track" that they can follow only because they walked it before the race. The spectators see nothing more than the gap in the trees where the runners disappeared.

About fifteen minutes after the first runners run into the trees the lead runner emerges out of the forest and dashes to the finish. Over the course of the next eight minutes or so all the racers stumble in, some vomit, and then all jog around slowly to keep from seizing up.

That's it! That was all Dad saw, runners disappearing into fiery trees, then nothing for a long time until we reappeared in the distance and vomited from exhaustion. After the race, often a two-hour drive from home, I had to ride the team bus back to school while Dad followed alone in his old Ford Taurus.

running on paths
cut into tree-lines
avoid puddles that will make shoes slow
tired now but more tired still at the end
acid filled muscles start to seize.
only the man in front pulling and the man behind to push.

———————

We moved to America from Switzerland in 1980. I was twenty-eight, married with two children. Genie was pregnant with John.

I was born in Switzerland to American missionaries. I grew up in a chalet on the edge of a Swiss village. I was the youngest of four, the child of Protestant fundamentalists. Mom, Dad, my three older sisters, and I were outsiders. The villagers resented our foreign presence, not to mention the invasion of their pristine alpine community by the American young people who flocked to our mission.

My parents, distrustful of the Swiss, and perhaps overprotective of me ever since I had polio—I wore a leg brace—home-schooled me until I was eleven and illiterate. Then they sent me to boarding school in England in a last-ditch effort to "do something about that boy." After graduating from Great Walstead, a wonderful English boys' "prep-school" (primary school), I was sent on to a dreadful British boys' "public school" (a private high school) in Wales. That was the school I ran away from.

I went back to the mission and hung out. My compassionate parents did not force me to return to Wales. I did schoolwork at home with various tutors and learned a lot, mainly about the sixties, pot, and generally doing nothing useful, from the students and back-packing hippies passing through.

———————

I got tired of high school before I even started. Then came the realization that I did not want to go to college right away and that I didn't identify with too many of my college-bound fellow students. I didn't like the direction of my personal life either.

I felt that after graduating from high school, and with no firm idea of what to do with or at college, I was going to continue the whole saga of drinking all weekend, occasional pot smoking, only doing work when I had to, only getting a job when I realized that I was going to have no money for beer. I saw that I'd just keep spending a good portion of a small life chasing girls whose lives seemed just as small as mine.

The military had always appealed to me, less as a career than as an idea that began in those childhood war games charging through the poison ivy. I read history and saw Churchill and Eisenhower shaping events at the head of vast armies when the outcome was doubtful. I read nineteenth-century novels such as *Foray and Fight,* which was about the exploits of the British in places like Macedonia.

When the barrel-chested Marine recruiter showed up in dress blues and bedazzled my boy I did not stand in the way. John had talked to the Army, Navy, and Air Force recruiters, too. Maybe their offers to tailor their services to his individual needs did not impress him. "An Army of one!" was not a slogan likely to inspire my son. John had always been a team player. This was one reason he made such an awesome defender in soccer: opponents had to get past him to reach the goalie, and John would be damned if anyone would get to *his* goalie!

John's eyes lit up when he was sitting across from the USMC recruiters at our kitchen table. He seemed to understand these stern clean men with their painfully straight backs and insanely flawless dress-blue uniforms in some basic way that I did not. This was a team with a purpose. John and his friend's talk of "well, I'm not sure what I want to study" could not have been more different from the resolve that radiated from these trim steely men.

Unlike the other services the Marines did nothing to sweeten the pill. When Genie, looking concerned and somewhat drawn, turned to one and asked, "But when he's done with the Marines, I mean, what will he *have?*" The recruiter replied, " 'Have,' ma'am? I don't understand you."

"I meant what will he, uh, get out of it?"

The recruiter sat up a little straighter and his cheeks flushed. "He'll be a United States Marine, ma'am!"

There were no promises of college funds, "signing bonuses," great "civilian opportunities" in later life. All the Marines offered John was the promise that if he joined the Corps he would find standards that had not been lowered. Nor had the Marines adopted the kinder, gentler training policies of the other services.

Men and women were still trained separately, the women by female "DIs" (drill instructors) the men by male DIs. A young man wanting to measure himself against the Marine Corps' fabled tradition of maximum endurance was not cheated of the experience. "Boot camp's still tough as hell," said Staff Sergeant Dubois, the recruiter. When he said this, I saw John's eyes sparkle.

After Staff Sergeant Dubois left, John said quietly, "I'm not sure I want to go into the military, Dad. But one thing for sure, if I do it'll be the Marines. Otherwise what's the point?"

I shared some of my family's intellectual interests but also had a taste for pop culture where my older brother and sister, who had been partly raised in Switzerland, didn't. I loved science fiction, fantasy literature, history, and television. (Dad didn't approve of TV and cut our cable with a pair of wire clippers when I was fourteen. He decided we'd become "addicted" after an all-night session of *Fawlty Towers* we'd watched till dawn.)

I felt truly American with or without TV. I have never lived anywhere else. I was the first of Dad's children born in the USA. I have always been independent, but maybe not in a typical teenage "rebellion" sense of the word. (I never dyed my hair or got pierced or tattooed.) In general, and in my own way, I did what my parents told me to do. However, specific instructions aside, I was perfectly willing to find my own direction. I did not ask my mother or father for advice very often, nor was I particularly concerned with their opinions regarding the direction of my life. I respected their views and listened, but I always liked the idea of making my own way. I decided to join the Marines without asking permission.

I was ignorant of the Marines. I had no picture of how things would go once John joined. I vaguely imagined John leaving for boot camp, then being sent off to the ends of the earth the day he graduated. I was having an easier time imagining flag-draped coffins than visits to John's base or ninety-six hour passes and trips home. Why the hell was John going into the Marines?

It had been hard enough sending my two older children off to college. The normal separations of life were nearly unbearable, let alone the prospect of my youngest son, my baby, going into the Marine Corps. It was unexpected, so deeply unsettling. Everything John had ever written or made became precious. I took his childhood drawings out of the moth-eaten suitcase under my bed and looked at them for the first time in years. I reread his old poems.

All I knew was that lots of Marines got killed in Korea, Vietnam, and Beirut. I didn't want John killed. I also knew that I wanted him to go to college. I knew that it was hard to do what I'd done: carve out a career without that "piece of paper." The idea of John going straight into the Marines after high school was disheartening. It was also embarrassing. Wasn't the military there to help poor kids make something of themselves?

My daughter Jessica went to NYU (New York University), my son Francis to Georgetown's School of Foreign Service where he won the highest academic award the school gives. I did not relish the prospect of answering the question, "So where is John going to college?" from the parents who were itching to tell me all about how their son or daughter was going to Harvard. John didn't even want to go to college first, then to officer training.

I didn't know any other parent at Waring whose son or daughter was going into the military, let alone as a plain old enlisted recruit. Waring was a small school for gifted liberal arts students that placed an emphasis on French studies. It was attended by the sons and daughters of middle-class and upper middle-class parents, a few of whom were amiable old hippies who had long since traded their VW bugs for BMWs and SUVs. Waring was not as snobbish or insanely expensive as the superwasp schools in our area such as Groton, Philips Exeter, and Choate. Nevertheless in the circles we moved in—at Waring and elsewhere—on the Volvo-driving, higher education–worshiping North Shore (north of Boston, that is), a son or daughter going into the Marines was something unheard of.

I was proud and pleased by the academic successes of Jessica and Francis. They were easy to talk about. In fact, Francis started to teach at Waring while he decided whether to go to grad school. Jessica married a talented composer and jazz pianist she met in New York while she was at NYU and went to live in Finland, where she studied art and ceramics and was raising their two lovely children.

Everyone at Waring loved Francis, and Waring parents had no trouble understanding Jessica. Finland, jazz, and ceramics were all okay. But the Marines have never been mistaken for a politically correct Scandinavian country. The very words "boot camp" were pejorative, conjuring up "troubled youths at risk."

"But aren't they all terribly *southern?*" asked one parent, speaking of the Marines. The filmmakers of *American Beauty* made the villain an ex-Marine, complete with Nazi memorabilia and a terminal case of homophobia. The movies were the only place most of my friends met any Marines, unless you counted one or two harmless old boys pottering around the local country clubs, relics from the One Good War.

It would be unlikely that any of my friends in Boston, New York, or Los Angeles would actually know any Marine serving. These days our kind did not mix with such people. It would be far more likely that they would have a daughter working for the Miles Foundation—I happened to read a piece about this foundation soon after John signed up—whose mission was, according to the *Times* article, "to study sexual violence in the United States armed forces." In our community, a son or daughter getting a job monitoring the military about alleged sexual impropriety would be considered a far more respectable career choice than actually serving.

––––––––––––

When I decided to join the Marines, I knew Dad would back me up. He always had. But I felt alienated from many people who would not or could not understand my decision to do something that seemed more quantifiable to me than striving to get into some "prestige" school. My graduation "speech" consisted of three poems.

> civilians are "slow"
> and "messy."
> Marines are "fast"
> and "ready"
> civilians are "me"
> Marines are "us"
> who is stranger?
> me or us?
>
> this is the summer
> before the Marines

and I am
sitting in my green chair
I can smell the Merrimac River;
marsh grass rotting
and hear the clanking
of sailboat masts.
pushups and screaming
will come later,
now I
can only see my dog,
basking in summer sun.

I go to school with people who do not understand
why I have chosen the Marines.
these are not things I can explain.
these are feelings,
the guts of my brain,
and I cannot scoop them out and hand them around
so that friends will understand me.
I lead a divided life.
I go to functions with Marines
who cannot conceive of the place that I come from,
or why I want to be one of them.

Everyone congratulated me on the poems, but I could tell they thought I was crazy and not the eccentric Woody Allen–kind of crazy either.

———————————

The graduation. Lots of expensive cars and clothes. Afterward John spun my flaxen-haired four-year-old granddaughter, Amanda, around on the bright green lawn, his academic robe whirling as I fought back tears at the thought of how few weeks were left before induction. Tears or not, I chuckled at the memory of the stunned faces of the other parents when John said from the podium—in answer to the question asked of each graduating student about where they would be next year—"I'll be the spear-point of American foreign policy."

Everyone else named a fancy college. John was a popular student. If I read the anxious glances of some parents rightly, they were hoping John's decision to join the Marines would not be catching.

My best friends, "The Boys," all came down from Salisbury and Newburyport to Waring for the graduation. They had not been to the campus before and looked around wide-eyed at the kids who went to such a privileged school. (They mostly went to the public high school or a couple of less than up-scale Catholic schools in southern New Hampshire.)

James, my best friend, said, "You stood up and said, '*Yeah*, I'm going into the Marines, what of it?' and sat down. It was awesome!"

2

At John's graduation I was nervous about not fitting in. I kept my tweed jacket on despite the heat, stayed for John's sake, and wandered the shady woods and green lawns. Everything was fine. Then John missed his own graduation party going out with his new girlfriend, Erica.

In the last months of high school John connected with Erica. She was tall, blonde, and going to another private high school nearby. Erica lived in Amesbury, a small town on the banks of the Merrimack River five miles from where we lived.

Only gradually did it dawn on me that John was spending more time at Erica's house than at ours—a lot more time. I felt hurt. With previous girlfriends John had always "hung out" at our place, as had all of John's friends, male and female. His absence couldn't have come at a worse time. I was counting down to the day he would leave home for the Marines. I missed John and knew I was about to miss him even more. A heavy blanket of mourning was settling over me.

That summer I was tense enough to fight back when Dad tried to discourage me from seeing Erica all I wanted, not to the point where some teenagers fight, screaming and yelling, but saying that I would do exactly what I wanted to do despite what my father said.

I was nervous about going into the Corps. Obvious reasons aside, being with Erica was a welcome distraction from my growing jitters. She chattered away and had a car.

Dad was giving me long hugs and acting as if we'd never see each other again. He looked at me as if he was at my wake. He nagged me about being home more. I wanted breathing room and Erica was fun to be with. I liked Erica. She gave off a sense of innocent sweetness. I enjoyed her company.

John knew I was sad so he tried to carve out a few father-son times between marathon Erica sessions. How did I use these rare moments? More fool me, I wasted the time we did have complaining to John that I was not seeing more of him and dragging him down into my growing pre-Marines depression.

"Why do you want to be with some girl who doesn't even want to visit our family? Why won't she ever come to dinner? I've called to invite her a dozen times and she always makes the lamest excuses," I said, as we drove down I-95 to a movie one afternoon.

For a while John beat around the bush. Finally he came right out and told me, "Erica doesn't like you, Dad."

"All your friends like me, damn it!"

"That day you took us to lunch . . ."

"In Boston? To the North End?"

"Yes. Remember you joked about colleges?"

"Sure."

"Well, she was offended."

"Because I *joked* about colleges? You're kidding?!"

"She takes college very seriously."

"And so she won't come over?"

"Yes."

"All I'd said was that it didn't matter what school she got into, they're all equally ridden with grade-inflation and stultifying political correctitude."

"Dad?"

"Yes?"

"She just doesn't have a sense of humor about anything to do with school."

I felt foolish giving John a rough time over some girlfriend. In every way John's choice to join the Marines was so very sensible compared with my own erratic teen behavior. But his Last Summer (this was how I was thinking of it, capital L, capital S) at home was no ordinary summer. My emotions were getting raw. When Jessica and Francis went to college, it felt safe; the Marines didn't.

I wished I could have had a chance to talk with my father about what I'd put him through and how best to deal with this horrible Last Summer. He had died in 1984. I would have loved to have asked my Dad how he put up with me when I was John's age, why this whole Last Summer/Marine/girlfriend obsession was undoing me so thoroughly. Mostly I wanted to tell Dad I was sorry, that now I understood why he yelled at me so much as I presented him with one crazy fait accompli after another, getting Genie pregnant, getting married at seventeen—and I was pissed at John?!

After running away from boarding school, and living a weirdly bohemian life—considering I was back at the mission—I declared myself an artist and added an easel, paints, and brushes to my stash of wine and food I kept in my attic "pad." My sweet parents indulged my painting and paid for art supplies.

I must have been a teen nightmare for my pastor-missionary father. I'd drift around the edges of the spiritual activities, a longhaired wraith in my paint-spattered jeans, studiously *not* participating in the Bible studies, prayer meetings, and church services. I grew up fast as I hung out with the nineteen and twenty year olds who came to the mission as "seekers," clandestinely listening to the Stones and Hendrix, drinking wine, and smoking dope with some of them, the as yet "unsaved" ones in the fields that stretched up to the woods behind our chalet.

I'm not sure where I was headed but I know that Genie saved me. Whatever John was looking for in the Corps, I found it by falling in love.

I met Genie in 1968. She was from San Francisco and traveling with her older sister Pam. They were visiting Pam's friend who was staying at the mission. Pam had just graduated from Berkeley and Genie from high school. The trip was a graduation present from their parents.

Pam and Genie walked into our chalet's gloomy little wood-paneled front entrance hall just as my parents and I were sitting down to the evening meal with thirty young people in the communal dining room. I heard a knock. I poked my head around the doorjamb and drank in the most beautiful girl I'd ever seen standing in the dim glow of the old Venetian lantern that served as the hall light. Genie's long legs, voluptuous figure, and sparkling hazel-green almond eyes stunned me. She literally seemed to shine. I bolted from my chair and hovered around as solicitous as a good headwaiter.

I proposed to Genie two days after she walked into our home, or rather while on a rambling walk through the forest tramping along over a crisp golden carpet of new-fallen larch needles under the watchful gaze of my beloved alps, towering white and clean, the first dusting of snow on peaks spiked against the cobalt sky. Genie laughed at me. She kept on laughing at me. It took me a year to talk her into marrying me.

My parents loved Genie. And she liked me well enough to stick around the mission. I instantly shaped up in terms of my behavior in order to be worthy of this goddess-girl. I quit smoking because I wanted her to quit; I worked a lot harder at my painting because I wanted her respect. I went so far as to try and convert Genie to born-again Christianity in order to both save her soul and to get her to marry me. Young marriage was no problem within our Calvinist denomination. What would have been a problem was to marry "an unbeliever."

All the while, and illogically, given my efforts to get Genie to "accept Jesus," I was having glorious, frequent, and utterly unprotected sex with my very own San Francisco hippie princess. The sun had set and the moon, mountains, and stars faded away. There was only—Genie—body and soul!

She was three months pregnant when we married in 1970. In 1980, when Genie, the children, and I moved to the States I found work in the bottom-dwelling strata of the movie business and wound up directing four low budget features—mostly horror and action films—and a handful of documentaries. I had always dreamed of making movies, ever since I'd crept into many a forbidden film as a child.

After we moved to the States, I was trying to figure out what, if anything, I believed. What I believed, that is, beyond survival and my next paycheck. In the first year or two after we moved, I used my parent's contacts and made some documentaries for several religious groups. At the same time I was feeling less and less attached to my religious roots. My ventures into the secular movie business were not much more satisfying, though I was lucky enough to get one directing job after another making small feature films.

"If you hate these crummy movies you're directing, why not write something you like?" asked Genie.

"Such as?" I asked

"What about all the stories you always tell the children about your vacations in Portofino, when you were a kid? Those are a lot more interesting than all this crap. Write a novel."

"What will we live on?"

"We'll figure something out. Don't give up."

It took years to feel somewhat at home in my country. Having a son born in the States made me start to feel more like a real American. At first I felt foreign, although I was an American, according to my passport. Perhaps, as with many emigrants—in my case an expatriate who had "emigrated" back to his own country—I began to find my place through my children. My sense of belonging grew up along with John, Francis, and Jessica as they pulled me into local activities from parent-teacher meetings to town-team soccer.

Compared to me at the same age, John was the picture of good sense. I was jealous and complaining because John was spending "too much time" with Erica, mostly at her house, and acting perfectly reasonable. By the time I was the age John was when he was about to start boot camp—almost nineteen—I had been married to Genie (and living in our cramped chalet-basement apartment at the mission) for the better part of two years. We had a beautiful little girl, Jessica, and I was painting pictures for my second art show (mostly large expressionistic works à la Erich Heckel with a touch of the textures of Rouault).

"Erica is selfish, she's ruining your life!"

The typical response in my head to my dad ran something like this: "Why do we have to spend every second of this last summer together? Wasn't the previous eighteen years of being together and talking every day enough to cement our relationship?"

Instead of answering Dad, I would just wait until he ran out of steam. Perhaps we knocked heads so much that summer because he was taking my relationship with Erica more seriously than I was.

My relationship with my father always seemed strange to the people who knew us well enough to get a glimpse of how things worked. I could screw up one morning, get Dad into a rage, and that same day go and have a pleasant, even memorable, afternoon with him. My strategy when Dad went ballistic had always been to play along with whatever he said and weather the storm. "Yes . . . no . . . yes . . . yes . . . no."

"You have to lighten up. Why would he want to be around the house when all you do is get on his case about some silly girl?" said Genie.

"But what's the point? I just don't get it." I said.

"You don't 'get' the point of girlfriends?" Genie laughed. "*You?*"

Genie gave me her if-this-is-how-you-behave-now-imagine-what-it'll-be-like-living-with-you-when-you-get-old-and-senile! look and shook her head sadly.

"This is a hell of a thing," I said, "I just don't know how to say good-bye to John."

"That," said Genie, "I do get."

Every week I would go to "poolee" functions. All the recruits in the area (the current "pool" of recruits) would get together with the recruiters. These events usually had something to do with preparing for boot camp. For instance, we would go and take the basic swimming test all Marine recruits have to pass. Or we might take a physical fitness test or go for a long distance run. Mainly the recruiters wanted to keep track of us, not let us slip from their grasp as the summer wore on.

As the poolee events unfolded, I started to realize that the dedication to the mission was what made the Marines so attractive to me. The idea of being a part of something, "the mission," as defined by the Corps, that was bigger and more important than I was, was compelling. It was refreshing to belong to something that looked beyond the individual to a simple ideal, the accomplishment of the mission at whatever cost. "In the end," the Marine recruiters told everyone, "You're important because we can use you." I liked their honesty.

Of course I knew the Corps was using these little excursions to get into my boy's head more deeply, to indoctrinate him with the belief that he was joining this great family, the Marine Corps, a family that would never let him down as long as he gave his all. But it was a relief when the recruiters made John do things. At least on those days John was not with Erica. I had begun to dislike her heartily. Part of my dislike of Erica was because of her standoffishness toward our family, and part of it was plain old jealousy. I already missed John.

When I was seven I was bitten by a dog who had just had her puppies taken away. Now I understood how the robbed mother felt. Erica avoided our house as if it was a leper colony, and by doing so was robbing me of my son's last moments at home. From what the recruiters said, they didn't like girl-friends either. I talked to Staff Sergeant Dubois, and he said it was "always the girlfriend" that got the potential recruit "screwed up," talked him out of joining, dragged him (or her if it was "the boyfriend") back into big sloppy civilian America just as the Marines were inviting the potential recruit to accept the Corps as his or her personal savior.

One night John said, "Wake me at six, will you Dad? I've got to go up to Andover for a Marine thing, and if Erica calls tell her I left early so she won't blame me for not calling. She doesn't like the Marines and I get sick of arguing."

I nursed this triumph all day. I was still on the man-to-man track with John and he'd asked me tell a small lie to Erica. Then that night my triumph turned to ashes. Dinner hour came and went. At eight I called Erica's number.

"John's here. We just finished supper. What a great young man," Erica's mother said brightly.

"May I speak to John please?" I asked in what I hoped was a cold voice.

"Hi, Dad," said John a moment later.

"John, where have you been?" I asked.

"Over here."

"I cooked supper. Rosemary chicken."

"You knew I had the Marine thing, right?"

"Sure, but you said that went till around six."

"Then I drove over to Erica's. I haven't seen her all day. She was very upset."

"How was I supposed to know where you are?"

"I figured you'd call over here if you needed me. And you did, so now you don't need to worry," said John calmly.

"What about us? What about the chicken? I *slow-roasted* the chicken, damn it!"

"Sorry."

"Well, have you eaten? You could come home now."

"Dad, Erica's parents are serving dessert. I need to go."

"*To hell with them!*" I roared.

I heard John trying not to laugh.

"I want to talk to her father," I said.

"About what?" John asked suspiciously.

"You just put him on the line."

"No, Dad. You're sounding too crazy."

"I'll just call back until he picks up."

"What do you want to tell him?"

"That if he's so nice why does he have such a rude daughter?"

"No, Dad. If you do that I'll never speak to you again. You know that."

"Okay, not that. But I want to talk to him."

There was a pause and lots of rustling.

"Hello?" said Erica's father in his soft, preppy voice.

"Hi, Trip," I said, trying to sound grown-up or at least reasonably sane. "I wanted to ask you if you were concerned that John and Erica might be spending too much time together."

"Concerned?" said Trip in that oh-so-sensible manner of his, that voice he used to mouth the canned ready-made pious platitudes, the kind of "visualize-world-peace" nonsense you saw on bulletin boards in front of day-care centers.

"I mean, you know, we don't want unexpected grandchildren and all that," I said, "I mean is everything okay with them being together *morning, noon, and night?*"

There was a long and shocked silence. When he spoke again Erica's father's voice had gone up an octave and he seemed ready to sob.

"My daughter has a *bright future* ahead of her! She and I have had *many talks* about making *wise choices*. I trust her ability to make *wise choices!*"

"Bright future." "Wise choices." Everything this man said sounded as if it was an outtake from a bad high school commencement speech.

"Is that right?" I asked, "But since they're practically living together and

John needs to go off to the Corps without getting anyone into trouble, I was just concerned."

I never used words like "concerned." I have loves and terrors, triumphs and abject failures, but not "concerns." *This* was what happened when you talked to Erica's tepid parents for more than ten seconds. Two minutes into the conversation you started using insipid words like "concerns" and "wise choices" and sounding as if you worked for Planned Parenthood.

"Erica is a very mature young woman who makes wise choices," said her dad.

I wanted to scream, "I'm not talking about 'wise choices,' pal! I'm talking about rutting like crazed weasels!"

But what I said was, "I remember being that age and 'choice' had nothing much to do with anything." I tried to chuckle in a fatherly, tolerant, or at least waspish Groton-Harvard way.

"I appreciate your concern," Trip snapped frostily, "but all they do is participate in the community of our family life."

After I told her about my conversation with Erica's dad, Genie shrieked, "You called Trip and told him you thought John might get Erica *pregnant?*"

"I didn't 'call him.' John just happened to put him on the line after I called to find out why John hadn't come home."

"And you said you hoped Erica didn't get *pregnant?*"

"Not like that. We were just talking about, uh, wise choices."

"Are you out of your mind? How can you insult him that way?"

"It wasn't an 'insult,' just one, uh, father talking to another."

"You're soooo crazy!" Genie stared at me dolefully and shook her head, "*Crazy!* John is over there for dinner and you call up and say, 'Oh, by the way while you're all having dessert keep an eye on my son in case he gets your daughter pregnant.' John will never speak to you again."

"Of course he will."

"The only reason you're so pissed off is because he missed your rosemary chicken," said Genie and smiled.

"Maybe, but I feel lonely."

Genie put a comforting arm around my shoulders.

"Remember that essay he wrote about your cooking?"

I nodded and could not help but smile. Genie disappeared upstairs and moments later reappeared with one of John's junior high compositions called "Touchy Food." Genie started to read a little of the piece out loud:

> Eating my father's food is a delicate process. It can only be undertaken with the greatest care and concentration. I have often thought it akin to crossing a five-lane highway blindfolded. The slightest sign of disinterest or dissatisfaction can trigger an attack of ultra sensitivity. . . . Don't get me wrong! I *love* my father's cooking, and in no way intend to cast aspersions on *anything* that he has ever cooked in his entire life, and no I will *not* eat on the way home from school.

We laughed.

"His teacher insisted on being invited to dinner after she read it," said Genie.

"I grilled her a salmon filet, lightly hickory smoked it right on the grill served with steamed fresh asparagus."

That night I walked down to John's room and peered through his door. It was as "shut" as it ever got, which meant it was ajar. John's door never closed properly since I'd knocked down a wall that hadn't been touched since 1835 when the house was built. (The wall was between what had been the old dining room and living room. I wanted to make a larger, sunnier room.) The floor above sagged two inches, and the children laughed at me for months.

Pale sky over the top of the trees cast enough light on John so I could pick out his features. A long white foot was sticking out at the bottom of his bed from under the cover. His lithe arm above his head framed his face. I tiptoed forward and knelt. I shut my eyes. Would John be gone when I opened them?

3

The day John left for Parris Island I woke before the alarm went off. It was set for three A.M. I had to get John to the Andover recruiting office by four-thirty. It was a twenty-minute drive. John was going from there to Boston and then on to South Carolina.

That night I did not yell at John for coming back from Erica's at two A.M. I was so forlorn that the sight of him seemed to be an apparition when he finally stepped through the door. I was just glad to get a hug and to walk up and sit on the edge of John's bed for a moment as he stretched out.

We left the house at three-thirty A.M. I'd promised the recruiter that I'd have John at the recruiter's office by four sharp. When he got up John asked me if we could swing past Erica's and pick her up.

"What?" I asked. "We won't have time. I promised Staff Sergeant Dubois I'd get you there on time."

"I told her she could come. Please."

My heart sank. I felt angry, then sad, and then resigned.

"Well, if she's coming, I'll go get her now while you shower. Then we won't be late," I said.

"Let's just get her on the way, Dad."

"No, because if she's not ready we'll be late. I'll get her now."

"Suit yourself," said John.

We didn't say much and I found it strange to be in a car with this girl who'd done her best to avoid Genie and me all summer. She acted as if there was nothing that needed to be said, that the fact she'd refused to come over to our house to dinner, even once, was something normal or at least not worth mentioning.

"Good morning, Erica," I said.

"Good morning," Erica sniffed.

"Well, this is a sad day," I said.

"Thanks for coming over to pick me up," said Erica.

"Don't mention it. Glad you can come along."

Then we were at my front door. John was hugging Genie and she was crying, not sobbing, just steady, silent tears. John was telling Genie he loved her.

When I mentioned to John that he could sit in the backseat with Erica, he elected to sit up front with me. Better yet, as we pulled out of our drive and I reached over to give his hand a squeeze, John didn't let go but enfolded my hand in his big paw, then held on as if he was four and we were on the way to the dentist.

This, I thought, is what the last twenty minutes of my life will be like. It will suddenly be over before it even seems to have started, the way John's childhood has just suddenly ended without warning, the way we've arrived here early when every extra minute would have been precious, the way the Last Summer ended before we did any of the things I'd hoped to do.

By the time we pulled in at the recruiter's office, made ghastly orange-green by the parking lot vapor-lights, Erica was melting into a smear of tear-streaked jelly in the backseat. John was sitting next to me so straight his head was firmly pinned to the roof of the car near the burned patch where Genie, at four o'clock one Easter dawn, on the way home from the Greek Orthodox midnight Pascha service, set our car on fire with a lit candle.

As Orthodox, we believe it is a blessed thing to carry a lit candle home on Easter, as a token of the flame that miraculously appears in Christ's Tomb in the Holy Sepulcher in Jerusalem each Pascha. The Holy Fire lights the bishop's cluster of candles without aid of human intervention. The flame is then passed hand-to-hand to the thousands of pilgrims who come from all over the earth to participate in the resurrection in that sacred place. In a reen-actment of what is happening in Jerusalem, in each Orthodox Church, the priest emerges from the altar in the darkened sanctuary with a single lit candle. Then the worshipers, armed with unlit candles, pass the flame of faith, life, and hope from hand-to-hand. After a few moments, the church, pitch-dark an instant before, is ablaze with light. Faces glow with joy. Sleepy children are woken up just in time to stare wide-eyed at all the dancing points of flame and light their candles.

It took several years of Greek Orthodox Easters to get the hang of transporting open flames in moving cars. (Keep the flame *low!* Heat *rises!* Do *not* hold your flame up so that "the early commuters can see our nice candles.") In 1990 our family had to learn the unusual skill of lit-candle-in-automobile-transport the hard way when, after falling in love with the liturgical life of Christianity's most ancient body, and to the consternation of my mother, I converted to the Greek Orthodox Church. (In their own time, Genie and the three children joined me over the next few years.)

"Converted" is the wrong word. I became Orthodox to embrace the fullness of faith in a mystical, less rationalistic way than provided for by the dry Calvinist fundamentalism of my childhood. In any case, John was the only one of our children to grow up in the Church. (Francis was a teenager and Jessica about to start college when I began my pilgrimage.)

John loved our church: the bright icons, Father Chris, the welcoming Greek men and women, the candles and incense—"You even get to play with fire here!"—and asked to serve at the altar the second Sunday he accompanied me, before we had even joined.

John served at the altar from nine years of age until the Sunday before he left for boot camp. Watching him Sunday after Sunday draped in his gold-and-white robe (until he outgrew it and was given a plain dark blue one), back straight, tenderly assisting a mother with her baby, as she and the baby were served communion, carrying the tall golden cross in the various liturgical processions, keeping the censor lit and pouring forth its smoky gardenia bouquet, was one of the profound joys of my life. Knowing that John would no longer be at the altar made his last Sundays all the more poignant.

John's hand had gotten colder as we drove. I tried to block out Erica's sniffing sounds coming from the backseat as I willed my son to be safe, to be comforted, to do well in his quest. A horribly brief moment later I was in the office and the time for regrets was done.

There was another recruit there. He looked like I felt, doomed, sick, and pale. The deathly neon in the office was perfect for picking out his night-of-the-living-dead pallor. Both boys were in simple clothes, stripped down for this, their last journey as civilians. They had one little bag each. The rules were strict: no tobacco or personal effects, nothing but the clothes on their backs. The Marines would strip their recruits down when they arrived at Parris Island and give them everything they needed from their military-issue socks up. John's bag had the family pictures he was allowed to bring and a prayer book.

I looked at John as he shook Staff Sergeant Dubois's hand and thought, *what is John trying to prove?* The last Schaeffer to wear a uniform was my grandfather on my father's side and he'd been in the U.S. Navy. There were no American flags around our home, no eagles above the mantle.

"Why do you want to do this?" I asked more than once during our Last Summer. "I don't really know," John answered. Sometimes he'd say, "I want self-discipline." At other times he'd mumble he didn't know what he wanted to study or that he was sick of school. He was mostly mute on the subject and looked slightly hunted when pressed to explain. The way John came to the Corps, sidled up to it, became mesmerized by the Marine idea, reminded me of the character played by Richard Dreyfus in *Close Encounters of the Third Kind*. I thought of the scene where Dreyfus carved the shape of a mountain in mashed potatoes after somehow getting the "message" of what the mountain—to which he was being mysteriously drawn—looked like.

Even when he spouted reasons right out of the recruiter's handbook— self-discipline and pride, for instance—I could tell John wasn't convinced. He wasn't lying either. It's just that something bigger than he could explain had seized hold of him. The best answer I got from John was "I just do."

---

tired, I could sleep for days.
holding two hands
my father next to me and Erica behind,
all fading into dirty parking lot dawn
on the way back to a different life than what I want
with warm beds and writing and study.
not what I want.

I never understood how my father was so calm when he took me to the recruiter's office that night. I think that maybe he had resigned himself to the fact that this was an inevitable landmark for both of us. Dad was silent almost the entire way to Andover, making the occasional remark and reassuring me that he would write. At the end there was a hug and a handshake.

"I'll miss you, boy. I'll write every day."

"Okay."

"I love you, John."

"I love you, Dad."

The Marines don't let recruits call home, let alone allow parents to visit. Letters are the only means of communication until after graduation from boot camp. If a man has not gone through Parris Island himself, there is no point of reference to his son. John might as well have been headed for Tibet.

After I dropped Erica off, I drove home alone. It was dawn but the overcast sky kept the road dark. I lost my way twice on a road I'd driven a thousand times. I had never experienced pride and fear as one emotion before. *Oh, Lord Jesus, please protect my boy and bring him home safe again!* was all I could think as I peered forlornly into the gloom while trying to remember where I lived.

4

here we go
the yellow footprints
the smell of alcohol on razors to shave heads with.
boots and cammies, skivvies and skivvie shirts, tooth brush and
shaving razor.
now we are naked.

My first days on Parris Island (PI) were a blur. That is how I will remember
them for the rest of my life, a dark, brooding, olive-green blur of moving half-
focused shapes and distant shouts.

When the recruit first arrives on PI, it is two A.M., and he (or she) is on a
bus. A DI storms onto the bus and yells, "You have enlisted in the United
States Marine Corps, you are now subject to the Uniform Code of Military
Justice. *Now get off my bus!*"

Red-eyed recruits stinking of sweaty fear, and some of the farewell alcohol
their friends fed them the night before stumble off the bus. They—we—had
been up for twenty-four hours or more. You do not sleep the night before
coming to PI or when you travel there (unless you are very drunk). You twist
and turn. You are so stripped of every emotion that you can barely hear above
the ringing in your ears as the bus drives down the long dark causeway onto
the island. Most of the recruits sobered up as we rolled over the causeway. The
rest certainly got sober as soon as the DI stormed our bus.

You arrive in the pitch black of darkest night. You have left the world in
the dark and been taken to a place that seems to have no connection to the
land—let alone your life. All I glimpsed from the bus was dark water, then
shadows of pine trees.

You are on the bus, then there is screaming and you step into the hot damp air of South Carolina, and there, smaller than you imagined them, are the famous yellow footprints stenciled onto the clean-swept pavement and lined up in rows to form the recruits into the shape of a platoon. You step gingerly onto the footprints in front of the in-processing building. At night it looms, intimidating, a dark, low, three-story pile of red brick but you barely glance at it or anything else. Everything comes down to taking the next breath.

When I stood on the footprints, I jammed so close to the next recruit that my chin was practically on his shoulder. There was plenty of space all around us on the gritty hardtop, and an empty road behind us faded away under the overhead hot water and steam pipes. The way the footprints were painted on the pavement deprived us of all personal space. We were crotch-to-ass in neat rows. We were all facing the same way. We were a knot of disheveled and fearful boys, ragged, and, speaking for myself, aware that we were a sorry spectacle compared to the Marine DI who paced and strutted around us.

I caught a few words of the "welcome" speech after we scurried onto the yellow footprints:

> You are now aboard MARINE Corps Recruit Depot Parris Island, South Carolina, and you have just taken the first step toward becoming a member of the world's finest fighting force—The United States MARINE Corps!
>
> You should be standing at the position of attention, that means your heels are touching; feet at a forty-five degree angle; thumbs along the trouser seams; palms rolled inboard; fingers in their natural curl; head and eyes straight in front; and your mouth shut! This is the only position from which you will speak to any MARINE sailor, or civilian personnel during your stay on Parris Island. . . .
>
> You are now subject to the Uniform Code of Military Justice . . . First: Article Eighty-six: "Unauthorized absence." You will be where you are supposed to be, at the proper time, and in proper uniform . . . Article Ninety-one: "Disrespect." You will be respectful to all

MARINES, sailors, and civilians aboard this depot . . . Article Ninety-two: "Disobedience of a lawful order." You will do what you are told to do, when you are told to do it—without question. . . .

The MARINE Corp's success depends on teamwork. Teamwork, therefore, is an essential part of your training. . . . You will live, eat, sleep, and train as a team. *The word "I" will no longer be part of your vocabulary!*

Over the course of the rest of the first night, we recruits filed into the receiving center at a dead run. It was a red brick and cinder block building filled with classrooms and one-piece stainless steel desks. Once inside we were given a last no-questions-asked chance to rid ourselves of any "contraband" (tobacco, drugs, condoms, pornography, and any other items not needed in training). Then our heads were shaved and cut, nicked, and scraped (the barbers are not gentle), and we received our first uniforms (sweats and cammies).

The "in-processing" that went on for three more days merged into a sleepless marathon of uniform fittings, medical exams, and paperwork. The cammies and skivvies, "hygiene gear" and "covers" (hats) all added up to a lot of "trash" (all personal issue) that had to be hurriedly tried on. Then came the rifle issue and the first encounter with the "Rifleman's Creed" that, in the next weeks, we would learn by heart and soon be yelling at the top of our lungs. (There are some slightly different versions of this creed but this is the one we learned.)

THIS IS MY RIFLE. There are many like it but this one is mine. My rifle is my best friend. It is my life. I must master it as I master my life.

My rifle, without me, is useless. Without my rifle, I am useless. I must fire my rifle true. . . . I must shoot him before he shoots me. I will . . .

My rifle and myself know that what counts in this war is not the rounds we fire, the noise of our burst, nor the smoke we make. We know that it is the hits that count. We will hit . . .

My rifle is human, even as I, because it is my life. Thus, I will learn it as a brother. I will learn its weaknesses, its strength, its parts, its accessories, its sights, and its barrel. I will ever guard it against the ravages of weather and damage. I will keep my rifle clean and ready, even as I am clean and ready. We will become part of each other. We will . . .

Before God I swear this creed. My rifle and myself are the defenders of my country. We are the masters of our enemy. We are the saviors of my life.

So be it, until victory is America's and there is no enemy, but peace!

After seventy-two hours I was finally allowed to sleep. A DI led us to a squadbay. I was so numb that all I remember is that there were beds.

It was a temporary DI's job (as opposed to the four permanent DIs we'd soon meet) to take charge of recruits from the moment they stepped off the bus through their first week on PI and processing. Our short-term DI was Sergeant Davis. He was a very big black man. All I can remember out of my fog of fear is that he was broad and black and had a voice that reminded me of a bulldog growling. It was his job to shape us into raw recruits who were fit enough to be taken over by the four DIs who were to guide us through all of our training.

We were so dazed we practically had to be led by the hand. Sergeant Davis seemed harsh by civilian standards, but, as we were to find out, measured by recruit training standards, he was the only person who would be nice (relatively speaking) during our entire stay on the island. This shape-up process, to instill minimum discipline, had to be accomplished in the space of our first few days on the island. It was a very tough job for one Marine to deal with some ninety plus raw, scared recruits. A few spoke almost no English, others were near having a nervous breakdown before they even got going with the real training, and still others were facing discipline and a structured life for the first time.

This preliminary introduction to life in boot camp was vital. If we had been dumped straight into the hands of our permanent DIs, they would have killed our little "gaggle-fuck" of civilians who were at a total loss as to how to even form up into an orderly platoon, standing at attention. As it was, Sergeant Davis had the responsibility of waking us up at 0500, getting us ready for the day, and taking us through each preliminary cycle of paperwork and fittings, as well as trying to teach us how to form up on line and the rudiments of marching and "sounding off" (yelling all responses to DIs at the top of our lungs).

My first week on PI was taken up entirely in processing, filling out life insurance forms, the paperwork for the GI Bill, getting vaccinated, and being marched from one place to another in the heat of the South Carolina sun. Each day we would go back and fill out yet more paperwork, some of it having to do with the disposition of our bodies and assets if we were killed.

paper work, preparing for pain,
undisciplined "gaggle-fucking."
bald flock that we are
all over the island
so many needles it feels like I got hit in the arm with a bat
preparing for true pain and panic.

On the first Saturday I was on PI, we took what is known as the IST (Initial Strength Test). The IST determined if the recruit had the basic level of physical fitness to even begin training. The requirements were a joke: three pull-ups, fifty-five crunches in two minutes, and a mile and a half in thirteen minutes. Those of us who passed were then introduced to our permanent DIs, who would be with us all the way through training. Those who failed (about ten recruits) were put into a special platoon to train them to train, PCP (Physical Conditioning Platoon), better known as the "pork chop platoon," a place for the fat and weak to get less fat and strong enough to begin the real work at hand. (This slim-down conditioning could take as much as six months, meaning that three months of boot camp stretched to almost a year for some recruits.)

Those of us who made it through the IST spent the rest of the first week walking (I wouldn't call it marching) all over "main side," which is the area of the base where everything from uniform issue to hair cuts to inoculations and medical care took place. I was put in Platoon 1093, 1st Battalion, "B" (Bravo) Company. At the end of processing we were taken to our permanent squadbay to await our DIs.

Our squadbay, like all the others on PI, was a long cinderblock room. The floor was polished brown-green painted concrete, the walls plain and white. On each side of the squadbay was a row of twenty-five or so metal "racks" (bunks), giving us the capacity to sleep our eighty plus recruits. At one end was the "DI House" (the DIs' office and quarters, a small, spare, cramped room). At the other end were the showers and "heads" (toilets). At the foot of each rack were our "footlockers" (metal trunks). Running down both sides of the room at the foot of the racks was a ruler-straight painted black line on which we recruits would always "get on line" (stand at attention in a row, heels on the line) when ordered to do so.

In front of the DIs' house, at the end of the squadbay was the "quarter-deck" (nothing more than a ten by fifteen–foot patch of concrete floor, named for the place on a ship where ceremonies are held), where recruits would be punished. Painted on the floor in front of the DIs' door were foot-prints to stand on when banging on the doorpost, on a painted handprint (three times), when a recruit needed to speak to a DI. On the walls and con-crete columns that supported the roof, Marine mottoes were stenciled, chiefly: CORE VALUES: HONOR. COURAGE. COMMITMENT.

There were other signs posted through the squadbay, in the showers, and in the head, listing everything vital for us to know: the muzzle velocity of the M-16A2, the procedure for treating a "sucking chest wound," rules of war and first aid, all with their own rhymes or "ditties" (memory keys) to rein-force learning.

Over the sinks: VULNERABLE PARTS OF THE BODY: Temple, eyes, ears, nose, throat, neck, torso, arms, groin, legs.

Over a toilet: WEAPONS OF OPPORTUNITY: Rocks are outstanding weapons of opportunity. The E-tool is a very effective weapon.

On the wall next to the showers: GENERAL ORDERS:

General Order 1
To take charge of this post and all government property in view.

General Order 2
To walk my post in a military manner, keeping always on the alert and observing everything that takes place within sight or hearing.

General Order 3
To report all violations of orders I am instructed to enforce.

General Order 4
To repeat all calls from posts more distant from the guardhouse than my own.

General Order 5
To quit my post only when properly relieved.

General Order 6
To receive, obey and pass on to the sentry who relieves me all orders from the commanding officer, officer of the day, and officers and noncommissioned officers of the guard only.

General Order 7
To talk to no one except in the line of duty.

General Order 8
To give the alarm in case of fire or disorder.

General Order 9
To call the corporal of the guard in any case not covered by instructions.

General Order 10
To salute all officers and all colors and standards not cased.

General Order 11
To be especially watchful at night and during the time for challenging, to challenge all persons on or near my post, and to allow no one to pass without proper authority.

Like every other piece of "knowledge" to be memorized, there was a ditty (memory key) to the General Order. This was posted over the metal urinal trough that served the entire platoon.

GENERAL ORDER MEMORY KEY
1. To Take
2. To Walk
3. To Report
4. To Repeat
5. To Quit
6. To Receive
7. To Talk
8. To Give
9. To Call
10. To Salute
11. To Be

Over the towel racks:

THE FIVE TYPES OF WOUNDS: KEY WORD *CALIP*
C-Crush
A-Abrasion
L-Laceration
I-Incision
P-Puncture

On the day we were formed we were not studying our new surroundings or learning memory key ditties! We sat on the cold concrete floor in rows and stared horrified at the DIs, mesmerized by the waves of threatening vibes that coursed out of the very tough men, these DIs who were just about to be launched on us. We sat while the DIs filed in and the series commander, Captain Card, administered the DI oath:

> These recruits are entrusted to my care. I will train them to the best of my ability. I will develop them into smartly disciplined, physically fit, basically trained Marines, thoroughly indoctrinated in love of the Corps and country. I will demand of them and demonstrate by my

own example the highest standards of personal conduct, morality and professional skill.

After administering the oath, the series commander left and the senior drill instructor spoke to us for several minutes. "Training here is tough. . . . We will accept nothing but the best. . . . There is only one way off the Island, the causeway. . . . Do not try to swim off the marsh . . . sharks . . . tides . . . we'll send the dogs after you." Then he told the DIs to "take charge."

From that moment on we were the creatures of the DIs and belonged to them heart and soul. For the next hours everything was a stomach-churning vague swirl of chaos and fear, recruits flying to get "on line," DIs everywhere, in everyone's face testing, poking, screaming, "BACK UP! TAKE YOUR SWEET-ASS TIME!" seeing who would crack in the very beginning of training, who was weak, who was strong. The DIs shouted, pointed, zeroed in on us, spun, stamped, moved on to the next recruit, chewed him out, turned back to another.

"OH, GOOD TO GO, YOU WANT TO BE ON YOUR OWN PRO-GRAM DON'T YOU?"

"No, sir!"

"WHISPER TO ME TOO."

"NO SIR!"

"Louder."

"*NO SIR!*"

"IF I HEAR YOUR VOICE DROP BELOW THAT VOLUME FOR THE REST OF THE TIME YOU ARE ON MY ISLAND I WILL SMOKE YOU UNTIL YOUR HEART POPS."

"AYE SIR!"

That is how I remember my first experience with DIs, yelling and panic and lost voices that would return stronger and deeper as time passed in training. The DIs who were "forming" us that day would become better known to me in the next weeks. My senior drill instructor (our SDI or "Senior") whose job it was to be "fatherly" to us was Senior Drill Instructor Staff Sergeant Marshal. He was short, black, wide, and the most brutally strong person I have ever encountered. He was a hurricane bottled up inside a powerful body that could barely contain him. He could do forty-seven dead-hang pull-ups at the age of thirty-four. Senior Drill Instructor Staff Sergeant Marshal's career path had taken him from the Marine infantry to the famed Silent Drill Team. (The Marine unit that performs flawless drills movements at official occasions, from wreath-laying ceremonies to White House receptions.) Then Senior Drill Instructor Staff Sergeant Marshal became a prison guard in a military prison. From there he was selected to become a DI. We lived in mortal fear of him. He told us that he had hung a prisoner off the catwalk of the prison with his bare hands. (No one died but, according to our SDI, "There were no more problems with this guy.")

Next in authority was Drill Instructor Staff Sergeant Matson. He was tall and had a somewhat detached look on his long horsey face. He glanced at us with a distant malevolent stare, as if we recruits were mere flies and he was planning to pull every single one of our wings off one by one.

Then there was Drill Instructor Sergeant Alvarez. He was the most energetic of all our DIs by far. He was "on" all the time and could play "fuck-fuck games" (endless screaming and harassment of every description) with the platoon until he ran us all into the ground and we'd roll over, some crying and all suffering complete muscle failure. Then he would go run ten miles just to show us how weak we were, having *already* done us in, push-up for push-up, right along with us nose-to-nose. His stamina was a constant source of amazement to us. The gap between Sergeant Alvarez's willpower and ours seemed insurmountable.

Last was Drill Instructor Staff Sergeant Perry. He was just plain mean. Being mean was his job. Perry got the task of being the "Heavy Hat." In other words, the "bad cop" to the "fatherly" Senior's "good cop." Perry would "smoke" a recruit (in other words push, punish, and bully him) until the recruit collapsed or until the recruit cracked or Perry got bored. In the beginning of training the recruit usually cracked first. (The DIs did not use physical violence. However, punishments were severe and involved endless exercises. These "smoke-checks" could go on for what seemed like hours.)

I didn't know anyone in the platoon. Nor did I want to. I was just surviving breath-to-breath, chow-to-chow. No names registered, not even faces; everything was happening too fast. We weren't given any chance to settle in.

Total disorientation was the point of the first weeks of training, and the program of stupefying bewilderment succeeded.

The first few letters we recruits sent our families were form letters. We sat on the "deck" (floor) behind our footlockers and filled in the forms. We new recruits were expected to be so out of our minds with fatigue and disorientation that we would be incapable of writing coherent thoughts that our families could understand. We were sleep deprived and scared-into-numbness and certainly not thinking straight. We were so exhausted that we had to even be instructed on how to fill in the blanks on our form letters. We sat left leg over right, "Indian-style"; rather, were told to sit this way, the "only way" to sit when filling in form letters in SDI time (the free time at the end of each day), while the DIs strode up and down the center of the squad bay ("the DI highway") and went through the letter with us.

"In the next space you put your nasty little name, your first name being 'Recruit' and your last being whatever your nasty little families gave you when you popped out of your nasty mothers and started screaming. Good to go?"

"YES SIR!"

"Questions, of you to me?"

"NO SIR!"

"Don't say 'no sir' if you don't have a question. How the hell am I supposed to hear the one recruit that has a question with all of you sounding off? If you don't have a question than just sit there and keep your cock-holsters shut!"

"AYE SIR!"

"OH, GOOD TO GO, WHAT'S YOUR NAME, THING?"

"RECRUIT PETRIN, SIR!"

"TALK TO ME ON YOUR ASS? YOU THINK THAT BECAUSE WE HAVE YOU PUT YOUR FOOTLOCKERS ON LINE THAT YOU RATE TO *SIT* ON THEM?"

During the first weeks of boot camp, there were no letters from John. He did not write anything beyond the two form letters the Marines sent for him to announce his arrival and on which he filled in the blanks.

COMMANDING OFFICER
RECRUIT TRAINING REGIMENT
MCRD
PO BOX 16001
PARRIS ISLAND, SC 29905-6001

I HAVE ARRIVED SAFELY AT PARRIS ISLAND, SOUTH CAROLINA
MY NEW ADDRESS IS:
RCT *JOHN SCHAEFFER*
PLT *1093 1ST BN B CO*
PO BOX 11004
MCRD PARRIS ISLAND SC 29905-1004

FROM JUNE 1ST UNTIL NOVEMBER 1ST IS HURRICANE SEASON. IF MCRD PISC IS THREATENED BY A HURRICANE, YOU CAN CALL 1 800 343 0639 ENTER THE NUMBER SEQUENCE 1-3-1 FOR UP TO DATE INFORMATION. INFORMATION ON FAMILY DAY AND GRADUATION EVENTS CAN BE OBTAINED AT THE SAME NUMBER BY ENTERING THE SEQUENCE 1-3-2. FURTHER INFORMATION CAN BE OBTAINED AT (www.parrisisland.com)

(Give this to Erica please? Thanx)

Form Letter #2

Dear *Mom + Dad*   Date: *99 08 20*

I have arrived at Parris Island and have been assigned to Platoon *1093* which is comprised of *85* recruits from various parts of the country. Our Senior Drill Instructor's name is *SDI SSgt Marshal* he is the one who is responsible for our training here. We will live and train together for the next three months until our graduation date on *Nov 12*. There are 4 Drill Instructors assigned to my platoon and I am told there will be at least one with the platoon each day we are here. I will send you their names later. Because of the balanced diet we will be on, it is recommended that you not send packages containing food items to me. I am enclosing my address again to be sure you have all the information needed to write to me. Be sure you address all mail to me just as I have it below:

REC SCHAEFFER PLATOON 1093 BRAVO CO, 1ST RTBN MCRD PARRIS ISLAND, SOUTH CAROLINA 22905-1004

5

Since I'd never been a Marine I only knew what I'd read and what I'd heard from Max and Asher Boucher, the only childhood friends John had who were Marines. They were ahead of John on the Marine path. They were friends from Newburyport who went to the public school. Genie and I had been close to their parents, Cathy and Danny, for many years. (Cathy was an artist and also owned a gallery, and Danny was an engineer.)

After John left I called Danny and Cathy for any news they had of their son Asher. He was about seven weeks ahead of John in boot camp. Max, Asher's older brother, was already a Marine officer. Danny and Cathy who also had no military, let alone Marine, connections had been mystified when their boys joined up, the little brother following the big brother into the Corps.

The Bouchers understood what Genie and I were going through and had recommended several books. One book that was particularly helpful was *Making the Corps* by Thomas E. Ricks. It became my Bible for the first weeks John was on Parris Island. The dog-eared volume sat on the kitchen table, open at the relevant day-by-day account of training. I followed John's activities and would try and direct my prayers accordingly while imagining John doing whatever *Making the Corps* said he'd be doing on that training day. I would call Danny and pump him for news of Asher and how he had come through the first weeks of training. I also e-mailed my niece's husband Rodman Miller (he lived in Switzerland), who had been a Marine officer long ago and received many an e-mail in return, telling me what a great thing John had done and how proud I was going to be.

Writing to John was a poignant exercise. There was something so unequal about writing to him from the lap of luxury and creature comforts when he had essentially died and gone to hell.

I found myself eating less and avoiding John's favorite foods, unable to suck down the homemade Tuscan pizza and other meals he loved while sitting next to his empty chair. For the first time in his and our lives, John was beyond my help. Ever since John quit the track team at St. John's Prep, just before he left that school for the Waring School, I had a nagging doubt as to whether he would stick out the challenges of life. Did John have it in him to become a Marine? I knew a lot of recruits were sent home. Would he be absolutely devastated if he failed? I felt sick.

To Recruit John Schaeffer
August 26, 1999
Dear John,
Mom and I miss you a lot, know you are busy. We'd like letters however brief whenever possible since we have no idea how your day-to-day life is going, good or bad. On the other hand we know that your plate is more than full. Speaking of which we hear from Rodman via e-mail quite a bit. Your going into the Marines seems to have revived a lot of old memories for him. He's very anxious to help you out. He is writing to you and e-mailing us long letters about his own time in the Corps.

Asher Boucher sent us a note of encouragement via his mom and dad. He is going to drop you a note, wants you to know it gets better and to hang in there.

We are so proud of you and so is everyone else. Keep up the good work old boy.

Love
Dad.

P.S. Have you been getting all the mail? I sent three or four letters before we had the correct platoon number. Hope you got them all. Also are you well? Are you sleeping? Are you out of your mind, or hanging in there? Tell us how it is. Love, Pop.

I scribbled a note on the flyleaf of my Field Training manual:

My name is "This Recruit"
I have no discernable features
No hair, no possessions
Nothing to set me apart,
I move in unison with 85 other "this recruits"
Drill Instructor Staff Sergeant Matson (he has a name), said, "The Constitution doesn't apply to you in the same way that it does to civilians. You signed that away when you came here."

Most of life consists of learning the "ditties" to get through the day:

"Sir, Condition One weapon is magazine inserted, round in chamber, bolt forward, safety on, ejection port cover closed, sir!"

Training started intense and slow. We recruits had been demoted to being toddlers who had to relearn everything. Nothing we knew was right. We did not know how to put on socks or tie our shoes. We did not know how to shower or shave or even how to piss. We thought we knew but our knowledge was a stumbling block, worse than nothing, civilian.

We could not move onto the next part of training until we completed each element (no matter how small), to the satisfaction of our DIs. From memorizing the Articles of the Code of Conduct to putting on a sock in the "correct way" or putting on both socks in the "wrong" order became an ordeal. Any infraction or deviation from the plan would cause severe punishment. Then the recruit or the whole platoon would have to start the activity all over again from putting on socks in the "right" order to making the rack (bed) "correctly."

In the beginning of training, every single little action, no matter how simple, took hours. Our time was spent divided between the squadbay, classrooms, and "drill." (Drill is marching and doing the drill movements such as "port arms"—holding the rifle directly in front of the body at an angle from right hip to left shoulder—and the other exercises you see on a parade deck.) We had to learn how to take care of our basic needs both in the squadbay but also in the field, as well as master the classes and the field training that went with them.

We were given pages to add to our two loose-leaf Field Training Manuals (the "Red Knowledge Book" and the "Green Knowledge Book") as intensive classes began. These classes covered the Law of War, the Code of Conduct, Combat Leadership, Basic Field Skills, Camouflage, Cover and Concealment, Day Individual Movement, Techniques of Unaided Night Vision, Night Individual Movement, Field Sanitation, the M40 Gas Mask, Tactical Weapons of Opportunity (i.e., rocks, sticks and anything else you could smash the enemy with when your rifle isn't handy), First Aid in Combat, Introduction to Field Firing, Application of Marksmanship Fundamentals, Field Firing Positions and Reloading, Presentation of the M-16A2 Service Rifle, Daylight Target Detection, Low-Light-Darkness Engagement Technique, Firing with the Field Protective Mask, Supported Firing Positions/Selection and Use of Cover, Multiple Target Engagement Techniques, Moving Target Engagement Techniques, and Range Determination.

There was also endless physical training or PT: miles of running; thousands of repetitions of exercises; pugil stick fighting (an extension of bayonet training, wherein we fought other recruits with six-foot long padded clubs); many a "confidence course" (we slid down ropes from high towers, crossed water on rope bridges, and climbed high, intimidating structures); and endless "humps" (marches while in full combat gear and carrying heavy packs) to the DI's barked cadences as blisters formed and the equipment got heavier with each step.

Drill and more drill became a kind of slow-motion torture. We stood holding our rifles four inches away from our bodies for hours, forty inches side-by-side, feet taking even steps, thirty inches each, "striking the ground with your heels so everyone glides," shoulders back, head straight. We learned about heat and sand fleas and how to hold back a groan as they bit and we couldn't move, even to swivel our "nasty eyeballs."

No matter what we were doing, it had to be done with the utmost speed and perfection. Every action became a trap set by the DIs. Just the act of entering the chow hall, eating, and leaving was an excruciating process requiring intense concentration. There was a "right" way (the recruit way) and a "wrong" way (the nasty civilian way) to do everything. We would learn the right way or die trying and collapse in a pool of sweat having just done more push-ups than we ever believed possible.

"Without the aid of reference, identify the nine principles of the Law of War!"

"Discipline in combat is essential. Disobedience to the law of war dishonors the Nation, the Marine Corps, and the individual Marine. (A) Marines fight only enemy combatants. (B) Marines do not harm enemy soldiers who surrender. (C) Marines do not kill or torture prisoners. (D) Marines collect and care for the wounded, whether friend or foe. (E) Marines do not attack medical personnel, facilities, or equipment. (F) Marines destroy no more than the mission requires. (G) Marines treat all civilians humanely. (H) Marines do not steal. Marines respect private property and possessions. (I) Marines should do their best to prevent violations of the Law of War, SIR!"

"The first article of the Code of Conduct?"

"Article One! I am an American, fighting in the force which guards my country and our way of life! I am prepared to give my life in their defense, SIR!"

"What does it mean, Yates?"

"This means this recruit is an American fighting for this recruit's country! SIR!"

"Article Two?"

"I will never surrender of my own free will! If in command, I will never surrender the members of my command while they still have the means to resist, SIR!"

"Article Three?"

"If I am captured, I will continue to resist by all means available! I will make every effort to escape and to aid others to escape! I will accept neither parole nor special favors from the enemy, SIR!"

During the first few weeks, it could take upward of an hour to get dressed. I got the feeling that, left to themselves, the DIs would have liked to take three or four times the amount of time allocated to teach us every last thing they knew from how to properly address an officer to how to properly tie our boots, where the laces went, how to polish that boot, to the fact that the M40 field protective mask has one main part and eight components, Head Harness, Inlet Valve Disk, Nosecup . . .

If we were lucky we would wake up when the "fire watch" (the recruits on watch at night) began calling, "Five minutes to lights! Five minutes to lights!" out of the back "hatch" (door). They did this countdown so all the platoons could coordinate and all the lights for all the barracks in the whole company went on at the same time. "Four minutes to lights!" Then a few minutes later the final countdown began, "Four, three, two, one, LIGHTS! LIGHTS! *L-I-G-H-T-S!*"

If we didn't wake during the countdown we would be screamed into terrifying wakefulness by the DIs who would charge into the squadbay. We leapt out of the rack to stand "on line," toes all neatly on the lines painted down the floor at the head of the rows of bunks. "Get up, up, UP!" We'd be shivering on line, clinging to the cold concrete deck of the squadbay, clad only in our PT shorts and skivvie shirts and shower shoes.

The first thing we would do each morning was "count off" to ensure that everyone was there and that no one had gone "UA" (unauthorized absence) overnight or killed themselves. (Suicide was a real possibility especially early in training.) In the beginning of training, even counting off often took ten to fifteen minutes because we were not fast enough or loud enough in yelling out our numbers so had to do it again and again. Then after we finally managed to count off fast enough and at the right volume—screaming—we would get dressed. Rather we would *try* to get dressed and find that we knew nothing of dressing and had to be taught how to dress.

Each item of clothing was to be put on in unison with all the other recruits, a kind of synchronized swimming exercise only with socks, skivvies, shirts, cammies, and boots. And in everything, speed and "correct attitude" was of the essence while the DI counted down the seconds.

> left sock, right sock, trousers and strip
> begin again
> get it right or we'll start the day
> on a bad note and go from there
> fuck-fuck games are not constrained by time
> get it right and feel the pride of not hearing anything,
> silence is glorious.

Boot camp was about following simple instructions and doing neither more nor less than you were told to. Improvisation was *not* something highly valued in boot camp. When we got dressed we would be told: "Put on your left sock NOW!" All you had to do was put on your left sock. Some recruits would not be able to do it in the time we were given. Some would try to get ahead and start putting on their right sock as well, at which point we'd all have to be punished collectively for this infraction of the DI's precise instructions. Then we would all take our left sock off and start over.

"Oh, okay, I guess I said take our sweet-ass time. Carr, take off your left sock NOW!"

"AYE SIR!"

Once we all put on our left socks correctly, we would do the right sock, then move to our trousers, each individual item put in its place. If we screwed up badly enough we would strip all the way down and begin again.

"Oh I guess I said to pick up your blouse there Marshal, okay we can be late to chow, I've got all day to play these fuck-fuck games with you, strip!"

"AYE SIR!"

"All of you, you think Marshal's the only one?"

"AYE SIR!"

In the beginning of training it took anywhere from twenty minutes to an hour to get dressed. Each day a little more was expected of us, we had a little less time to get dressed, and every requirement was a little bit tougher until we were as close to perfection in the little things as we could be. The Marines call it "attention to detail."

Above all, there was the "right" and "wrong way" to respond to the DIs. The right way was to sound off loud and clear. The wrong way was to mumble, or not sound off so fervently that you practically spit out your lungs, screaming, "SIR, YES SIR!" or "AYE, SIR!" to every command or question. There was a right way and a wrong way to look at a DI too. "Are you eye-balling me, recruit?" the DI would yell, if you made even fleeting, inadvertent eye contact.

We recruits were not Marines. We had no right to look at one full in the face, much less look into the eyes of our DIs. We were civilians, wanna-be Marines, not fit to breathe the air shared by our DIs, let alone look at them in the face! We did not rate eye contact:

"Are we drinking buddies?!"

"NO, SIR!"

"Do I know your mama?"

"NO, SIR!"

"Are we friends?"

"NO, SIR!"

You could not look at anything when you were marching, except the back of the recruit's head marching ahead of you. Worst of all was a glance at any female or female platoon that might be marching past. I had never seen a recruit reduced to jelly so fast as one who had a couple of female DIs march over to him from their female platoon, called the male recruit out (while our own DIs watched with approval), and descended on him in full fury.

"Were you eye-fucking my recruits, you nasty thing?"

"NO, MA'AM!"

"You have just disgraced your platoon and your Senior!"

"AYE, MA'AM!"

"PUSH, NOW!"

"AYE, MA'AM!"

The evenings involved not rest but learning how to maintain our rifles, shining our boots and brass, and showering. We were issued towels with the M-16A2 and all its parts printed on the cloth with the correct names of each part: upper receiver, firing pin, bolt cam pin, charging handle, bolt carrier, buffer, action spring, hand guards, extractor, extractor pin, bolt, firing pin, lower receiver, and sling. We endlessly took our weapons apart, laid them out on the towels, and reassembled them after each piece was laid out correctly, and cleaned.

We got thirty-second showers and twenty seconds to shave and brush our "nasty fangs" as we were rushed, a naked jumble of eighty-plus recruits, through the showers. Half would shower while half shaved.

"Port side shower! Starboard side shave!"

"AYE, SIR!"

"Article Six?"

"I will never forget that I am an American fighting for freedom, responsible for my actions, and dedicated to the principles which made my country free! I will trust in my God and the United States of America, SIR!"

"Port side shave! Starboard side shower!"

"AYE, SIR!"

All doors had been removed from the toilet stalls. The walls were lined with twenty or so showers, the water running into a common drain. There was no need for privacy. We were recruits and did not "rate" a closed door when we defecated. We were there to learn we were a platoon—not a collection of individuals and learning went on all the time. While we sat on the can, we memorized the knowledge posted next to the toilet paper roll: "*Illegal Conduct*. It is recognized that war is, by its very nature, the darker side of human behavior. The laws of war attempt to eliminate repulsive acts in dealing with combatants as well as noncombatants. Illegal acts: A. To fire on an enemy who has thrown down his weapon. B. To threaten, torture, or treat inhumanely any person you capture. C. Pretending to surrender then shooting at the enemy."

The final portion of each evening was scheduled as personal time called "senior drill instructor time" (SDI time). In the beginning of training, we didn't always "rate" (deserve) SDI time, and so our free time was taken up with fuck-fuck games, such as rifle drill moves with our forty-pound foot lockers, wherein we would hold the locker in the same position you would normally hold an eight-pound rifle, while muscles ached and numb fingers clutched the locker. We did a "port arms" (normally the rifle is held diagonally over the chest, barrel over left shoulder, stock in front of the right hip), and "order arms" (the hand grips the top of the barrel on top of the front sight post, stock rests by boot, thumb on trouser seam), with those lockers again and again until tears were shed and recruits were standing in puddles of sweat. Or we did other "IT" (incentive training punishment exercises on the quarterdeck) until we rated a little time to ourselves. As a result of all this extra "incentive" time my parents never received any letters for the first couple weeks of training, other than the form letters.

> do it faster now
> and no running your nasty mouths
> stop picking at your face
> now now NOW!
> 10, 9, 8, 3, 2, 1, you're done.
> work as a team or I'll kill you!

From the instant after "taps" (lights out and bedtime) two recruits were put on fire watch in each squad bay, until "reveille" (lights on). They would work in one-hour shifts, counting the number of rifles, footlockers, seabags, and recruits in the squad bay. The fire watch also cleaned the head and squadbay and checked the locks on the rifles, seabags, and footlockers. Each recruit's rifle was padlocked to his rack every night. (We were all issued combination locks for our rifles, seabags, and footlockers.) The fire watch was relieved every hour by two fresh recruits.

We all took our turn at fire watch and would pace the dark squad bay, our red-filtered flashlights (red filtered to prevent loss of night vision) sweeping the sleeping forms in the racks, checking that all the weapons were secured and recruits in their bunks, hearing the murmurs and whispers of deep troubled sleep while snatches of the knowledge we'd learned that day floated from murmuring lips.

Fire watch was not, as it may seem, a stupid or pointless exercise in a solid concrete, unburnable barracks. We needed guards to prevent recruits from going UA or from committing suicide. Thoughts of suicide or running away came to some recruits in the first weeks before we were "adjusted" during the time when we did not yet "rate" anything at all, not even the right to draw breath without the DI's express permission. At one point or another every recruit looked over the hazy marsh to the lights beyond and just wanted to get the hell off.

———————————

We were letter-less. I was starting to panic.

"I bet *she's* getting all the letters!" I told Genie after John had been gone about ten days.

"Nonsense! He'll write. He's busy."

"I thought the Marines were into family. Why don't they make him write?"

"He will as soon as he gets a minute."

"Do you think he's written to Erica?"

"How would I know? Anyway if that comforts him. . . . What are you saying? That he can't write to his girlfriend?"

"I wish we were secular Jews," I grumbled.

"What?" exclaimed Genie and laughed.

"If we believed less we'd be happier. I wish I was like Frank Gruber. Can you convert to being a secular Jew? Do you think Frank is tortured by all these doubts and longings? I'm sure he's nicer to his son than I am to mine."

"Frank is a nice man."

"And I'm not?"

"I just mean he's more sensible than you."

"I bet he'd fret plenty if Henry was in the Marines."

"But Frank wouldn't have spent Henry's last summer yelling about some girlfriend."

"I'm not disagreeing. That's my point. Frank is a happy secular Jew! The less you believe the better off you are."

"You know you don't really think that."

"Maybe not but I think it all goes back to being a missionary kid."

"What does?"

"This thing with high expectations, this overanalyzing everything, this idea that everything has to be part of some *mighty plan* to follow God's will for your life or a test or something! You know what?"

"What?

"I'm sick of God!"

"All because John hasn't written?" Genie laughed.

"Well, why the hell hasn't he?"

"Because he's in boot camp! He's getting screamed at by rabid Southerners. Quit whining!"

"I know. I know! Don't you hate the way our generation whines? I hope John doesn't turn out like me! I wish I hadn't yelled at him so much this summer."

"At least it wasn't in a southern accent," said Genie and smiled. Genie kissed me. "Just be nice."

"Okay," I muttered glumly as I went to check if the mail had come yet. None had so I did the next best thing to reading a letter from John, I wrote to him to fill in the silence. Half a conversation was better than nothing. I tried to come up with a cheerful little letter that spoke of everything but the howling emptiness I was feeling.

To Recruit John Schaeffer

August 28, 1999

Dear John,

I went to a movie today up at Cinemagic in Salisbury. Fun movie. My old friend Barry Mendel produced it: "The Sixth Sense." Bruce Willis can be quite good and there is a boy, aprox 10–11 who is great! Won't give away the plot. We'll get the tape when you're home.

Danny Boucher called. Danny was explaining to me that if you wrote at all, besides the first form letters, it would put Mom and me way ahead, since the first weeks are terrible. He said it was a while before he got any letters at all from Asher. I know from what I've read, though I only "know" in theory not know the way you do now, that you're fully occupied! But as Ash said in a letter to his Dad, "John Schaeffer must be in a world of confused shit and pain about now like I was seven weeks ago."

Needless to say we all pray for you non-stop. Jessica keeps e-mailing wanting to know how you are. I tell her that when I hear something I'll fax her a copy. Genie called her parents, gave them your address, so you'll keep getting mail. Speaking of prayer, did you get the little crumb of Andithero I sent down? [Holy bread taken after communion in the Greek Orthodox Church.] It comes with everyone's love at church.

It's hot, muggy here so I can only imagine how it must be there! I never asked but is the place you sleep air conditioned? How is it going? Are you in hell? Is there a glimmer of hope?

Love you lots and miss you big guy. Wanted to sneak into another movie today after watching "Sixth Sense" (I paid for it since Barry will get a few cents of my five bucks I trust!), could have but didn't have the heart without you there. Then again maybe Marines can't do that, so I'll have to reform my ways and become a paying customer!

Much love
Dad

P.S. Enclosed addressed stamped envelopes, when you can write use them, may save you a little time.

6

Blessedly two letters arrived the next day! They were over a week late. (The PI mail tends to be slow.) John had been at boot camp three weeks before we got the first hastily scribbled note. Of course it was old news but still very welcome. It gave me a strange feeling to be so out of sync. By the time the letters arrived, I knew John was much further along in training than the first letters indicated. This fact made him seem even farther away, as if I was hearing his voice calling me from down some long dark tunnel.

Dear Mom + Dad
Only have a few minutes so this has to be brief, it's Thur morning and we woke up at 4. We just came back from chow. Yesterday was exhausting but I got through it. My temporary DI is Sgt. Davis. Anyway it's not so bad here and I'm doing fine. I have to go.
Love John

Dear Mom + Dad
Tomorrow we pick up our real DIs, we met our senior DI (Marshal) today very imposing and impressive. He was on the silent drill team for 3 years. Very prestigious. Anyway I'm scared but I will write and tell you how it went.
Love John

P.S. How's Erica?
P.P.S. Give my love to all.

To Recruit John Schaeffer
August 30, 1999
Dear John,

It was *great* to get your letter, made our day. We understand you don't have much time to write but do when you can. We will keep sending Jessica your letters via fax, so everyone will get your news. We read the letters over the phone to Francis.

Let me know what else we can send, anything you need. We love you a lot and admire you for what you're doing. Hope things are tolerable as you close in on week three big guy.

Love,
Dad

---

today is church day
relative rest for us
recruits
flames shoot out of glass
and communion wafers pass from chaplain to mouths full of "nasty fangs"
prayers that we send to God
with our sweat saying, look at our dead
are we not worthy, because I will be one of these, are we not worthy?

Appeals to a higher power took on a frantic note. At night during "devotional time" (just before lights out), we prayed, either one recruit speaking for all or in small groups. We asked God to protect family, to protect self from injury, to put the DIs in a good mood. We even prayed to God to make time go faster. I heard all these prayers said in fervent tones. We knew that the only way we were ever going to get out of PI was either on a stretcher, in disgrace on the bus home, or walking across the parade deck.

Prayer and church on PI provided a tie to home for some, but for many it was also an opportunity to hedge bets. If graduation could be achieved with the help of some omniscient power, so be it. If you didn't believe in God before you went to boot camp, you sure as hell found Him when you arrived!

The vast majority of us gladly went to church weekly, though we were not forced in any way to go and could have rested in the squadbay. I attended Catholic Mass because it was the closest thing to the Greek Orthodox liturgy I could find. In church we prayed to a deity that many had only just formed a desperate faith in. We prayed for strength not only to graduate, but to just make it through the next day or even hours. We prayed for friends whom we had no way of seeing or checking up on, and our families, whom we only knew existed because we got their letters. We prayed as the smell of our thousand bodies rose to heaven with our prayers, another silent petition, as if our sweat and fear might earn us special privileges with God. (We were clean but after a few weeks the sweat never really washed out of our cammies.)

The recruit chapel was a modern brick and wood structure with a wide open, Protestant-style sanctuary, a high wood-paneled ceiling, and large, square, stained-glass windows running all along the lower walls at eye level. The stained glass appeared weird. It depicted different Marine battles and themes. Allegories of specific combat engagements were mixed with heavenly visions.

It was not until I went to PI that a stained-glass window, featuring a Marine using a flamethrower with the dead and wounded scattered in the background, seemed to mesh with my everyday religious life. Near the "Flamethrower for Jesus" window (as I thought of it) was another stained-glass panel that illustrated the last sentence of the "Marine Hymn": "If the Army and the Navy ever look on Heaven's scenes, they will find the streets are guarded by United States Marines!" Two Marines stood outside the gates of heaven looking out into a crowd of civilians, and members of all the other armed services gathered in front of them waiting to get in.

Church was the one time everyone on the main side of the island—male, female, newly arrived, or just about to graduate—was gathered in one place. A new recruit entering chapel for the first time—bald and scared—saw a sea of drab olive green and brown cammies, sleeves rolled tight and high on each arm. Above the cammies were the tired, taut faces of hundreds of recruits. Sitting in their platoons next to the raw recruits were new Marines. Their confident faces seemed to shine. They had just completed their training and were on their way home.

As a new recruit I glanced nervously at the new Marines with their proud "high and tight" haircuts. (Near graduation, heads are not shaved, and hair is allowed to grow in enough so that the new Marines can have a real haircut for graduation.) These supreme beings had just completed the Crucible (the final fifty-two-hour test before becoming a Marine) the day before and would shortly be leaving the island. They would be moving on to MCT (Marine combat training or ITB, infantry training battalion), then to their MOS (military occupational specialty) schools. Glancing furtively at them, it was almost impossible to imagine how these Marines could have earned the title when each day I was made more and more aware of just how inadequate I was.

Recruits knew so little about what would be happening to them in the next week of training that church became a place to seek advice and information. We new recruits tried to position ourselves near a platoon that was ahead of us in training. "Stay motivated" was the phrase most often spoken to us recruits by the new Marines.

It was usual for any recruit further along in training to tell a junior recruit to "stay motivated," even if they were only separated by a week in training. The fact that you were a few days ahead of another recruit made the recruit junior to you eager to receive whatever wisdom or encouragement you could provide. Any information was welcome! The fact that a recruit had made it even a few days further than you proved that it could be done and gave his or her words weight.

After a few weeks on the island, it was easy for a recruit to tell where another recruit or platoon was in the training cycle. The demeanor of the recruits became different week to week as they progressed through the phases of boot camp. A sense of bearing was slowly being instilled that another recruit could spot. Gang-bangers, mamma's-boys, college drop-outs, homeless derelicts fresh off the street, farm boys, city kids—black, white, brown, and all shades in between—began to look more alike than different. A sense of resignation prevailed. The recruits further along in training seemed to reflect the attitude: "I know whatever comes next is going to suck. Screw it! I might as well do it anyway! I can take it!"

Recruits huddled together and traded information all through church in a running whispered conversation that the DIs called "the recruit underground."

This exchange about what came next in training was interspersed with fervent and heartfelt prayer. The distance from where we were standing to actually earning the title of Marine seemed impossible without the intervention of a higher power.

In church we heard sermons and sang hymns that blended Marine Corps training and the way of salvation. We sang "The Marine's Hymn," "The Battle Hymn of the Republic," and "Amazing Grace" in the same services. We gave thanks for having made it this far and begged God for the strength to take the next step. It all made sense. Religion in boot camp was a reminder of home and whatever faith the recruit was raised with. It also began to make sense parallel to the ideals that were being installed in the recruit in training: honor, courage, commitment, teamwork, the welfare of other Marines before self. At almost every turn on the paths that crisscross PI were memorials to Marines who fell on grenades to save the lives of their fellow Marines or who did other selfless heroic acts. The idea of being faithful and obedient in the little things, for instance, putting on your socks right or keeping your rifle clean, was presented to us as the route to heroic action and obedience to the command to make the ultimate sacrifice.

On Sunday morning after church, if we rated free time, I wrote to my family and to Erica and organized my footlocker. After that there might be a few minutes to talk to other recruits. It was on Sunday mornings that some personal bonds began to form between recruits as we "relaxed" just enough to focus on the faces near us. By the third or fourth Sunday, I started to get to know who everyone was, recognized faces, and began to talk to the recruits around me. These conversations started slowly, a comment here and there, a joke, usually whispered to the recruit next to you. Sometimes conversations begun on Sunday mornings carried over into the week during SDI time in the evenings.

The person to whom I talked most was Reyes. Recruit Reyes was a short Columbian Hispanic from Miami with a wide friendly brown face and intense black eyes and a fairly good command of English, although he did have a heavy accent. The thing that first brought us together and made us realize that we had something in common—besides the suffering and experiences we were sharing—was our unbelievable and inexplicable desire for Burger King BK

Broilers. (Perhaps not inexplicable: we were starving and both losing pounds we did not have to give.)

Reyes and I shared dreams of sinking our teeth into a chicken sandwich and spoke in detail of the taste we anticipated. We vowed that when we got through and graduated we would eat a few together.

To everyone who asked, I said I fully supported John for taking the Marine path. On some days I felt as if the whole thing was a huge mistake, that the distance between the life he'd lived, the books we'd read, the good food we'd eaten, my rather lax discipline at times—the yelling notwithstanding—and the new and tough reality John had entered into might be too great for him to bridge. His idea of a good time was to curl up in the living room in front of the fireplace and reread his favorite bits of *The Hobbit*. How would my tall runner-poet who let the fish he caught go and his teammates win become a Marine? What sort of a person would he be when the Corps was done with him? What did the military life do to men?

I began to think about all the men I'd ever met who had served in the military. Most of them were men that I liked and admired. I was comforted by the pleasant childhood memories that came flooding back related to the men I knew who served. Perhaps, I thought, John will become like them— if he makes it.

I knew the Marines cut over 10 percent of the recruits on Parris Island and that many more failed to pass various tests and were dropped. Perhaps, I thought, as I sat bolt upright in the middle of the night, John is already on a bus home! Perhaps he got off in some ragged southern town and killed himself because of the shame of failure! Maybe he's still on Parris Island but barely coping, so plunged into depression that at the first opportunity he'll kill himself! I was already wondering how I'd explain to the Bouchers, Rodman Miller, my mother, and all those I'd told about John joining the Marines why he'd been cut.

I expressed my fears to Genie. We both worried. On the other hand I tended to worry less about John getting hurt than Genie did. Or rather I felt that physical pain and hardship would "teach him something." What it was meant to "teach" I'm not sure. Maybe to use the pull-up bar I'd built for him at the start of the Last Summer, to clean his room, to argue with me less?

The best I can express what I hoped John would learn on Parris Island was how to succeed where I had failed. The closest I could come to expressing what my failure was, was to admit to myself that I'd always felt apart from others as if I had climbed in windows when others used doors. This sense of not quite belonging, of having taken a weird and individual path in all things, left me feeling ragged and incomplete, unofficial, and outside the "system."

I wanted John to be a complete person, to be as unselfconscious as I was self-aware, to feel as included in his time and place as I felt excluded from mine and, above all, to not wallow in introspection but to be a natural man easy in his own skin. That was what I'd sensed in the men I knew who had served.

My friend John Kohn, the most decent man I ever met in the movie business, was a veteran from World War II as well as a movie producer and screenwriter. I knew him for over ten years before he happened to mention that he had been a gunner on a B-17, and that he flew many missions. He was one of the kindest and most humble men I have ever met and not at all like most successful movie producers. My friend Bill Jadden was the same. He served in the Navy during the war. Bill was a businessman living in Switzerland who was very kind to Genie and I in the early years of our marriage. John was a liberal and a Jew. Bill was a conservative and a Protestant. There was a lovely steadiness and generosity about both men I treasured.

I fondly remembered the soldiers on the U.S. Army base in Frankfurt, Germany, where my mother took me to once a year in the late fifties. We traveled by train to the Army hospital to get my "bad leg" checked by the American Army doctors. (My mother did not trust the Swiss doctors.) Each year I was issued a new leg brace that held my withered limb in a steel grip, two bars running from my knee to my foot attached to a thick clumpy boot *à la* Forest Gump.

For a seven-year-old boy, the trips to Germany were fraught with drama. Germany was the place "we" had fought in, died in, liberated from the Nazis. Most of the war stories I knew were about defeating "the Germans." It was thrilling to take the train through Germany, to hear German, to know that these men, perhaps even the friendly conductor on the train, had so recently been the enemy.

I remember waking up in the middle of the night and peering out of the grimy sleeping car window onto the platform, hearing the hiss of steam and seeing carts piled high with luggage being slowly wheeled past by blue-smocked porters, each wearing a brass number badge on his chest. The only light in the sleeping car compartment was a dim blue bulb that came on automatically when the main lights were switched off. I remember waking thirsty, and my beautiful mother, who was sleeping in the bunk across from me, sitting up and giving me bottled water to drink. She forbade me from drinking from the tap over the small sink in the sleeping compartment, saying, "The water in these German trains isn't safe to drink . . . yet." The word "yet" implied that the war's end was still fresh as the unpatched bullet holes pocking the German stations we passed.

"Mom, did they fight in *this* station?"

"Yes, dear. They fought everywhere in Germany."

"Those are bullet holes, aren't they?"

"Yes dear."

"Was this where our guys were?"

"I don't know dear. Maybe the English fought them here."

"But some of our guys got killed, right?"

"War is a sad, tragic, and sorrowful thing."

"But we won!"

"Yes, dear. But it's still a terrible thing. Now try and get some sleep dear."

"Look! Is that an *American* Army truck?!"

While we were in Frankfurt we were the guests of a friendly Army sergeant from North Carolina named Bill. Bill, like many of the other soldiers, airmen, sailors, and Marines who visited our mission from time to time, had served in World War II. I was also meeting soldiers fresh back from Korea. The "Army guys" told me stories of what they'd seen in Korea and in North Africa and Italy, France, Germany, and the islands in the Pacific. They told their tales in quiet dribs and self-effacing drabs in an unfussy manner.

I was proud to put on the old Army jacket "my sergeant Bill" brought me once when he visited our mission. Years later I still had a few Army trophies, hats and badges and such, to contribute to John's boyhood sand dune war games. I never thought about what it was that made those "Army guys" so attractive to me until I tried to understand John when he decided to become a Marine.

I remember eagerly pumping a veteran from the Korean War for information when I was seven or eight. We were sitting in the kitchen of our chalet, and he was peeling carrots with big, severely scarred hands.

"Mom said you were a prisoner of war."

"That's right."

"She said you got wounded."

"Right."

"What happened?"

"We did our job I guess."

A much more forthcoming witness to war was Mr. Brabey. He was one of my teachers in boarding school who had fought in the First World War. I arrived at Great Walstead, Lindfield, Sussex, years behind the other boys in schoolwork. I was plunged into math, English, history, geography, and Latin classes before I even had a grasp of reading in English. Math in particular was a trial. I was handed over to Brabey for extra tutoring. He was an ancient teacher, living in a damp, closet-size room next to the school kitchen that smelled of mildew and the lifelike models of animals he made from plastic wood.

Brabey had been a stretcher bearer in World War I. He was bald, short, and fat with a kindly face, pudgy triple chin, and a fringe of yellowing white hair around his shining pate. He had a tuft of nose bristles to match his fringe. His face and hands were the color of boiled lobster, a bright reddish-pink that only the perpetually chilly English seem to be afflicted with, along with such cold and damp-related ailments as chilblains. "Old Brabey," as we boys called him, dressed in baggy heather-colored tweeds and smelt of undergarments somewhat past their prime.

I spent many a gray afternoon listening to harrowing tales of life in the muddy, rat-infested trenches. Each lesson in trench warfare ended when Old Brabey would shout furiously that I was distracting him from teaching me math.

"But, sir, I have not tried to distract you, sir."

"A lie is a terrible thing, Schaeffer!"

"Yes, sir."

"It's a hard world, boy, as you shall soon find out and . . . *Schaeffer!*

"Sir?"

"Wipe that grin of your silly FACE! Do you think this is *amusing?* I weep for you boy! I *WEEP!*"

"Yes sir."

After this ritual exchange, Old Brabey would give me an ineffectual "slap" on the side of my head with his large soft hand. The moist, fleshy blow, more a friendly cuff than a slap, hurt no more than being gently bumped with a damp doughnut.

"I shouldn't have *struck* you, boy! Ah, me, my addled brains! A-d-d-l-e-d BRAINS! You make me see red, boy, but you're a good lad at heart."

"Thank you, sir."

"The fact that you're thick as clotted cream is not your fault, lad!"

"Thank you sir."

By way of apology Old Brabey would always offer me a "digestive" (the quintessential English cookie), as if this was the most magnanimous gesture imaginable. I'd sit staring out the high window at the lawn and distant sodden cricket pitch soaking up yet more drizzle, the view made wobbly by the wavy Victorian glass panes, while munching hungrily, visions of men on stretchers, brains blown out mingling with the view of the English countryside.

"He died the worst death there was lad: *gas!*"

"Yes, sir."

"Choked his life away before me, ME a HELPLESS stretcher bearer and not one thing I could do for my *own brother!*"

"Yes, sir. Sorry sir."

"Have *you* ever seen someone die in a gas attack, lad?"

"No, sir."

"Well, I did! My own brother! Clarence, poor Cla . . ."

Old Brabey would start to sniff and dab at his puffy eyes with his inky handkerchief.

"I'm terribly sorry, sir."

A tear would roll down his florid cheek and hang trembling from his yellowing nose whiskers, then splash on my notebook. The pale ink would run.

"They called the next skirmish a 'world war' but it was nothing!"

"Yes, sir."

"*Nothing!*"

"Yes, sir."

"The Great War was the most terrible cataclysm ever to befall our noble race!"

"Yes, sir."

7

few days into the second week of training, we recruits of 1093 were
able to rate enough SDI time to write slightly longer letters. We were
still confused. I referred to myself as "this recruit" in my letters out of
habit. Of course the letters were scrawled and messy, given that the precious
minutes were ticking away as I frantically wrote.

I knew there was no way to actually describe the fear. So I told my parents about what we were doing but not the fact that the main "activity" of boot camp, at least for the first half of training, was just getting through the day, the fact that time had stopped, that there was no end in sight as I stumbled from chow to chow, Sunday to Sunday.

> Dear Mom + Dad + Francis + Jessica,
> Well it's Wed. and I think the last second I had to myself was on Sat.
> I think that's when it was but I can't remember. We got picked up by
> our real DI's and it's been really tough since then. I've been made the
> 4th squad leader and it sucks. I've been on the quarterdeck once and
> the pit once for other people's shit (and that's since yesterday). This
> recruit hopes he gets fired soon so that he doesn't have to do that all
> the time. Sgt Perry the "heavy hat" says, "I'm gonna burst your little
> heart" but SDI SSgt Marshal is slick. I have to go but I have a request,
> SDI SSgt Marshal said we could get Power bars and Gatorade in the
> mail. Could you send me a box of each? Thanx,
>
> > Much Love,
> > Rec. Schaeffer
>
> P.S. I probably won't have much time to write until I get fired.
> P.P.S. Here's a poem.

the DI's don't remove you
the weak will weed themselves out of this life
if you don't belong here you will know

We were on SDI time from the moment we finished our last required exercise and were done for the day. We would be assembled in our crossed-leg position on the floor of the squadbay for mail call. This assembly began by us standing in a big semicircle around our SDI. Two recruits would get footlockers to stack up so that our SDI could sit on them. He would stand in front of us while the recruits arranged his footlocker seat behind him. When he was seated he would command the rest of us to sit.

"READY . . . SEAT!"

On that command all of us would drop to the deck faster than gravity could take a civilian to the ground under any circumstances. We would freeze in whatever position we hit the deck.

"AHHH-DJUST!"

We would briefly unfreeze and adjust our position, then bellow, "RIGHT HAND, RIGHT KNEE, LEFT HAND, LEFT KNEE, BACK STRAIGHT, MOUTH SHUT, AYE SIR!"

During the yelling of our posture-when-sitting-on-the-deck "ditty," we would suit action to words and settle into the "Indian-style" required posture of left over right leg on the cold deck. Then our letters and packages were handed out.

All packages would be opened for inspection, and any items, such as cookies, candy, or printed matter, deemed inappropriate (comics, porn, or any books other than Bibles or other religious texts) would be confiscated. If the SDI took a dislike to any particular item, including some comment that might have been written on the outside of an envelope, by way of a joke at the expense of the Corps, the recruit who had received it would have to "pay" and start to push, run, climb, hop until the SDI told him to stop.

Several recruits had Marines for older brothers who had decided they would help toughen their little brothers by scrawling something like, "Is your DI really a pansy?" or "Real men go Army" on the envelopes of their letters with the predictable result.

Our Senior was a health nut and told us early in training that if somebody were to send us "healthy, nutritious food," say power bars, that he *might* allow us to eat it and that we could also get powdered Gatorade which he would give to the platoon at night, *if* he thought we were worthy of such a high prize and rated his respect. More often than not the power bars we received ended up being eaten by our DIs. (Our SDI gave us the Gatorade when we had it.) All other food was tossed as "nasty civilian trash."

My father's supply of power bars mostly fed the DIs, not me, though I never mentioned this fact in my letters since Dad seemed so pleased to be able to do something for me and, after he got my request, sent down power bars twenty at a time. What the SDI approved (that was not picked off by the other DIs first) was thrown into a general footlocker that contained all power bars and other healthy treats that our families sent. The SDI announced that until we rated these treats we would get none. Later in training, he said we *might* rate.

Since I got a lot of mail, a letter a day from Dad, letters from Mom, Erica, my sister, brother, and friends, soon I had to "pay" with a little extra sweat and pain at every mail call. This payment helped even things out in regard to the recruits who got little or no mail. As in everything else on PI, it was best to just do your job and not get noticed or singled out, even by getting more than the average amount of mail. A few weeks into training, as soon as the SDI called out my name for a letter, I would just start pushing and go on until he was done handing out mail. He would throw whatever letters I got at me while I pushed.

Because earning SDI time became a merit and speed challenge, we, as nasty new recruits not yet adapted to life on the island, did not have much free time. The stress of always being able to measure our failures by how little time we got, if any, really began to tell on some recruits. Since teaching us how to do things quickly and well under stressful circumstances was the DI's main job (not to mention weeding out the "turds," those "unworthy of the title of Marine"), they would invent endless tasks—"fuck-fuck games"—that almost drove us crazy, for instance, the "gear party."

A gear party took place when the DIs ordered us to empty all our gear, Alice packs, seabags, helmets, boots, uniforms, underwear, shoes, foot lockers, sheets, blankets, and mattresses, and to toss it all on a huge pile in the middle of the squadbay. Occasionally the DI sent a couple of recruits to the top of the pile to "reenact the flag raising on Mount Suribachi" made famous by the Iwo Jima memorial.

We spent frantic hours trying to find our gear mixed with the identical gear of eighty other recruits, remake our racks and get "squared away" only to have to rip everything apart again if we'd done it too slowly. Our platoon record was about five hours of gear party, during which we remade our racks and squared away all our gear ten times or so. All the while we were running around dazed, confused, and under a barrage of insults from the DIs. "Any day now! *Any day!* Take your sweet time!" Of course the only way to achieve any order was through teamwork and by trying to keep our heads.

"Combat requires constant and exhausting anticipation of the unexpected!"

"AYE, SIR!"

During our first couple of weeks on the island, there was a suicide attempt in one of the other platoons. A recruit tried to slit his wrists with a shaving razor. It was one of the Gillette Tracers that we were all issued in our first few days on the island so all the cuts were double, twin-bladed shallow slashes. Of course the suicide attempt recruit was "gone" from his platoon right away.

Another recruit went UA and headed out across the wide marsh toward the bay that separated us from the mainland. After hiding in the long reeds all day, he realized that he would be unable to swim the mile or so to shore and crawled back to his platoon. The DIs switched that recruit to another platoon, gave him another chance, and he did, in fact, graduate boot camp with us as a Marine.

At the time, had I thought about it (I didn't), I would have realized how much compassion this demonstrated within a system that allowed for severe punishments, restriction, extra duty, and possible prison time for going UA. The Corps hands out NJPs (non-judicial punishments), for much smaller offenses than going UA. Fines, imprisonment, loss of rank, and so on all add up to a severe result even for a relatively small slip. The fact the DIs gave the UA recruit a second chance showed that if the DIs thought a recruit might eventually be worthy of the title of Marine they were willing to bend the rules to accommodate his mistakes early in training.

Our main fear was the fear of not measuring up. Not measuring up was a real possibility. By the third week of training, seven members of our platoon had been sent home, several others were recycled to the pork chop platoon, and a couple were too injured or sick to continue and were in the hospital or on light duty waiting to be recycled back into training with another platoon. Several other platoons on the island in other companies had recruits who had been NJP'd for offenses ranging from attacking a DI to stealing and were spending time in the brig.

Keeping recruits in line was a full-time job for the DIs and also the various recruits chosen to help lead the platoons. In boot camp a platoon has its own interior command structure: one "guide," the leader of the whole platoon who carries the "guidon" (platoon flag); four "squad leaders," responsible for the four squads compromising a platoon; and three "fire-team leaders" per squad. Thus, accountability (and the ability to keep an eye on everyone) is broken up into very small groups, allowing a platoon to be a more flexible unit and to accomplish more objectives.

I was made the fourth squad leader in the first few days. I think it was because of my height. DIs usually chose the bigger recruits for leadership positions until they figured out whom they really wanted. I didn't last long as a squad leader, about five days. I hated every second of it.

When you are a squad leader, if someone you are in charge of screws up you will get smoked alongside them. It usually goes much worse for you than for the other recruit. The DIs remember your face and how many times you've been punished so the punishment gets a little longer each time. You do not want the DIs to know you too well!

A DI wishing to punish a recruit in the squadbay orders him up to the quarterdeck outside the DI house at the end of the bay. If the recruit has his rifle, he will hold it out at arm's length and either run in place or stand at attention while the DI stands in front of the sweating recruit "encouraging" him. "Is that all you've got? Show me something! I'm gonna pop your heart today!" The rifle weighs approximately eight pounds, but it gets heavy pretty damn quick.

If the recruit does not have his rifle, the DI will often make him go through a series of exercises: push, run, climb, hop. One push-up is followed by two steps running in place then one "mountain climber" (running in a push-up position with your feet coming up to your hands with each "stride") and one "side straddle hop" (jumping jack), all at a very fast pace and repeated endlessly. After about ten minutes these exercises become excruciatingly painful. After twenty minutes they are almost unbearable. After half an hour there is muscle failure. There is no set time limit. Even if you are in excellent shape, the DI will work you long enough to turn you into a quivering mess.

The solo "smoke check" on the quarterdeck is painful; however, it is vastly preferable to the alternative: "fuck-fuck games" for the platoon as a whole. These can range from doing drill (rifle drill movements) with your footlocker to the entire platoon being sent to the pit because of one individual recruit's error. (The pit is a giant sandbox that stands just outside every company's barracks. It takes up a space that is about fifty feet by fifty feet, and the perimeter is lined with telephone poles lying along the ground.)

In boot camp, being a squad leader is a good way to get yourself "smoked" a couple times every day during all of training until muscles are burning, breathing hurts, and you feel as if you're pumping acid through your veins— all because one of the members of your squad has committed some sin that you yourself were barely aware of, such as using the first person when addressing a DI. The entire platoon can see you suffering since smoke-checks are always public though if one platoon member is caught staring, he is more than likely to end up alongside you.

"Is what's happening on the quarterdeck interesting to you, Yates?"

"NO, SIR!"

"Oh, well, if it's so interesting why don't you go on up there and take a LITTLE CLOSER LOOK!"

"AYE SIR!"

If the recruit's crime is considered to be so heinous that something a little more palpable is in order, he is taken to the pit, or "the beach" as it is popularly known among recruits. For instance, this might happen if you or one of the other recruits under you fails to sound off properly or, God forbid, makes his rack a little wrong or shows anything by way of "attitude" that can be construed as a general "lack of motivation" or, worst of all, "lack of discipline." Showing a "lack of discipline" was a good way to get your whole platoon pitted. Getting your platoon punished was the worst thing that could happen to you, other than being dropped back in training.

A recruit who is responsible for the platoon being punished, while not necessarily blamed by the platoon (unless it has happened before for the same offense), will be emotionally crushed for several days afterward. This sense of shame comes from the fact that the platoon has become the recruit's entire life. He has nothing outside of it by which to judge himself.

As training days pass, a recruit's motivation to perform comes not from a desire to succeed as an individual, but from a desire for the good of the whole platoon, the only people who truly understand him and would die for him at any moment. The brotherhood of the platoon is what makes life on PI bearable. Training ceases to be an individual challenge. It must be done as a group, or it becomes meaningless and worthless. This is why being recycled is every recruit's greatest fear. To be dropped back in training, for whatever reason, is the severing of every bond that has kept you from going insane. It is the immersion into a completely new universe that is a total mystery with its own dynamics and life, unknown recruits, unknown DIs, unknown laws.

When the whole platoon is punished for an offense, the pit is usually the chosen instrument of destruction. An entire platoon doing push-ups can just fit in the pit hip-to-hip, sucking up the sharp Cheddar smell of years of sweat and vomit.

If a visitor took a stroll around PI, he'd be sure to see a platoon getting smoked in their company's pit. On some days they would be freezing, on others about to pass out from the heat or being made to fill their pockets with damp, filthy sand to ruin uniforms that they would then have to wear for the next week. They would all be doing punishment exercises—"Push!" "Run!" "Climb!" "Hop!" "FASTER! FASTER!"—to the limit of their endurance and well beyond, until complete muscle failure left them exhausted, facedown, and swarmed with biting sand fleas.

If any recruit were foolish enough to scratch those bites or do anything at all to make himself more comfortable, say try to blow the swarming fleas out of his nose, then the smoking would begin all over again. On PI suffering is not the point: taking the affliction the right way is the point. In combat, utter self-discipline and absolute stillness is required to survive and accomplish the mission.

PRINCIPLES OF INDIVIDUAL MOVEMENT:
We have learned many lessons concerning war fighting from over two

hundred years of experience. The following principles of individual movement are time tested . . .

When not changing positions remain totally motionless . . .

To observe lift your head slowly but steadily and without abrupt movement . . .

Carry only necessities...

Do not disturb birds or animals that could give away your position . . .

"In combat there are no second chances; you twitch and you'll get the whole platoon killed! Pain is good! Push! Run! Climb! Hop! FASTER!"

"YES, SIR!"

At the Bravo Company barracks, the sun beat down on the pit all morning. To be pitted in the morning was to suffer heat exhaustion. The coming of the afternoon shade brought no relief. With the longer shadows came the sand fleas.

Sand fleas swarm when their home is disturbed. Sand fleas get in your eyes and ears and nose and leave little red welts, sometimes blood, on all of your exposed skin. DIs will make a platoon stand in the pit in the evening at the position of attention and suffer the fleas without showing how maddeningly itchy the bites are. Any recruit who twitches or swats a sand flea demonstrates the very "lack of discipline" and "lack of bearing" that the DI has been railing about and watching for with eagle eyes for days, ever since these "nasty recruits," the "worst recruits I've ever seen," were put in his charge.

There are two methods to getting through boot camp. The first is to never volunteer for anything and hope that you don't get noticed or singled out. The second is to try to do everything you can to be noticed with the intent of ending up in a leadership position. I took the first approach: Do your job; get through the day one moment at a time, week-to-week, Sunday-to-Sunday, chow-to-chow. I had no interest in leadership positions in boot camp. Perhaps I lacked the proper spirit, but survival was my main goal. Getting noticed was *not* a good way to survive.

All of us squad leaders and the platoon's guide managed to get ourselves fired on the same day. Our Senior was very unpredictable and tended to make wide, sweeping changes according to whim. He called us all out of formation one morning and screamed "YOU'RE FIRED!" No explanation was given. We were ecstatic. Everything seemed instantly so much better with only our own sins to be punished for.

> stuck in the limelight
> waiting for the end of each day
> hoping only to hit the rack without the pit
> hoping to get fired.
> so much easier with only one responsibility,
> hope for the end of sand fleas and not to spill my sweat into the pit,
> "the beach"

With John gone, bound to me only by the slenderest of all-to-short hasty letters, I would daydream about our times together as if memory and worry could bring John closer to graduation, and back to us. The regrets even over small incidents wherein I felt I'd treated him badly loomed large.

Near the end of the Last Summer, Genie, Francis, John, and I spent ten days staying with friends in the Bahamas. Our dear friends the Maillis family owned a seaside mango farm spread over sixty or so rocky acres next to a glorious white beach. It was our farewell vacation, and, we knew, the last family vacation we'd be likely to take together for a long time.

We swam, ate mangoes standing chest-deep in the limpid water, and snorkeled to our hearts content while watching the fish, the Maillis boys (ages six and up, brown, almost amphibian), and each other floating weightless in the turquoise water. The only sad moment during that pristine vacation occurred while fishing.

At dawn, after an all night fishing trip, we tied up to a giant ocean buoy where the tuna were biting. The big fish liked to gather in the shelter of the buoy's anchor chain that fell hundreds of feet into the deep cobalt-blue ocean trough that lies about thirty miles off Nassau. Moments later the tuna began to hit our lines, and we caught several thirty-pound fish. Then a big tuna grabbed and ran with John's bait. John fought "his" tuna for about twenty minutes as the sun rose over the ocean. The fish made several spectacular runs that set John's reel to singing out the high-pitched whine that signals a hit by a monster.

We all knew the fish was at least sixty pounds or more, judging from the run it made and the way it bent the rod in comparison to the thirty-pound tunas we'd already caught. We floated on the wine-dark sea as John fought his fish and waited as the tuna made run after run. After about half an hour I got impatient and dropped my own line into the water and soon had a bite. We were both fighting powerful fish just as the sun rose and paved a path of fiery red to our boat.

Mine turned out to be a thirty-three pound male dolphin-fish (not Flipper, this was a fish!)—a beautiful bullet-headed golden-blue creature that raced under the boat in a streak of quicksilver lightening. My line snagged John's!

I should never have put another line in the water while John was in his big fight. In fact, the Maillises had quickly pulled their lines out as soon as John had his fish hooked. It was John's line that broke as it sawed across mine. His huge tuna got away! I landed my dolphin, a nice big fish but nothing like the tuna John hooked that had bent his deep sea rod like a toy bow and strained John's powerful arms until I heard his tendons popping.

Once he was on Parris Island, I could barely look at the photograph of John, Francis, and me standing with my damned fish. Predictably John had said he didn't care and he congratulated me.

All vacation John made a point of keeping the other fish he did land, and he went diving with the sons of our friends and shot a few fish out on the reefs with a Hawaiian sling spear. Maybe John had decided that since he was about to become a Marine it was time he killed something. He had always let the "stripers" (striped bass) he caught in our river go.

To Recruit John Schaeffer
August 31, 1999
Dear John,
I have a few questions. I know you have little time so, borrowing Mom's multiple choice format, please finish these sentences.

[*John's answers are in italics.*]

The thing I *like* best about my DIs is *When the PLTN is doing well they relax.*

The thing I *dislike* most about my DIs is *when we do badly and we get to the pit.*

What scares me most is *getting hurt and having to be recycled to another PLTN.*

The recruit I admire most is *Rec Yates, a 20 year old who was here 2 years ago but had to leave with stress fractures 9 days before graduation now he's back and is still trying. As the Marines say, "Never give up!"*

My worst moment so far was *Training Day 1 when I realized I had 64 left to go!*

My best moment so far was *the end of today because its 1 day closer to the end.*

I'm most lonely when *I wake up.*

I'm happiest when *I go to sleep.*

The most punishing thing so far was *3 hours (total) in the pit today with the whole PLTN.*

At meal times I *eat.*

Church is *very strange non-denominational stuff.*

As time goes by I *wait for the end.*

I wonder what I've done by joining when *I get hungry.*

I feel like I've gone to another planet when *I can't refer to myself in the 1st person.*

After almost three weeks I'm *ready for grad.*

The funniest thing I heard/or saw was *the SDI lose his mind and toss a rifle the length of the squad bay (40 yards) sparks came off.*

Looking forward to getting the above. Please fill in and send back.

Love, Dad

John wrote this note on the back of my "questionnaire."

Today was rough, I think the PLTN spent more time in the pit than out. I'll be very strong when I get back but still the day ended so it wasn't all bad.

I can move the rifle in drill pretty well now but I still need to work a lot at it.

Love John

P.S. Envelopes, paper and stamps please.

8

drill or kill
either you drill or I kill you
it was our motto
given to us by DI SSgt Matson
and it served us well
drill or kill
drill or kill
inspection arms or the pit
say your ditties

Up until training day thirty-one, the platoon drilled every day. "Close Order Drill," the ultimate test of drill abilities, is the execution of the simpler drill moves a civilian might see at a parade as drill teams move as one up a parade deck with their rifles while doing "port arms," "present arms," "right shoulder," "left shoulder," and other drill movements.

For the first month and a half of training, drill is basically the life of a platoon. There is nothing recruits hate more or take more pride in. A recruit eats, sleeps, and breathes drill until it is completely automatic and he or she stops even noticing numb bruised hands, arms, and shoulders, the result of standing at attention, hours each day, with your rifle held in the same position and slamming repetitively into the same spots on your body again and again and again.

Drill is pain and fear of making the least error. There is no faster way to get an irate DI in your face screaming his lungs out until his spit mixes with your sweat and begins to run down your face than to make a mistake in drill.

To shame your DI, say while drilling in front of other DIs or to do badly in the Series or Company Drill competitions (wherein each platoon competes with others), is to buy yourself hours of the pit and keep your DIs genuinely angry with you for days, if not weeks.

Drill teaches no specific skill, say how to shoot, but the most basic lesson of all: the reflex to obey each command and the self-discipline to control your body at all times. There is no way to look good in drill if even one person is not doing his job flawlessly. Yet there is no greater individual thrill than hearing the "crack!—crunch!—crack!" of eighty heels striking the deck as one and knowing that your own boot has done its part in producing this sound of perfect harmony, "Marine Thunder."

"Failure to follow simple instructions is going to get somebody killed in the Fleet! Understand?"

"YES, SIR!"

"Pivot! Align to the right! Don't close up! Cover forty inches!"

"YES, SIR!"

"Drive your heels! Lean back and DRIVE YOUR FUCKING HEELS!"

"YES, SIR!"

"If there was a rank lower than recruit that's where you'd be! You are the nastiest gaggle-fuck of sorry-ass civilians ever to set foot on this island! Why?"

"NO EXCUSE, SIR!"

"You must be from West Virginia! Is that why you're all just about retarded?"

"NO, SIR!"

"Sit down!"

"AYE, SIR!"

"ON YOUR FEET!"

"AYE, SIR!"

"You are pissing me off! Close order drill means moving from the WAIST DOWN. You're frigging DITTY-BOPPING! We drop ten percent of recruits!"

"AYE, SIR!"

"You ain't hurt enough yet!"

"AYE, SIR!"

"I wanna hear eighty-three bolts slide at ONCE! I wanna see eighty-three rifles come to port *together!* YOU HAVE ONE MORE CHANCE TO FIX IT!"

"AYE, SIR!"

Drill becomes such a big part of a recruit's life that a recruit will often wake up marking time or doing port arms in the rack. Sometimes he will not wake up and just do drill in his sleep. While on fire watch as I would patrol the squadbay, I'd often see four or five recruits doing drill in their sleep. I woke up several mornings with my arms tired from holding my pillow rigid above me at port arms.

As my parents sent me more and more letters and told me stories about friends and other family members, my old life seemed increasingly distant. It would take me a few minutes to recall who someone mentioned in a letter was and what they were doing at my house with my parents or why we even knew them. The faces were the first things to go. Soon I couldn't remember the names of friends either, and this didn't bother me. If something wasn't affecting me directly, I had a hard time caring about it.

Sun 29th

Dear Mom, Dad, Jessica, Francis, I'm on SDI time here. I got fired as squad leader a couple of days ago (I can't remember what day) but yesterday I was in the pit 3 times (twice with the entire platoon) and on the quarterdeck once. It's called IPT Incentive Physical Training. I'm averaging quite a few push-ups a day and every time you get IPT you're worked to the point of muscle failure, so I'm pretty sore today.

Anyway I've 59 more training days to go (not including Sundays because we don't really train at least not hard on Sun.).

This last week I took classes. It was on using the bayonet. I was using upper body blows (actually we got two of those classes). We also learned about USMC rank and structure.

Actually it's not that bad here. I wouldn't say it's killing me by any means.

I love you all, give my best to everyone at church.

Love John.

P.S. Poem for you.

food, killing, drill
my world has become this

as I drift from "fat and nasty"
to killing machine
outside the chow hall screaming
"READY TO FIGHT, READY TO KILL, READY TO DIE BUT
NEVER WILL!"

To Recruit John Schaeffer
September 1, 1999
Dear John,

Mom and I were so happy to hear from you. We were especially pleased that you said that though PI is tough you're okay. From the sounds of the amount of push-ups you're doing you will be tough as old leather when you get home! Good poem!

Max is coming by this afternoon with Monique. I'm going to ask him how often there is mail-call for you guys, so I get a better idea of when you get our letters & boxes. By the way let me know if you want your Gatorade in powder form or mixed in bottles like I sent down. I'll do whatever works for you. Has the first box arrived? There is more on the way.

Everyone asks about you constantly, from the people at church, to Frank Gruber in LA. Needless to say we pray for you all the time, literally every little while through the day. Mom and I are so very fond of you and proud of you for confronting this challenge.

We love you,
Dad

I began to be unable to identify with many of the ideas and daily privileges that seem as obvious to a civilian as they are foreign to a recruit: the right to a shower when you needed it, food when you wanted it, the right to sleep when you were tired, to think, to ask questions, to scratch an itch, to be addressed politely in the first person and be called by your name and the right to leisure, to a time in the day when you could relax and let down your guard, "be yourself."

As a recruit I found out that being yourself was not good enough. We recruits became aware that certain constitutional rights did not apply to Marines, such as the right to free speech. PI was like living in a Third World country far outside of any democracy. In this new country there were rigid customs we knew nothing about and yet had to obey. None of the rules were explained to us, unless it was an issue of safety. "Issues of safety" included never coming within one arm's distance of a DI. This rule was in place due to the fact that recruits occasionally lost their minds and made the unwise decision to attack a DI. I saw enough recruits get the wind knocked out of them by an elbow to the solar plexus to be very conscious of my surroundings and of keeping my distance from the DIs.

Other mysterious boot camp rules included: When passing a superior ranking officer or noncommissioned officer from behind, you must pass them on the left and say, "By your leave, good morning/afternoon/evening sir (ma'am)!"

Usually we only discovered our mistakes moments after committing the error, when we had a DI screaming in our faces and realized that we had just made a serious error about something that we did not understand moments before.

"WHY THE HELL DIDN'T YOU RENDER THE PROPER GREETING TO THOSE FEMALE DRILL INSTRUCTORS?"

"SIR," panic creeping into the recruit's voice, "THIS RECRUIT DOESN'T KNOW THE PROPER GREETING FOR MORE THAN ONE FEMALE, SIR!"

"WHAT?! ARE YOU STUPID?!"

"NO, SIR!"

"WHAT'S THE PROPER GREETING FOR ONE FEMALE?"

Tentative gulping.

"GOOD AFTERNOON, MA'AM!"

"SO WHAT'S THE GREETING FOR *TWO* FEMALES?"

Hesitation.

"GOOD AFTERNOON, UH, MA'AMS, SIR?"

"NO! YOU'RE ABOUT RETARDED SON!"

Panic.

"GOOD AFTERNOON, UH, WOMENS, SIR?"

"NO-O-O-O! GOOD AFTERNOON *LADIES!* PUSH, PUSH NOW!

NO, DON'T TAKE YOUR BLOUSE OFF! PUSH, UP, DOWN, UP, DOWN, HALFWAY UP, STAY THERE!"

Resignation.

"AYE, SIR!"

Letters from a world in which there was not someone waiting to scream at you for a mistake in keeping a rule that you were unaware of seemed so strange as to be almost unbelievable. Our world—push-ups, screaming, classes, and drill—began to make sense to us. We began to understand our lives when we saw how much better we performed knowing that the consequence for mediocrity was discomfort on a scale that few young American men of our age, at least in our time, have ever had the privilege of experiencing.

> moving further away from luxury
> learning things that begin to make sense to me but not to you
> Dad, Mom.
> tangible correction,
> something much needed when learning the right way to do everything, the right way to walk, talk and especially the right way to greet women

It was rare we made the same mistakes twice. We retained more from our classes than I ever saw any group of civilian students retain. The mixture of fear, chanted ditties, memory keys, tests, shouting answers in unison again and again, and severe punishments for the least failure to get the job done worked. I could have finished high school in a year and gotten into any college in America if the teaching methods at either one of the high schools I attended had been as intense and efficient as Marine boot camp.

In the beginning, our quest to do the job right was mostly due to the fact that there could be no satisfaction in a job that was not done well because the furious DIs would work us until it was done correctly. After a while we began to expect nothing less than perfection from ourselves in every detail of boot camp life, from executing the perfect port arms to addressing all officers correctly and learning how to disassemble, clean, and reassemble our rifles while blindfolded. We consistently passed our knowledge tests.

Doing something well was the only experience of quality that was left to us. To do the job given us as well as possible was the one choice we could make and claim as our own. Our errors, no matter how small, irked us. We began to police ourselves. Soon we were as tough on each other as the DIs were on us. We polished, dusted, swept, and mopped whatever we were assigned to clean until the brass and squadbay walls and floors shone. If our work wasn't good, it was a mark on the reputation of the platoon and an embarrassment to each one of us personally.

The only thing that kept bringing my mind back to civilian memories was food or rather the lack thereof. I could still picture food long after people's faces began to fade from memory, and I dreamed of my parents' cooking. The dreams were so vivid that I could "taste" the food as I slid dream slices of hot egg pizza into my mouth. Egg pizza is a kind of Tuscan pizza with chopped hard-boiled eggs on it, along with capers. It has been my favorite ever since my parents took me to Italy when I was twelve, and we spent a great two weeks in Tuscany. (Dad has always loved Italy since, as a child, he was taken on vacation to Portofino each summer by his parents.) I "tasted" olive oil and sun-ripened tomatoes picked from Dad's garden, my mother's thin, chewy pizza crust. I would wake with the distinct flavor of the meal in my mouth—until I realized that it tasted more like rough linen than anything else and that I had been gnawing on my pillow long enough to soak an entire side in spittle.

Naturally I kept quiet about my "nasty" civilian dreams, except to laugh about them (quietly) with Reyes. Dreaming of food was a reminder that there was still a way to go in purging myself of the last of my old civilian ways.

A civilian had become a different species to us recruits, a "nasty filthy" being who had no concept of hardship and looked only to the next meal and a comfortable bed. Civilians were "fat and nasty" as we began to say, unintentionally mimicking our DIs. Civilians had no idea what it was to suffer hardship like ours or to hold an M16-A2 service rifle and be ready to take someone's life, a person so far away that you could not even see their face.

We knew that we as Marines would be more likely to be put in a lethal situation than most other Americans. We imagined killing.

"Marines have seen action in over forty major engagements and campaigns since 1775, that's combat about every four years. What are the odds that you'll be put in a situation where you have to decide whether it'll be your buddy or the guy who's trying to kill him? Yates?"

"Pretty damn good, SIR!"

"Damn right, so it's essential you are not only prepared to kill but that you become proficient with your weapon, whether it be your rifle or your body, good to go?"

"YES SIR!"

"So it would behoove you to clean your rifle in your spare time and make your body stronger so that when the time comes and it's between your buddy and the enemy you and your weapon are ready, good to go?"

"YES SIR!"

It was typical of John to say in his letter that boot camp was not as bad as he'd thought it was going to be. "Anyway it's not so bad here and I'm doing fine," was exactly what I would have expected him to say whatever was really going on.

"Surviving danger and letting the adults and womenfolk worry is one of life's male pleasures," I said to Genie, as she sat reading in the living room. "Perhaps us men, us boys, need some little corner where we can still do things that make women squeamish."

"Because you're so big and brave?"

"Mock all you want but you know that's probably why I understand all this manly Marine's stuff."

"I'm sure you do," answered Genie with a small sigh.

She was getting used to the fact that John's boot camp experiences and my reading all I could lay my hands on about the Marines had awakened in me some slumbering wanna-be martial beast. I might not have served in any military, and I might clutch my car keys as I raced through dark parking lots, rehearsing what I'd do if I was attacked—and hoping I'd get to the car before I was—but having a son at boot camp had the effect on me of a testosterone shot into the carotid artery.

"I always loved to show my mother my gaping cuts suffered doing yard work or from my adventures in the woods, the worse the better."

"That wasn't very nice."

" 'Nice?' We men aren't about '*nice!*' Was Churchill nice?!"

"He was to his dogs, he was a weepy old boy and easily moved," said Genie, without looking up from her book, "just like you."

"He went to boarding schools just like me! He was a man!"

"He hated every minute and missed his mother horribly and so did you."

"Maybe, but he was made of good stuff!"

"Canings didn't make him that way."

"Never mind all that! The point is little boys are *not* girls! I'd squeeze the most blood I could from whatever the current cut or scrape was before I'd come in and show it to my mom. We men glory in tests of strength!"

"You must have been a very difficult child."

"I remember comparing my welts with the other boys after 'whackings' and assuring them that no tears had been shed."

Genie put her book down and looked resigned.

"We were all lined up outside the headmaster's study door and took our turns being given 'six of the best' with his old and devastatingly pliable size thirteen tennis shoe."

"Silly."

"There! You just *don't* get it!"

"Beating children?"

"As each boy stepped through the dreadful portals—a high mahogany door leading to the head's oak-paneled study, smelling of stale digestive biscuits, mildew and cold tea—"

"The Brits are so grubby."

"No argument there. The boy ahead of him would come skipping out while fastening his trousers with shaking hands and grinning. He would be smiling with glee at our discomfort as he whispered a lurid description of what torments he'd just suffered—"

"So you went to school with little masochists?"

"—a description we hardly needed since we could hear the whistle and thwack! of the springy rubber landing with a fleshy slap and counted off the strokes with sinking hearts."

"I need to go put the bread in the oven."

" 'Old Sparky's in rare form! It's six of the best lads, *trousers down!*' the first boy out the door would tell us gleefully. The rest of us twelve-year-old miscreants would groan and shuffle our feet over the cold black and white marble floor as the line of quaking boys moved up to the door."

"And the point is?"

"The very awfulness of the punishment and surviving it was glory. I *understand* John's pride in surviving boot camp!"

"So you understand it better than the women recruits down there?"

"I didn't say that. Men and boys are different than girls, that's all I'm saying. You don't see the pampered progeny of today's bewildered parents comparing notes on their last so-called time-out! All they do is negotiate with their children. It's pitiful. There should be a bottom line, literally."

"The bread *must* go in."

"There is no glory in surviving psychobabble! There is no joy to be wrung from the constant negotiation that passes for 'discipline' in households and supermarkets, where ineffectual parents try and cajole good behavior from rotten-little-Lord Fuckoff!"

Genie had left for the kitchen. A moment later she popped her head around the door.

"How about a glass of wine?" asked Genie.

"That would be nice," I said meekly.

To Recruit John Schaeffer
September 2, 1999
Dear John,
Molly [Genie's sister] called, is buying, *Making the Corps,* wants to read about what you're up to. She mentioned she wrote to you. You have a lot of people who love you a lot pulling for you. I read Francis your last letter. He was so pleased to hear that you were okay, as was Jessica.

I seem to get up earlier all the time! Today I was writing by three A.M., nuts, huh?

Anyway when I'm up early I watch the clock, think of when you'll be getting up, try and pray you through the start of the day. At about that time I'm standing on the porch deck, looking at the first light in the sky, having my second cup of coffee and thinking of you, proud of you. You're a great son.

Love,
Dad

In rereading the letter I notice how while sincerely rooting for John I was also trying to compete with him, trying to send the message that the old man is still in the game. "I seem to get up earlier all the time! Today I was writing by three A.M., nuts, huh?" Let's hear it for the old man.

9

Our Senior spent Labor Day with us. We spent the morning drilling and marching to our senior's powerful melodic voice calling out cadence. Then we all formed up to march somewhere; as usual, we didn't know where.

We never knew where we were going until we got there. Informing a recruit of the schedule is just not done. It might give a sense of stability or independence if recruits knew what to expect from the day, the hour, the moment. We marched all the way out to a part of the island that we had not been to yet that was reserved for "permanent party," Marines and their families stationed on the island. We stopped in front of a large building.

Because I was standing at attention, I was unable to read the sign that I could barely see in my peripheral vision. A recruit, if he values his life, will never move at attention, let alone swivel his eyes or turn to see something, neither will a Marine, for that matter. Moving at attention is just not done.

We fell out into a line and moved up the steps of the building. Finally I was able to glance around at my surroundings, and I saw that we were at the Parris Island Museum. This was to be our celebration of the national holiday. We were allowed to move through the exhibits at will for about half an hour. The freedom to move and think unsupervised gave me an odd floating sensation that was unpleasantly disorienting. After being so closely watched, yelled at, and directed in every detail of my life since stepping onto the yellow footprints, the idea of having a free half hour made me nervous.

While looking at the exhibits, I felt I was honored to be associated, even as a lowly recruit, with the great military heroes who were remembered there. Medal of Honor winners were listed, their acts recorded, and their pictures displayed. Their bravery made me feel I belonged to something that was truly worth the effort and pain that was required to achieve the title that every one of us wanted: Marine.

Weapons and uniforms of different time periods were on display. There was even a board that showed movie stars such as Gene Hackman and Harvy Keitel who were Marines. (There are no ex-Marines: "Once a Marine, always a Marine.")

Even in that relaxed atmosphere I could feel my body maintaining the rigid posture that had been drilled into it. It was uncomfortable to try and relax and I was unsure of what to do when the direction that I was walking in had not been picked for me. Where should I look? How should I walk? What position should I stand in? Where should I put my hands as I read the Marine Corps bits and pieces of history?

"Every Marine a rifleman. The first Marine officer to receive the Medal of Honor in World War II, Captain Henry T. Elrod, was a pilot, his aircraft no longer flyable, he died leading Marines as infantry on Wake Island."

"Lieutenant Clifton B. Cates, destined to be the Corps' nineteenth commandant, reported during a World War I battle: 'I have only two men left out of my company. I have no one on my left and only a few on my right. I will hold.'"

"Colonel David M. Shoup, who would be the twenty-second commandant of the Corps during the desperate fight on the Pacific atoll of Tarawa reported: 'Casualties many; percent dead not known; we are winning!'"

"Our third president, Thomas Jefferson, designated the Marine Band as the 'President's Own.'"

"Unlike the other services' emblems signifying defense, the Marine emblem, the eagle, globe, and anchor, symbolizes distant service to represent our nation's interests in 'every clime and place.'"

"The historian T. E. Fehrenbach, writing of the Marines in the Korean war, wrote: 'The man who will go where his colors go, without asking, who will fight a phantom foe in jungle and mountain range, without counting, and who will suffer and die in the midst of incredible hardship, without complaint. He has been called United States Marine.'"

"April 9, 1942, there were one hundred and five Marines on the Bataan Death March."

"February 19, 1945, 4th and 5th Marine divisions assaulted Iwo Jima, raised the flag on Mount Suribachi."

"January 20, 1968, North Vietnamese opened battle against the 26th Marines for Khe Sanh."

"A wounded Marine in France, during World War I, was asked by a French nurse if he was an American. 'No ma'am,' he replied, 'I'm a Marine.'"

We were allowed to move at will through the exhibits, spending a little time looking at each item, until the word was quietly passed (we spoke in whispers out of respect for the museum and what it represented) that we needed to form up outside and prepare to go. Then our Senior led us back to the barracks. Later he let us almost take our time in the chow hall, to eat almost enough (but not quite), to actually be full for once.

That night we got to drink Gatorade from the ten-gallon cooler. Our Senior talked to us, told us stories about the silent drill team and how he stabbed himself in the leg with the bayonet at his first drill performance in Tokyo, and continued through the rest of the performance. He told us that when he was the drill master for the Silent Drill Team he would make them practice drill with thirty-five-pound lead pipes, so that when the time came to use the rifle it felt like nothing in their hands and they could snap to perfect port arms every time.

"Always practice harder than you need to and you will look sharp when the time comes and girls will want to fuck you."

Our SDI allowed us to relax in the sense that we did not have to sound off when we talked to him or asked questions that night. It is one of my fondest and strangest memories of boot camp, the day I got to relax.

> the day I relaxed
> never to be forgotten
> a day of honor
> and Gene Hackman
> girls will want to fuck me

The next day the memory of the half hour of freedom evaporated as the shouting began again at 0400. But the moment of respite had given me a chance to take stock. Boot camp was relatively easy as long as you did what you were told when you were told to do it.

Dear Mom + Dad, Francis and Jessica,
The DIs have sort of stopped screaming at me (in the face sense) seeing that I don't really lose my composure under that sort of thing. Thanks Dad!

Things going fine since I got fired, nothing interesting yet but since yesterday was Sunday I'm pretty rested today. By the way I saw the flame-thrower stained-glass window in the chapel it was very impressive.

The only really depressing thing takes place on Fridays. From our squadbay we can see the parade deck where graduations happen and every Thur and Fri. I see families and graduations so those are hard days.

Max's advice works though, just take it a meal at a time.

Love John.

P.S. Poem:

like clockwork the machine rolls on
spitting out Marines week by week,
a fresh batch every Friday
we're rolling closer, I can feel the wheels
molding me into Charlies
extruded through the machine.

Thursdays and Fridays—Family Day and Graduation Day—were the most depressing days of the week for every recruit on Parris Island. We watched the new Marines walking around the island in their "Service Charlies" (green trousers—skirts for the females—and a short sleeve khaki shirt) with their families. We saw them leave after graduation, having captured what we were all after, the title of Marine. They were getting away, and taking everything that we wanted with them.

The only upside was that we got to perform in front of an audience. There was no better feeling for a recruit than to march by a family of civilians and have them watch you with wide eyes while you performed a crisp drill movement right in front of them. There was pleasure in hearing the crack of rifle hand guards against palms to the rhythm of falling heels and knowing that some awestruck civilians would take the memory of that sound away with them.

The DIs liked to take us out on these days when we had someone to impress. We were always at our best on Thursdays and Fridays. The DIs took it a little easier on us on these days too. Their normal practices of almost maniacal fury, screaming two inches from the recruits' faces and pitting recruits mercilessly for hours, would have looked unnecessarily harsh to the parents of the newly graduated Marines. We had a term for not freaking out the civilians. We were told to be careful not to offend "congressional mothers against bullshit."

On Thursdays and Fridays when we were outside the yelling was a little less strident, and the fuck-fuck games grew a little less brutal. We hardly ever went to the pit on those days. Inside the barracks, out of the sight of incensed "congressional mothers," things continued as normal.

"TOO SLOW TULA, get on my quarterdeck, oh and get your rackmate, your squad leader, *AND* your fire team leader up there with you! I'm sure I can motivate one of them to square you away!"

"AYE, SIR!"

"You come here too, guide!"

"AYE, SIR!"

"I'm gonna pop your hearts!"

"AYE, SIR!"

"I'll have you crying like bitches inside of ten minutes!"

"AYE, SIR!"

"PUSH!"

My sense of foreboding was not related to a belief that the Marines would not care for my son. I knew perfectly well that recruits were looked after well, if for no other reason than the public-relations fiasco that ensued when a recruit was killed in training. Nevertheless the deadly ultimate purpose of the training, not just the daily hardships John was enduring, hovered over me. Worst of all, the more time he invested the higher the stakes got.

Out of the blue I would get a sinking lonely feeling, then have to think a moment to remember why it was I felt so uneasy. The view of our beloved marsh and bay, as seen from my office window, would change. The golden russet of the autumn marsh seemed to fade to gray as the harsh reality sunk in: even robust eighteen year olds are frail for all their bluster. The knowledge that John was being stripped down to his bones and rebuilt for the express purpose of being put in harm's way left me with the same uneasy heightened awareness that I'd had years before when trying to work or get to sleep while keeping a wary ear open for the cry, cough, or groan of a sick child. That John could go through all he was enduring and still might fail was a terrible thought. That he could succeed and then be sent to the ends of the earth and be killed was even worse, something too terrible to dwell on. I stuck to worrying about the more bearable challenges of boot camp and the possibility of failure there.

I knew what it was like to try and explain some fiasco, such as why I got stuck making a series of low-budget "exploitation films" when I'd set out to make "art." Still, none of my failures in the movie business cut to the heart of who I wanted to be. I had a fallback position: a good marriage, three children and a few successes along the way in my novels and other writings.

John was trying to earn a title that was nonnegotiable. There would be no second chances or substitutes. I could always write another novel if the one I was working on was rejected. If he failed he would have lost his right to be part of a unique—to him *the* unique—fraternity of warrior brothers. There is only one United States Marine Corps.

As the weeks of boot camp wore toward the month mark, any young tall man I saw with a short haircut got a second look. I missed John! The fact that he was being extruded from boyhood to manhood at an lightning pace— wherein the experiences, hard knocks, and maturing process of ten years was being packed into three months—left me dazed and feeling that I had lost con- trol of my ability to help my child. I found my greatest comfort in his letters. He still sounded like himself. His laconic personality was not yet breached. "The DIs have sort of stopped screaming at me (in the face sense) seeing that I don't really lose my composure under that sort of thing. Thanks Dad!"

I must have read and reread those lines twenty times. I could easily conjure up the image of John standing tall and impassive, eyes focused within as the DIs cir- cled piranhalike, trying to break down my serene boy. I could picture the some- what chagrined DIs once they discovered that they could not "get to" this recruit.

It warmed my heart to hear John's dry chuckle behind the words, "Thanks Dad" to grasp the implied forgiveness of my stupid yelling. It was a sweet gesture.

To Recruit John Schaeffer
September 4, 1999
Dear John,

We got your letter today from last Monday. Thank you. It makes our day to hear from you. Jane Vizzi* was here for the weekend so she heard your letter, wherein you mentioned that the DIs were yelling at you less because they can't upset you as I helped you prepare ("Thanks Dad!") for their tender ministrations to you! We all enjoyed the comment.

Jane is preparing for boot camp by running three miles a day, lifting, going to a rifle range and learning to shoot *and* taking kick-boxing lessons! She wants to be iron woman [a title given to the strongest female Marine in each female training platoon] and at twenty-six wants to give the younger girls "a run for their money." I told her she'd be the only recruit put on the bus home for being weirdly *over prepared!*

Well you're into your fourth week! Good for you. We think of you all the time. I understand how the Fridays when families are around must be tough. We miss you too.

Francis was up here helping Mom with the computer today when your letter came so we read it out loud and talked about you, all good, and got a laugh out of you saying my yelling at you had been good prep for Parris Island.

I hope all the mail is getting to you. You should be receiving a letter a day. Has the mail been coming through okay?

Lots of love,
Dad

---

*Jane Vizzi was a family friend of ours who had decided to join the Marines. Jane was an interesting case. She had been accepted into a philosophy Ph.D. program and had been working as a personnel director for a firm in New York. Jane wanted a "change" and a "challenge" and, inspired by John, though he was nineteen and she was twenty-six, had just signed up! We called Jane "the Bionic Nun" because she'd spent a year in the desert at the Greek Orthodox monastery of St. Katherine's, where she had converted to the Greek Orthodox Church. Genie and I met her after she happened to be at a lecture I was giving on Orthodoxy.

10

get a letter
watch to see what they do, looking at these pages
from so far away
holding them like they might get taken in the wind
if the breathing gets too hard
some get angry, some just cry
a few just read, like it was fiction.

Mail affected each recruit in different ways. For some, letters made us homesick. I saw many recruits slip off line, at one time or another, and behind a rack to cry after reading a letter or getting a few pictures of younger brothers or sisters. For all who received letters, they were a motivation to continue with training, to get back to the world, not to be civilians again, just to exist in a place other than the Island. Some recruits did not want mail, or felt threatened by it, wanting to cut all ties they had before they joined.

For me, mail was a mixed bag. My father wrote me every day, my mother and Erica wrote often. My father's letters made me feel somewhat homesick but also helped me to keep my chin up by making me realize that life off PI did exist even if memories of it no longer made sense.

Erica's letters began to annoy me as training wore on. She had started college and wrote me letters that seemed to be filled with typical teenage problems, like "Should I change my hair?" "Do you think people will like me?" "Do you think I'll find a roommate who will give me my personal space and like the CDs I want to play?"

I stayed in touch with her, but I felt more and more estranged with each letter received and sent. I did not want to spend time thinking about problems that were so small. In my letters to her I found myself repeating empty phrases that had completely lost conviction. Our short life as a "couple" seemed to get less meaningful by the day to me, a recruit sitting on his footlocker in the squadbay of 1st BN Bravo Co PLTN 1093, savoring a few minutes of hard-earned and precious SDI time. Ercia's many complaints about friends and their not "being nice" to her, or not "nice enough," became more and more vexing.

I was getting a chance to compare my feelings for Erica to the feelings the other recruits expressed for their girlfriends. Some of the other recruits had serious girlfriends, and a few of them were even engaged. Some of these loves fell away over the course of boot camp due to the distance or because of feelings of estrangement, like the ones I was experiencing. When I realized how some of the other recruits felt about their girlfriends, how they were prepared to spend the rest of their lives with this or that one woman, I was shocked to compare the feelings they spoke of to mine for Erica and to realize how I had just been playing around in comparison.

I was beginning to find my place. I had been searching for it, and this search led me to Parris Island. Erica seemed farther and farther away from everything Parris Island represented—a place where things truly mattered and where the intangibles could be seen and felt. Loyalty and friendship were earned and taught and rested on the respect of a common goal.

From the beginning Erica had opposed my joining the Marine Corps. In the end when it came down to it, I knew I would choose the Corps.

Our SDI talked about girlfriends from time to time.

"Susie Rottencrotch is NOT more important than the Corps! If you want her to stay with you through all the shit that the Corps is going to give you, then you have to involve her in the life of the Corps! She has to feel like she is part of it or your marriage will not last, good to go?"

"YES SIR!"

This is not to say that the Corps became the most important thing in my life. There were some things that I would choose over the Corps. I would not give up my family for the Corps.

I saw in Erica's letters everything that I had hated about myself: being too lazy to accomplish anything beyond waiting for last minute panic to kick in, hoping that a basic ability to bullshit would let me slide through. I remembered

Erica's parents and all the other old hippies (now wealthy fat, "nasty civilian" business people, many of whom still smoked weed and generally fucked around like their kids) and the rest of the "sixties generation" that filled trendy Newburyport and the rest of the North Shore with children tired as old men before they were fifteen. I did not want to be reminded that I might have been on my way to becoming one of them.

Dear Family,
Tomorrow is Saturday. It's 2 weeks from my birthday and life's getting kind of monotonous. A lot of times I can't tell what part of the day it is. This morning when I woke up and we got outside it was still dark. I thought it was nighttime. There are no clocks here, *anywhere*. And I had to figure out the date on my fingers.

I'm not really having any problems though, just boredom and wanting to take a break, but I'll get one on Sunday, after tomorrow.

Love John.

P.S. Give my love to everyone at church.
P.P.S. More power bars arrived, Thank You!

[Multiple choice questions Genie sent to John as a way to find out a few things he wasn't telling us. John's responses are in Italics.]

How often do you get mail? *Every day (except Sundays).*

Can you sleep? *Yes, like a log. I'd wander the earth but the DIs are watching.*

How do you feel about your cammies and boots? *I need a cigar to complete the outfit!*

How many in your platoon? *83 (actually 81, 2 more just dropped).*

What are the other guys like? *Some dumb, some nice.*

What's one good thing that has happened to you so far? *Chow time.*

What's one bad thing? *Skipping breakfast as a punishment (for the whole PLTN).*

Have you started pugil* sticks yet? *Yes (I kicked ass).*

The DIs led from the front and were with us every step of the way. We never did anything that they did not do with us. We marched to the deep, gravel-voiced baritone of our SDI as he called out cadence for us. On our humps he was with us step for step.

A "hump" is a march at a quick pace and may go for many miles. The guide carries the platoon colors, the "guideon" ahead or next to the platoon. The DI marches next to the platoon and calls cadence. The equipment is heavy and feet are soon sore. At each road crossing the recruits assigned to "road guard" duty stop the traffic, if any, and wait until the platoon has safely crossed before rejoining it. Cadence carries the tired body forward through the pine forests of the Island or through a moonless night, as the DI shouts-sings a line and is answered by a thunderous sung-shouted response from the platoon.

(DI) Everywhere we go-HO!
(Platoon) Everywhere we go-HO!
People wanna know-HO!
People wanna know-HO!
Who we a-ARE!
Who we a-ARE!
So we tell them
So we tell them
United States Marine Corps!
United States Marine Corps!
One! Two! Three! FOUR!
One! Two! Three! FOUR!
United States Marine CORPS!
United States Marine CORPS!

---

*Pugil sticks are a combat training method wherein the recruits fight each other with six-foot padded clubs meant to simulate bayonet fighting.

If I wanted to be—
If I wanted to be—
a doggy
a doggy
Then I would have joined—
Then I would have joined—
the Army
the Army
If I wanted to be—
If I wanted to be—
a fly-boy
a fly-boy
Then I would have joined—
Then I would have joined—
the Air Force
the Air Force
If I wanted to be—
If I wanted to be—
a Swabee
a Swabee
Well I would have joined—
Well I would have joined—
the Navy
the Navy
But I wanted a job—
But I wanted a job—
that makes you lean and mean
that makes you lean and mean
Live in the woods—
Live in the woods—
carry an M-16
carry an M-16
Eat hotdogs—
Eat hotdogs—
pork-n-beans

pork-n-beans
The Marine Corps
The Marine Corps
has all of these things
has all of these things
I said I wanted a job—
I said I wanted a job—
that gives you pride and joy
that gives you pride and joy
Now, the Marine Corps—
Now, the Marine Corps—
has all of this
has all of this
Now the moral of—
Now the moral of—
the story is
the story is
That when it comes to—
That when it comes to—
the armed forces
the armed forces
THE MARINE CORPS HAS GOT THEM ALL BEAT!

Equipment: pack, rifle, canteen bedroll, sleeping bag, and all the rest is strapped on, all thirty to forty pounds of it. (This was not bad compared to the amount of weight units carry in the fleet; however, it was still challenging to us.) The battle to be fought and won is the battle against dehydration, cramp, and fatigue.

"Drink water! All of your canteen, NOW!"

"YES, SIR!"

"Hold it over your head, open! There better not be a drop left!"

"YES, SIR!"

"Forty inches back to chest! Oh, don't want to stay close? AT&T NOW reach out and touch someone! Grab the recruit's pack in front of you!"

"AYE, SIR!"

"You call that alignment? AT&T NOW!"

"AYE, SIR!"

Those who fell out on a march were treated to the "silver bullet," the six-inch-long thermometer designed to be shoved up your rectum to measure core temperature and thereby let the Navy medic assigned to Marine units ("the corpsman") know if the recruit was dangerously over-heated and dehydrated or just tired or lazy. Woe betide the recruit that "took a knee," in other words collapsed and dropped out, if the DI deemed he was fit to march! Woe betide the other recruits that let him fall out, even in the dark of a night march through the woods, if they did not report to the DI and halt the platoon!

"We NEVER leave a man behind! You are responsible for the recruit marching next to you!"

A recruit who fell out during a hump and was unaccounted for was a pos-sible career-ending blow for the DI leading the march. If a recruit suffered heat stroke, he could fall out and die if nobody saw him and he was not accounted for. To come back to the squadbay with someone unaccounted for was a serious offense for all concerned, starting with the DIs, followed by the platoon's guide, the squad leaders, the man marching behind the recruit who fell out, and every man who might have passed him by.

Dear Family,

I got 2 letters from you tonight, aren't I excited, anyway as I said time doesn't really happen here. 1) request though or maybe more paper, envelopes and stamps, I need them. I'm running out fast. 2) Powdered Gatorade, power bars and granola bars. 3) For my *birthday* (This is important to me) Get Erica's school address and send her flowers with a message that says, "I'll be there soon." Anyway that's about it. Oh, I found out that I should be coming home with about $2,500 in pay. *Very* exciting.

  I LOVE you all, I have to go.

Love John

There were no watches allowed on PI. Only the fire watch had a clock, and they gave it back to the DIs after their duty ended. The only way any recruit could recall the time was to stop and try to remember which meal we had last eaten.

"Hey! Did we eat chow yet?"

"Nah man, it's still morning."

"Thanks."

When rendering the proper greeting to a DI we would often get in trouble because we could not remember whether it was morning, afternoon, or evening. The statement "GOOD MORNING SIR!" was often met with "MORNING? WHAT THE *HELL* TIME ZONE ARE YOU IN RECRUIT?" After hearing this we would desperately try different times until we got it right.

> writing letters to a place I can't see
> anymore,
> words of common sense dripping
> while I eat peanut butter flavored
> power bars and my ass gets cold
> on hard concrete

After mail call, on the rare occasions when our Senior was pleased with us, the footlocker now full of power bars (the ones the DIs hadn't eaten) would be brought out and one power bar each given to the recruits. We would eat, almost at our leisure, sitting left foot over right on the cold concrete barracks floor, savoring the clammy texture and artificial flavor of the vitamin-laden protein as if it was manna from heaven while our Senior sat in a chair towering over us, instructing us in the ways of life.

"When you get outta here you're going to want to buy all sorts of useless crap and get married to little Suzie Rottencrotch. Hold off. Wait until you make a little rank before you start doing all that sort of shit so you can afford it. And you're all too young to be getting married anyway. Besides, comin' out of here you're going to see just how many women are out there who want to nail you. There's sex to be had everywhere for the taking. Just make sure you know how old she is before you bang her, cause you can't nail sixteen year olds anymore. In the Corps you'll go to jail for that sort of thing, and fer chrissakes don't get any of 'em pregnant!"

The wisdom the Senior shared with us after mail call made for a weird mix with the news from home. I knew that my family existed and knew they loved me and were thinking about me, yet they seemed distant, cut off by the men training us, the fatigue and hunger. I knew what was happening at home and, if I concentrated very hard, I remembered ordinary life, sitting on the screened porch watching the sailboats on the bay, listening to Dad tell funny stories about producers who owed him money. I knew my brother Francis was on an annual school camping trip with his students in the forests of New Hampshire next to a lake. He'd written me a letter and told me he would soon be going. I could remember that annual school trip. I couldn't see myself with the Waring students and teachers anymore. Having "meaningful heartfelt discussions" about how wonderful it was to "express our emotions" through conversation "as a group" seemed so far removed from my life that I could only recall it as if I was remembering some movie.

"You got any family?"

"Yah, younger sister, hope I get outta here for her birthday. Long as I don't get hurt I should be all set."

"Yup, getting hurt and recycled that's the only thing that really scares me anymore, 'cept for the gas chamber."

"I'm not too nervous 'bout that, all I can think of right now is chow."

"Yup."

Dear Mom + Dad + Jessica and Francis,

Thanx! for the power bars and Gatorade, one thing though, the Gatorade has to be powdered. I was thinking today and never realized before how much of a nice thing sitting down was, or lounging or having nothing to do and a lot of time to do it in.

Jessica, tell Benjamin [her son and my nephew] to start working on his pull-ups. Give all my love to Dani [my sister's husband] and Amanda [her daughter and my niece].

Francis, could you do 2 things for me. 1st say hi to the school for me. 2nd, promise me a Chinese dinner, seeing as I've lost 5 pounds since I arrived.

Mom, are you taking your design courses again or are you too busy? Just think if Dad pisses you off, I've got that x 4 (seeing as I've got 4 DIs!)

Dad, all the best on your writing. No one has more faith in you than I do.

All my love, Your Son + Brother
Rec. Schaeffer

Worrying about family is one of the things that a recruit does constantly. Relatives die, brothers and sisters are born, and fathers and mothers get in financial trouble. Sometimes news from home was not good. Families would often keep problems from a recruit because they did not want him to be under undue stress, and the recruit knew it. Many recruits did not get mail, and being utterly cut off in a place with no sense of time, with no visits or calls, meant that there was no beginning, middle, or end to any day.

Our worst fears grew. A lot of recruits had plenty to worry about; many came from very poor families, many had been raised by single mothers. Even when there was no reason to worry, our harsh existence seeped into our thinking and fed paranoid fantasies of disaster at home.

nagging doubts of death in the family
motivate us to stay healthy
not let the DI's see how sick we get
or tell them how the injuries are only getting worse

Some recruits found out that their families were losing money, even their homes. Fathers lost jobs. It ate at us to be in a place where we were so helpless. Worries about home, that invisible mystical place, became another motivation to stay well, to keep from getting injured and to hold on, to graduate with the platoon at all costs. To try and get off of PI sooner rather than later became our paramount concern. Somehow we got the idea that there was no way our families could be functioning properly in our absence. Relatives and loved ones must be dying in rapid succession simply because we were not there to save them!

Our SDI knew what we were thinking, having gone through PI some sixteen years before. He informed us in no uncertain terms that: "If something fucked up is going on back home, your families can get in touch with the Red Cross and they'd get in touch with you. I don't want any of you crying like bitches 'cause you had a bad dream about Suzie or your nasty families gettin' creamed by a bus! Good to go?"

"YES SIR!"

"So stop thinking about it!"

"AYE SIR!"

Dear Family,

Well we are almost one sixth of the way done. It was a pretty long day, we had classes almost all day and we didn't pit once! A new platoon record! I haven't been quarter-decked or pitted for my own behavior in almost a week.

Time is passing and I find that one of the things I miss most is food. A good portion of my day is spent thinking of "meals I have eaten." Pizza, Chinese, turkey, BK Broilers, these things dominate my dreams. Anyway I gotta go.

All my love, John.

Poem:

food, pain
none of this will break me
you have shown this to me,
demonstrated it once and for all.
"fat bodies" will lose the pounds
and we will go hungry and sore
but neither this nor anything else
will crack our dazed veneer.

I believe that a recruit is intentionally fed too little as part of the mind games the Marine Corps plays to build mental toughness. I lost five pounds of muscle in the first two weeks of boot camp and ten more soon after. Tall and thin with no fat to give, I was shedding muscle, not fat, and got weaker, could do less pull-ups than before PI. I could not imagine what the "fat bodies" or "diet trays" (overweight recruits), as we came to know them, were feeling. Their rations were cut exactly in half!

A fat body had to spray paint two horizontal stripes on his skivvie shirts (undershirts) so that he could be easily identified during PT and in the squad bay. He also had to be weighed once a week to make sure that he was losing weight. On Sunday a DI would emerge from the SDI house (the DI's office) and rumble: "Where are my diet trays? C'mere, fat bodies!"

"HERE SIR!"

"Go get my scales from the big gear locker and get on the quarterdeck and weigh in! Scribe, write'm down."

"AYE SIR!"

After they were finished being weighed, the scale would be put away and the scribe would bring the list to the DI. Invariably there was always one recruit who had not lost enough weight. The DI would come into the squad bay and scream at him.

"WHAT THE HELL IS THIS HAPPY HORSESHIT, YOU ONLY LOST *TWO POUNDS* LAST WEEK, YOU BEEN EATING A DIET TRAY?"

"YES SIR!"

"THEN THE ONLY REASON THAT I CAN THINK OF IS THAT YOU'RE NOT GETTING ENOUGH PT! IS THAT IT?"

"NO SIR!"

"YOU KNOW WHAT'S GONNA HAPPEN TO YOU WHEN WE GET OUT ON THE RANGE, YOUR FINAL WEIGH-IN BEFORE THE PFT AND WHEN YOU'RE OVERWEIGHT YOU'RE GONNA GET RECYCLED AND GO TO PCP AND WHILE THE REST OF THIS PLATOON IS MARCHING ACROSS THE PARADE DECK AS MARINES YOUR JIGGLY ASS WILL STILL BE EATING A FUCKING DIET TRAY, *IS THAT WHAT'S GONNA HAPPEN?*"

"NO SIR!"

"THEN YOU BETTER GET SOME MOTIVATION IN THAT WEAK BODY OF YOURS! YOU LOOK LIKE TEN POUNDS OF SHIT IN A FIVE-POUND BAG! YOU BETTER BE DOING EXTRA PT EVERY FUCKING CHANCE YOU GET! I'M GONNA WEIGH YOU AGAIN IN TWO DAYS! IF YOU HAVEN'T LOST THREE POUNDS BY THEN YOU'RE GONNA BE MY SPECIAL LITTLE FRIEND AND WE'RE GONNA VISIT EVERY SINGLE PIT ON THE ISLAND TOGETHER UNTIL YOU LOSE EVERY SINGLE POUND THAT YOU NEED TO! I WILL THRASH YOUR LITTLE HEART UNTIL IT *POPS!*"

"AYE SIR!"

No fat body in my platoon ever failed to lose the weight he needed to. The thought of being run around the whole island alone with a DI on his tail was pure motivation! Weight dropped fast off the diet trays until the only indication of fat that remained were the flaps of skin hanging from muscle and bone.

I had dreams of food almost every night in the rack. I had daydreams of food during our hours of standing at attention in the squadbay, awaiting instructions, while a DI would walk around and wait for someone to move so he could smoke them on the quarterdeck.

The SDI was the only person who was allowed to discipline the platoon as a whole, but if a DI was upset, he would take us, ten at a time, to the quarterdeck until he had gone through the whole platoon and then he would start over. While we cleaned our rifles, he would move through the platoon and take the first ten. They would lay down their rifles and go up on the quarterdeck to be smoked. When the DI was finished with the first ten, they would come back and continue their cleaning (hands shaking with fatigue) while the next ten would repeat the process. This could go on for hours until we were all so tired that we could only do about ten of everything, push-ups, sit-ups, and climbing exercises before we were completely exhausted and ready to collapse.

Being smoked to exhaustion became routine. After a while we no longer cared. We avoided the quarterdeck or the pit if we could. However, when it came our way we did not mind. We knew that each of us would hurt the same. We knew we could survive anything the DIs handed out.

The burden of shared punishment and pain no longer irked us. We even joked about it. We knew that DIs could not break us. That was the point; our punishments and pain proved to us that we could not be broken. In the end we became unconcerned about punishments and just waited for it to be over once it started.

To Recruit John Schaeffer
September 7, 1999
Dear John,
When we get your letters everything stops. It's the best moment of any given day. After the Labor Day Holiday (I'm sure you guys took the day off, right?!) your letters came in, in a nice batch of 4. Jane was

still here and Mom, Jane, and I read and reread them. Then we faxed them all to Jessica.

We were very pleased that you'll have some good pay to come home with. That sounds great. With some money in the bank you'll have ready cash for what you'll need when you start your next phase of training, great!

I'm sorry you miss food, well glad from the point of view of a cook whose cooking is missed, but sorry for you. We, I, will cook you all of any and everything you want as soon as you come home! Francis is at the Waring camp now but when he's back he'll read your letters and I'm sure he'll be glad to make you out an IOU for all the Chinese food you want!

Today we picked the peaches and lots of the plums. We have too much of everything and are drowning in fruit. We'll be taking it out to friends and church and such.

Things on the writing front are as usual. I'm waiting for notes on the script and in the meantime reworking my new novel *again* (like Bilbo longing for home, "not for the last time!"). So we'll see. Keep praying something works out since I'd like to get some sort of deal squared away sooner than later.

We are all proud of you. Sounds like you did well with the pugil sticks. What else are you up to? You are prayed for round the clock. You are loved and missed.

Much love, Dad

11

eat drink sleep perform
not for yourself,
for the platoon
the only thing that matters
anymore.

On the island it was almost impossible for me to remember the bad things about home. I could not imagine my family in any but the best light. There could be no place worse than the island excepting hell, prison, or combat. Home was so sweet in memory. Conflicts with my father faded and were replaced by the ideal home that I wanted, a refuge without fights or tension. I recalled a reality at odds with having to become the catalyst of calm in order help my father relax or to let him wear out his emotions on me, exhaust himself shouting instead of stalking around the house, a bomb waiting to explode.

Families took on a mystical importance in the life of the recruit. The taken-for-granted people who were sometimes ignored became demigods to us recruits. I remembered the reading out loud at night, walks during the day, the small pleasures of a soccer ball kicked back and forth across the grass, the family trips to New York to see plays (we'd get up early and drive for four hours to a matinee then drive back all in one day), the many visits to the Metropolitan Museum of Art, Gardner and the Museum of Fine Arts in Boston, the way Dad would choke up at passages that moved him when he read out loud, my mother and her love, the way Dad loved her, would yell at her then apologize so profusely it made everyone laugh or the way he'd rant and rave about the way the Orthodox and Byzantines had gotten a raw deal from the

West. These things faded into nothing and became utterly unimportant. Chow to chow, one Sunday at a time. . . .

> discipline is the word for these days
> ignore the sand flea that just flew into your ear
> biting and licking the blood
> that should be feeding weakened muscle
> how do I
> express discipline
> to people who have never seen it?

Writing in detail to my parents was not what I had been doing thus far in my training. My letters merely filled in the smallest peripheral details of my life. There was no way to encompass any of what I had been feeling. I could only express the change in physical terms: "I've lost weight," "We got pitted again. . . ." I could find no words to describe the change that allowed a naturally active, fidgety person such as myself to stand at attention for three hours, not turning my head to the right or left by so much as a millimeter.

There were whole days where perhaps three words passed my lips that were not screamed in response to a DI's question. It was natural that when it came to writing letters, we recruits would not exactly be verbose, especially in ways that concerned our feelings, seeing as these no longer mattered. It no longer came naturally to begin any sentence with the word "I." All that mattered was group performance and accomplishment.

The change that was being wrought in us by our DIs was more mental than physical. Our minds were becoming tougher as we were slowly starved and exercised to exhaustion. A few became physically stronger, some stayed at the same level, many of us became weaker. Over the course of boot camp I lost fifteen pounds and five pull-ups. Yet more was expected of us every day, not only climbing ropes and charging over obstacle courses, but also in the area of personal discipline, often measured by what we would *not* do: itch, cough, move our eyes.

The consistent lesson was not the activity itself but the ability to cope with whatever was thrown at you next: hand-to-hand combat training; the art of gouging; stomping the life out of the enemy; "take-downs" taught by close combat instructors; drill and more drill; bayonet drill; the screaming of "KILL! KILL1 KILL!" while we impaled life-sized rubber dummies; the blows given and taken in many pugil stick bouts, one-on-one and in two-on-one combat; the confidence course; the fear of climbing over a forty-foot obstacle—all this was a far greater mental than physical strain. My mind could now push long after my weakened body gave up.

Dear Family,
It's Sunday morning. I'm waiting to go to the Catholic service (closest thing to Orthodox I could find). Today we got about fifteen minutes for breakfast, quite a luxury. I hate the breakfasts here, they serve scrambled eggs *every* day, there hasn't been a day since I got here that I haven't had scrambled eggs, oh well only 2 more months to go.

I don't know if I already asked this but could you send Erica flowers on my birthday? That would be a very nice present to me.

Love,
John

Dear Family,
Life continues, things are moving a little faster now, but more is expected of us every day. I now officially *hate drill*. It sucks.

We stood at attention for 5 hours (no joke) on the parade deck yesterday doing drill with the rifle, but on the plus side there's no more drill after Training Day (TD) 31. (Yay!) So there's 17 days of drill to go after tomorrow. Well I have to go.

All the best,
John
P.S. I have 2 more stamps and envelopes I need more, please.

To Recruit John Schaeffer
September 12, 1999
Dear John,
It's 2:15 A.M. Sunday morning. I woke up in the middle of a bad dream where I was, as Benjamin [my four-year-old grandson] would

say, "fighting the bad man." Since it's a little early for coffee by about a half-hour or so I wanted to write to you rather than just kick into the coffee-writing routine.

Yesterday afternoon we got your letter, the one where you mentioned standing at attention for five hours. Nuts, huh?

For me this is a time of waiting then waiting some more. My screenwriting agents in LA seem to function on the principle that you give a little encouragement, just enough to raise hopes, then slip into silence for long stretches to let hope fade. I'm in one of the silent stretches right now. So each day is a little battle to keep getting up and writing as if it all mattered even when I hear nothing. However the work itself is what counts since that is something I *can* do something about. One thing is great, knowing you are doing well. Mom and I are so proud of you, big bright spot in my heart.

Yesterday we drove up to Ogunquit ME, just north of Kittery Point and our beloved "Gray Beach." We went to the Ogunquit Museum of American Art to see a show of Steve Hawley's work. By coincidence Steve and Barbara were there along with Vincent and Angelina and Steve's mom and dad. It was lovely to see a big painting of Genie looking eternally beautiful. Everyone asked about you. Steve's dad, an Army colonel in WWII was pleased you're in the military, said, "That's a good beginning," to life I guess he meant. In any case Barbara said she prays for you every morning and they all send you their love.

Well big guy, wish I could see you or at least get this letter to you today but it will have to wait for the Monday post run. I love you lots, pray for you all the time and am so proud of what you are doing.

Love,
Dad

---

your families are too far
to see what you are becoming
there is no point of reference
on either side

except maybe those lights on the water
to make you think of real food
and what it would be like to be
in a place where choices can be made.

Each squad was assigned an area of the "house" to clean. Every morning
when we cleaned the barracks, we could briefly gaze from an open area at
the back of the squadbay across the bay that separated us from the mainland.
We saw lights reflected on dark water in the gloom. We dreamed about what
the people did who lived behind the lights and envied them for the choices
they were allowed to make.

Hushed conversation:

"Those lucky assholes, they don't have to be awake for another three
hours at least."

"Yeah, and I bet they haven't been eating the same breakfast every day for
the last month either."

"Hey, if we'd joined the Air Force we'd be graduating their boot camp
next week!"

"Yeah, and we'd all get to be raging pussies too."

Detail became more important to us every day. For my cleanup chore I
adopted a brass drain grate that was next to a low concrete balcony overlooking the marsh and open water. My drain was about eight inches in diam-
eter. Every day for three months I made "my" drain grate shine. It became
the one tangible thing that I could control in my life. As I knelt to polish the
drain I could glance over the river as the sky began to lighten. The view of
water, reeds, and the occasional great blue heron flying across the sky
reminded me of home.

Dear Family,

I've lost 11 pounds as of 2 days ago. Yesterday the platoon screwed
up pretty badly in drill and we went and did something called
"island hopping" which is running from pit to pit (there's 2 at every
barracks) and spending about 20 min. in each. We did that from
noon to evening chow, about 5 hrs. So I'm a little sore today and
probably a couple pounds lighter too. Things went well today

though: no pit calls whatsoever, and tomorrow's Sun! Yay, we haven't been allowed to eat power bars yet, but SDI SSgt Marshal says when we're ready we'll get them.

Anyway next Fri. we've been here for a month, and it's my birthday! (If I got the date right?) Time has sort of all molded together. If you took any single event that's happened further back than yesterday I wouldn't be able to place it within a week of the actual event on a timeline. It's all a blur.

I'm almost a third of the way done, and tomorrow it'll be 2 months to grad.

We were out running early this morning and I caught a piece of the Crucible ceremony, very powerful. Also I saw Asher go by in formation. We made eye contact but that's about it. I got a note from him about 3 days ago, very sound advice.

I still find myself constantly dreaming about food. The food here is mediocre, it's all edible but there just isn't enough to really take up space. So I would like to request first that when I get liberty the day before grad, that first we go to a Burger King (you *know* what I want) and then that we go to a real restaurant or maybe find a park and have a ridiculously large picnic. Second, when we get back, can we have pizza? I really crave that above all things, egg pizza. I actually woke up last night and I could taste the egg and cheese and tomato and basil and Mom's crust. I couldn't go back to sleep.

Tomorrow I go to church. What I've been doing is just reading the St. John Chrysostom Liturgy during the Catholic Mass, not quite the same as real church, but hey! Everything's screwed up around here (example: you have to leave the toilet seat up!).

Could you bring some pizza or a whole pizza? If not that's fine. I can wait an extra day maybe.

My biggest fear right now is getting injured and being recycled and having my graduation date moved back as a result.

All the best,
John

P.S. Have Francis tell me how camping went.

no morning wood
no waking up to a hard on
nothing, might as well just use it for pissing
whatever they did it killed my penis
those bastards

An interesting thing happened in boot camp that I had never heard of or banked on. *No one* got an erection in boot camp. Not a "chub," a "hard on," or even "morning wood" was to be seen in an entire squadbay of almost ninety recruits! All the other Marines that I have talked to since I joined the Corps never had or saw one either!

Whether our impotence was stress related or whether we were given some sort of chemical in the food or in the immunization shots that we received in our first week, not one of us got an erection. There was no midnight masturbation in the head or even the urge. I can recall no sex dreams or even thinking about sex the entire time I was on the island. Anyone that knows an eighteen- or nineteen-year-old male will know exactly how far-fetched that sounds, but it is completely true.

September 13, 1999
Dear John,
Today I booked flights to and from your graduation. I got us a rented car and hotel rooms too. We'll come down the day before, Nov 11 for Family Day and of course be there on Nov 12 for graduation. The night you graduate we're booked into a nice hotel in Savannah, GA, about 1 hour from PI. We'll find some good food that night or bust trying!

Love,
Dad

The very idea of looking as far into the future as graduation struck me as very amusing; I had trouble seeing past my next meal, and here Dad was booking flights for an event almost two months and a lifetime away! (The fact that he was willing to discuss *future* plans also showed me how much the graduation meant to him.)

Dad always refused to let my mother tell him where he was about to go speak or do a book signing until the actual morning of the event when he'd look at the ticket for the first time. (He would only pack moments before walking out the door!) Dad had a horror of discussing the future, and he hated to be drawn into planning anything. For him only the moment existed. The only plan he ever made was to get up the next morning and keep writing. "The past is dead, the future a blank slate, only the project matters!" Dad would say.

When we went on vacation, Dad refused to make reservations and would look for a hotel when he needed one. (Of course he could only get away with all this because Mom kept track of everything for us. For instance, she brought along the money, just as the DIs knew what was ahead for us.)

I had always laughed at Dad for his addiction to the moment-by-moment way of life, but now on PI it made sense to me. On PI this existential mode was drilled into us, adopted and believed. Looking past the immediate mission would only cloud our performance in the present and make the future that much harder. Live "chow to chow, Sunday to Sunday," or, as Dad always put it, "You just get up every morning and write that next chapter!"

We recruits saw only what was put right in front of us, realizing that as soon as we got over that hurdle there would be another waiting for us just on the other side and that if we loaded our plates with more than just the tough challenge of the moment, the "plate," in other words, our brains, would shatter.

There was never a time when you were done. A three-hour close order drill session would be followed by a five-mile run. Were we "done"?

"You ain't even started! PAIN! You have not experienced HURT yet! WAGON WHEEL! [Walking in a large circle sipping from canteens] NOW!"

"The more you sweat in peace the less you bleed in war!"

"No honor, no courage! I blame your nasty parents!"

"We will *drill!* You have been out here drilling for five hours! You ain't even started!"

It was during training week five and six that I decided to put my head down and just charge ahead, living only to get over the next hurdle. There was also a new realization: once I was over each hurdle I never had to go back; it was done. Drill was a killer, but a day came when it was done! Time could not go backward, even on PI, unless you were recycled. This was a huge discovery for me. You only had to keep running forward and eventually you would run headlong into graduation. At least that is what I hoped.

> full speed chewing,
> full speed swallowing,
> don't glance
> right or left
> eat now
> forks and spoons hitting trays
> swallowing.

Chow time was the most second-by-second part of each day. There was never enough time for everyone to eat let alone to plan ahead or think. We were not allowed to speak at all. The only voices that could be heard in the chow hall were those of the recruits in the chow line asking for a particular food: "Chicken, Recruit!" or "Rice, Recruit!"

Recruits on "Team Week" (a period of training which we had not yet reached) assigned to work in the chow hall served the food. The only noise was the "tic-tic" of metal spoons or forks hitting trays. We were only allowed to eat with one utensil. If the DIs were particularly pissed with the platoon we could only eat with knives. If you have ever tried eating rice with a knife, when you are starving and are only allowed a few minutes to shovel all the food down you can shovel, you will be able to understand what an excruciating experience this was. (Fortunately for me, platoons always march from tallest to shortest, and I was one of the tallest men in the platoon. Since I was one of the first in line, I got to finish my meals most of the time.)

The DIs on Parris Island constantly referred to the Marine Corps as "My Marine Corps," as in "I don't want trash like *you* in MY MARINE CORPS!" Each DI wanted to hold *his* recruits to *his* Marine Corps standard, a standard more rigorous than the Corps' official rules. Our DIs made sure that we all ate as quickly and as little as possible and only of the food they approved of. We were allowed to eat "pastries" (dessert) only twice in three months, though they were served every day. "We don't need any of that sugar shit in MY CORPS! I'll let you eat the pastries when you've earned them!" our SDI would bellow.

The platoon's guide would go through the line last, or first, depending on how the DIs were feeling. Whether the guide started to eat first or last made a *big difference* as to the rest of the platoon's ability to finish our meals, because as soon as the guide was finished eating, so was everyone else. If there was food in your mouth when he barked: "Get out ninety-three!" you either swallowed it or spit it out, if you hadn't finished chewing. If your fork was halfway to your mouth, you dropped it.

Fast meals, too little time to eat, and half-finished plates of food made for very hungry days. For the most part we got used to constant hunger though we never accepted it. We also never passed up an opportunity for a little extra food, if we could ever get it.

The trick to survival was to pile all the food on your tray onto the bread and eat it sandwich-style. Rice, liver, and the little salad that I could grab went straight onto the two standard-issue slices of white bread we were given and from there into my mouth, crammed in with one hand, FAST, before the bread got too soggy to hold together or the guide shouted, "Get out ninety-three!" (Diet trays only got one slice of bread and a completely different meal, and they suffered greatly.)

My desperate sandwich making had to be accomplished with one hand. My other hand (and every recruit's other hand in the chow hall) was resting on my left knee with the fingers extended and joined, my heels would be together with the toes at a forty-five-degree angle, and my back would be straight. The position of "sitting at attention" was enforced at all times while eating. The rule of eating with one hand was also enforced. (Try eating without being able to use a fork—presuming you are even allowed to use the fork that day and not just a knife!—to hold your food while you cut it, and try doing this fast as the precious seconds tick past.) A fast sandwich, made of whatever, sitting in front of you was the only way to go!

We were not allowed to drink any of the juice drinks or the chocolate milk in the chow hall. Our SDI did not approve of such "trash." We could drink a glass of milk, sometimes, *if* we drank an entire canteen of water first (one quart). "Dehydration is a killer! Do you want your piss to be the color of tea? DRINK WATER! DRINK IT NOW!"

competition coming
ditties ringing out

cracking eardrums
"Inspection Arms!"
"Snatch and tight and pull and port"
"Port.
"Guide to the B . . . C . . . T . . ."
"Arms!"
"Click, Pop!"
we are ready, nervous ready.

The platoons competed among each other in two official drill competitions. First in "Series Drill," which was a competition between the three platoons in either the follow or lead series. Finally all the platoons in the company competed. Each time they were judged by Drill Masters who graded on form, bearing, and the rhythm of each particular drill movement and whether the platoon was in sync. The Company Drill Competition was the final test of how well a platoon had learned our drill movements.

For the purpose of learning to stay in sync we memorized ditties. We would scream these as we did every single movement in the drill to keep us together:

"PORT ARMS!"
"SNATCH AND TIGHT!"

These ditties didn't necessarily have anything to do with the movement, but they kept us doing things in sync. We needed all the help we could get. Preparing for series drill competition was a brutal experience. The DIs and the SDI in particular had no patience for our mistakes. The competition was their chance to shine in front of the other DIs. Punishments took on a new severity during drill practice, especially on a movement called "Inspection Arms."

Inspection Arms was the most difficult movement we did. It is a seven-count movement, which goes through the steps of preparing the rifle to be inspected. During Inspection Arms the bolt of the rifle must be pulled to the rear from a very awkward position and be locked, held open for inspection. Invariably a few recruits failed to get it back all the way or in sync with the rest of the platoon.

"GOOD TO GO! Not *everyone* got the bolt back! Hold your rifles at arm's length away from you *now!*"

"AYE SIR!"

"Pull the bolt back and hold it *now!*"

"AYE SIR!"

We would stand in the hot sun, arms and fingers going numb with the muscle strain of holding the bolt back against the pressure of the spring for as long as it took for the DI's frustration with their weak, nasty charges to wear off. Then we would try the movement again, and again the rifles would be held out in front of us, bolt held back, each time a little longer until our arms and shoulders were on fire.

During preparation for the company drill competition, the pit also held new meaning for us. We would invariably piss off our SDI. (Remember he had spent three years on the fabled Silent Drill Team and had no patience for drill imperfections at all.) When our SDI drilled us, he would just take us straight to the pit and drill there. He knew we would never meet his standard of synchronized perfection, so we would practice in the pit. It saved him the time of having to march us to a pit from wherever we happened to be drilling.

Dear Family,

I have to be brief, not much time. Due to the hurricane off the coast of Florida, we are being evacuated to another base in Georgia to continue training. No need to worry, it isn't even raining yet, just pray it doesn't set back graduation. I will write as soon as I can, if you want more info, you could try the Red Cross but I don't know if that'll work.

All the best,
John

P.S. Get in touch with Erica and let her know, please.

12

the evacuation
school buses before the wind
half standing half sitting
waiting for the end
longing for cold concrete
only we would think this was rest

On September 13 all the recruits on Parris Island were evacuated to a logistics base in Albany, Georgia. Seven thousand men and women were moved. Our SDI informed us that we would be leaving right after morning chow. We packed all the gear we needed for the evacuation, jammed the rest into the big gear locker, and wedged our mattresses against the windows. We were told that we would be bringing our rifles. We were told we were going to Georgia and that we would be missing series drill. (Series Drill Competition was among the platoons in the same "series." In other words, the three platoons living in the same barracks in the various squadbays competed against each other.)

The recruits were transported in yellow school buses. We were on those buses for twenty-one hours. One of the biggest worries for the DIs was that in taking us out of the training environment we would lose the discipline and the cohesion that had been pounded into us thus far in training. Their efforts to thwart the problems that we might face began even before we left the island. We were given two MREs (plastic bags containing the famous Meals Ready to Eat with a shelf life of eternity or so) for the ride and told that we would be informed when we could eat them.

There were two DIs from different platoons driving us and the first words before we even started rolling was, "Get your heads down and keep them there!"

"AYE SIR!"

Down went our heads.

"None of you had better go to sleep either or I've got some games in mind to play with the likes of you."

"AYE SIR."

A perpetual state of crazed exhaustion being the lot of all recruits, within ten minutes there were at least two recruits asleep on the bus.

"Good to go, some of you want to sleep, obviously, seats are too good for you! Get your asses off those seats and stay in a sitting position *above* the seats! I better not see your dirty little asses touch those seats or there's some more games that I can play with you!"

"AYE SIR!"

I can't remember how long we stayed there, half-sitting and half-standing, crouching over our bus seats, but judging from the leaden feel of my shaking thighs, when we were finally allowed to sit back down it must have been at least a good twenty minutes later. The rest of the ride we sat with our heads down—awake until the DIs told us we could sleep.

We were sandwiched into our seats with our packs and weapons and not allowed to look at the slowly passing view. It might reconnect us to the nasty civilian world our DIs were working so hard to pry us loose from. No sights, no sounds of ordinary life were going to get to us if the DIs could help it!

"Keep your HEADS DOWN!"

"AYE, SIR!"

We were allowed to eat but not to talk. When night rolled in on the convoy, we were ordered to go to sleep. In those uncomfortable school bus seats, with our rifles over our shoulders jammed into our backs and with our full packs in our laps, it made for an interesting night.

The next morning when we arrived in Albany, Georgia, we were moved into the supply warehouses on base. We were housed on the concrete floors of these warehouses, and we ate MREs for the entire time we were there. The morning we arrived, a full twenty-one hours after we had left PI, we were ordered once again to go to sleep. This was more for the benefit of the DIs, who had been awake for a full two days. At any rate, we got another eight hours of sleep, which, as uncomfortable as it was on the floor, we needed badly after a full day and night on overcrowded buses.

Dear Family,

I don't know if you got my last letter so here's an update. I don't even know if this will get sent from here.

I've been evacuated to Georgia because of the hurricane. It's Wed and because of the civilian evacuation from Florida clogging all the roads north it took us 21 hours to finish what would normally be a 6–8 hour trip. Training has been suspended and our SDI says we can miss a week to 2 weeks of training before graduation gets moved back.

So it really depends on how much damage there is on Parris Island and what happens with the storm behind this one. Today's the 15th (payday) we get paid on the 1st and 15th of every month.

Well I have to go, hopefully this'll get sent. In the meantime we're living on the floor of a huge warehouse in Georgia.

Love
John

P.S. Pray.

P.P.S. Could you let Erica know? Thanx

P.P.S. I need more envelopes. Just send them to the normal address.

P.P.P.S. Imagine five weeks here and I still don't know one first name!

————————————

On the days when I was filled with doubts as to why John had joined and if it was a good idea or not, I'd try and figure out if I was to blame. Had I exposed John to too much macho bullshit? In Namibia, Africa, where I directed *Rebel Storm* out on the wind-sculpted sand dunes of the desert coast, my sons Francis and John, then fifteen and eight, used to hang out with the effects department and help wrap explosives in the miles of tape needed to make the bombs for our action sequences. (The "action" was mostly motorcycles chasing an armored vehicle with lots of bullet hits, explosions, and such, all boring to watch in the film but fun to do.)

My sons and I shared the satisfaction at Genie's nervousness. The boys were hanging out in the effects truck with a bunch of hard-drinking, chain-smoking, rough South African effects guys, lounging on hundreds of pounds of black powder, bales of primer cord, and blasting caps. When John and Francis took to hitching rides with the stunt men on their dirt bikes between setups, and flew over the vast five-hundred-foot dunes, our adolescent father-son, lets-shock-the-women joy was complete.

Maybe watching those swaggering stunt guys had given John the idea that weapons were "cool." Maybe they were the people that started him thinking smoking was "cool" too. We had numerous blowups about his smoking. The last one was two weeks before boot camp. I had heard the latch of our back door close with a gentle click. It was four A.M.

"You've been smoking, I can smell it!" I shouted. "You said you wouldn't smoke. If you go to the Marines a smoker you'll smoke for life, a short life with a cancer finish! Why do you smoke?"

"Smoking relaxes me so I can sleep."

"Take two Benadryl. Then you'll sleep."

"I'm not taking those. I might fail the piss test."

"The Marines don't care if you take an antihistamine!"

"I'm not supposed to take anything."

"Well if you'd stay home with me you'd sleep."

"How's that?" asked John and grinned.

"Being out with Erica all the time, and now look, I get up to write undisturbed and you come in and disturb me! Do you think in the Marines they'll let you wander around like this, all hours?"

"I'm not in the Marines yet."

"But all your bad habits will follow you down there."

"Would you rather I just lie in bed awake?"

"But why, John?"

"I like to hear the night sounds," said John quietly.

"What 'sounds'?" I asked.

"The flap of a big fish under the bridge. There were stripers feeding tonight. The peepers in the distance. Owls. I saw a fox." John looked at me for a moment. "Dad?"

"Yes?"

"What's wrong, Dad? Why are you so mad at me all the time these days?"

"You know perfectly well. I want you up in bed safe where I can see you when I get up to write, and I hate the fact you smoke. I like to look in on the way past and see you sacked out. When I look in and the bed's empty I get scared."

"I'm sorry."

John stepped over and hugged me. His skin was cold from the damp night air. He stank of those fucking Camels—goddamn the tobacco companies to hell! He went over to the kitchen table and scribbled a note, stuck it up on the hood of the stove. John gave me a pat on the shoulder. A moment later I heard the creak of the loose board on the back stair.

I walked over to the note and read it: "Mom, please wake me at 8:45. Love J."

I took the note down. John wouldn't need his mother to wake him. I'd do it. In fact I'd bring him hot chocolate in bed—even if he *had* been smoking, damn it!— just the way he liked breakfast, along with Genie's delicious French bread cut in pieces the right size for dipping. It was John's favorite.

I took the scrap of paper and tiptoed up the front stairs to my bedroom. Then I laid John's note in the suitcase I kept his childhood drawings in. I collected quite a little pile of envelopes and other scraps that summer with messages on them: "Wake me at 5, J," "Gone for walk, back soon, J" "At the Marines, Andover, see you at supper, J."

The note I liked best read, "Out with the Boys, call JP's if you need anything, Love you Dad, J." No one had made John write, "Love you Dad."

---

don't get hurt
sent back
to DI's who will kill you
with recruits who do not care
because you are not theirs
you have no bonds with them
left to drift in a cruel sea.

Injuries are a recruit's worst nightmare. An injury is the surest way to get dropped in training, or to get sent to MRP (Medical Recovery Platoon). MRP is like purgatory for a recruit. No training can be done. No progress can be made toward any goal. You simply sit and pray for a miraculous healing.

Since MRP recruits are still recruits, injured or not, they are treated like regular recruits, in other words, harshly, for the same reason that we were told to keep our heads down on the evacuation bus ride. The DIs don't want the injured recruits to get out of the recruit mentality just because some nurse has asked them how they felt or some civilian doctor might have nodded or smiled at them during an examination. This meant the injured recruits still got shouted at and had no special privileges. In fact I heard that life was made as boring as possible as a way to "motivate" recovery.

We heard about the life of injured recruits from our SDI who, in not too veiled terms, seemed to suggest that unless we were seriously injured we would do best to just keep any illness or injuries to ourselves.

"A recruit who gets sent to MRP might as well be dead; time stops for him! Good to go?"

"YES SIR!"

"He sits and waits while his platoon continues on through training, graduates and leaves PI as Marines, while he sits on his footlocker passing time."

After that conversation the number of recruits who went to sick call fell by almost half. One recruit went through the rest of training with a hernia all of us knew about but that no one ever revealed. We did not want to lose him to MRP. My foot had been hurting for several weeks and was deteriorating, but I kept my mouth shut.

When a recruit is healed enough to function, he leaves MRP and is sent back to another platoon at the exact same training day he left his own platoon. Because the training is identical from platoon to platoon, day-to-day, the recruit doesn't miss much in the way of training. However, picking up with a new platoon is terrifying. It did not happen to me, but I saw the terror in the eyes of the recruits that we picked up. They did not know the other recruits, who had of course already formed their bonds. The DIs went out of their way to prove to the newly absorbed recruit how much tougher they were than his former DIs.

The fear of losing your platoon was almost worse than death when you got far enough into training to feel settled and finally learn where you stood in the order of your new universe. Injuries began to prey on our minds. During devotional time, Reyes and I always prayed for the same things: for the platoon to do well, the DIs to be in a good mood, BK Broilers, and, above all, no injuries. The idea of being on PI late in training—alone with no one to support me or help me—began to haunt my nightmares.

The bond I began to form with Reyes was yet another motivation to not get injured. We both wanted to see the other safely through boot camp and to graduate together. As the training became more difficult and more dangerous, our fears of injury and being dropped grew, and we became more and more determined to hide whatever injuries we had. As a consequence I did not let myself limp.

To Recruit John Schaeffer
September 22, 1999
Dear John,
You know how I knock myself out doing jobs around the house! Well as I said I'm putting in this door. I'm feeling muscles I never knew I had after walking up and down the stairs hauling buckets of wet cement. The old knuckles are scraped and swollen, nothing like hammer blows while gripping a cold chisel to get your attention. There is a certain sense of panic that goes with tearing a gaping hole in the exterior wall of one's bedroom! I feel like I'm working against the clock. This sense of desperation is reinforced by rain! If the wind comes up I'm done. We'll be re-carpeting the bedroom and then some if the water pours in. In any case I'll let you know how it comes out. So far so good! (I'm not trying to keep up with you or anything! Just rebuilding the house with my bare hands!)

Tonight I'm going up to Salisbury for a planning committee meeting. The town wants to put some cell-phone towers up in the woods down Ferry Road overlooking the marsh. I shall go and do battle for our marsh!

You know the weird thing is that when we first moved to America I was uninterested in local politics. In Switzerland as an American I couldn't vote and you know how Europeans are about public causes, people just don't involve themselves or are fatalistic about the outcome when trying to fight city hall. Well, with you in the Corps suddenly I realized how much I've changed. Now I'm working to form a committee to stop Mass electric from putting up new towers to carry the high-tension wires over the river. And we've generated quite a few headlines in the paper. (This cell-phone deal is just a minor issue by comparison.)

I find that with you in the Corps suddenly I feel pretty damned like a citizen and want to have my say! I no longer am intimidated by the "old boys" up at town hall and went to the selectman meeting and said my piece last week. No more huddling indoors waiting for "someone else" to fix things.

Some of the old guys in town are really funny. One said—actually an old toothless woman in this case said—that the reason *she* opposed the new towers was, "because I just don't like his face!" She was talking about the engineer from the electric company! "There's just something about him that reminds be of a goddamned weasel," she said, to the hearty applause of the townies.

Maybe it's just my imagination but I seem to have gotten much more friendly with the locals ever since I put a Marines bumper sticker on the car. Does this make me "one of the old guys in town" now?

Autumn is on the way. The grass is green again with all the rain after a dry summer. The last of the tomatoes are picked. We'll be bringing in the geraniums and rosemary and hibiscus soon. Newburyport keeps looking richer. One more giant SUV and the whole place will sink into the river!

Much love,
Dad

Dear Family,
It's Tue night and I *think* this is the first letter I've written you since the evacuation. I'm *very* sorry but I just haven't had enough time *at all*.

We've moved back into the house (that means barracks) without a hitch and have really gotten down to the business of training. (This week we do swim qualification requirement.) I'm going through it okay and will continue to, Lord willing. Some people are not passing. If they don't qualify they get recycled in training to "Charlie" Co. (They don't graduate till *Dec. 23*) Wow! Pray that doesn't happen to me.

Next week's the gas chamber (Not fun). The DIs are actually allowed to use any means necessary to keep you in the chamber because if you panic others could lose it too.

I have to go.

All my love,
John

P.S. I saw Asher on Sun. He's graduating this Fri. and had to skip the Crucible because of the hurricane.

Asher Boucher had always been a friend of mine. Knowing that Asher had completed boot camp was one of the greatest motivations I had on PI. If he could do it, I knew that I could. When he had about a month to go in training, Asher sent me a short note. That had helped me quite a bit. It contained the only advice that really mattered on PI: "Do your best and sound off." Which is all a recruit ever needs to really know.

Asher was becoming a Marine and pulling me along with him. All Marines had become gods to us recruits. They bore the title that we were all reaching for so desperately. They had already done what we were doing and had pushed forward to the almost mythical Fleet Marine Force.

I saw Asher in church the week before he graduated from Alpha Company His hair already bore the characteristic Marine Corps high and tight haircut that all Marines leave the island with. (My head was still recruit bald.) I wanted that haircut! We were getting close, but there were still formidable obstacles to graduation from the swim test to possible injuries, and, of course, the biggest test of all, where the most recruits were dropped: the rifle qualification.

To Recruit John Schaeffer
September 26, 1999
Dear John,
Last night, Sat, Mom and I went to a party that Cathy and Danny Boucher held for Asher to celebrate his homecoming from Parris Island. He mentioned he'd seen you several times at a distance. Max was there so we talked Marine shop for a bit. It was good to feel a little closer to you for a moment.

Max did a funny thing to Ash three days before graduation. He sent a letter to Ash with a bunch of pointed remarks about Asher's "soda-pop DI," and "cream puff hard-hat" etc., on the letter. The predictable result was Asher had to pay. When the DIs learned Max was a Marine lieutenant they got the CPR first aid life-size rubber dummy and made Ash dress it up, call it "the lieutenant" and made Ash shower with it, sleep with it, walk with it etc. Ash graduated private 1st class meritorious. Apparently he did fine notwithstanding! Max says it was payback for "all my toys Asher broke."

After I write this I'm calling Jane. She called and told Francis she was getting nervous. She'll be down to PI Oct 4. So it seems we are keeping a constant stream of family and friends in PI. Max says for me to tell you to remember: small, shallow, controlled breaths in the gas chamber.

Looks like this stop-the-tower project is coming well. We've formed a committee. We meet upstairs at Michael's Harborside each Monday with our "board." What a mix of people! We've got multi-millionaire Debbie R. of the lingerie company over in town and crazy old Jimmy D. (the nutty ex-fisherman of Sweet Apple Tree Ln.), all in the same room!

You should have seen the old guy's eyes pop when Debbie suggested a lingerie show to raise money for "the cause!" Fr. O'Hara, the wimpy new Catholic priest in town is on the committee and he turned beet red! Old Jimmy then suggested that they hold the lingerie show in his marina shed! Then Debbie got incensed and reminded him that her models were "high paid professionals!" then he said "I bet they're *pros*," in that real low-down phlegmy gargle of his that carries a whole other meaning and the meeting almost broke up. I love all this! Down with Mass electric! Up with the people!

We love you a lot and are so proud of you. We pray for you *all the time.*

Much love,
Dad

P.S. Jane will be there soon stepping on the yellow footprints.

––––––––––––––––

Knowing that a friend, Jane Vizzi, was soon going to be having a tougher time than I was cheered me up to no end! On PI the difficulty and hardship of any event decreases in direct proportion to how many people are suffering with you. If there are one recruit and two DIs in the pit, that recruit will be "crying like a bitch" inside of an hour. On the other hand if there is a whole platoon and four DIs, one or two may crack if they receive "special attention" in the smoke-check department, but on the whole, the platoon could go for a day and never break.

In a large group you can hide a little and rest. You can pull each other along. "If he can do it I sure as hell can . . ." You watch other people and become detached from your situation by observing them as if they were some kind of show on TV you had nothing to do with, as if you were just floating above it all while they pushed until they collapsed.

Becoming detached from your own suffering and finding a way to live someplace other than in your tortured body is one of the only ways to survive PI. A recruit must learn to have a somewhat morbid fascination with the suffering of others as well as his own. Seeing how far a DI has the stomach to push someone, seeing how far each recruit can be pushed, watching yourself and finding your true limits becomes a game. To not be hampered by the old rules society used to impose on you, unwritten rules that made you stop exercise or work when it hurt, is the point. Pushing yourself until you couldn't do another push-up if God himself told you to becomes an end in itself. Just seeing how far you can go is the true test.

13

I got a hunger for that lanky frame, for the touch of my tall son, for his head and neck bowed toward me to receive my hug like some grazing giraffe bending to feed from the lower branches. I dreamed a prayer for John one afternoon. I was lying on my living room couch. The long shadows, cast by the failing sunlit maples were spilling through the windows. I woke hearing a prayer for my son spoken within me: "Let not my sins remove your blessing from my son!"

I remembered that somewhere in the Bible there is a passage that says that the Holy Spirit takes our imperfect longings and forms them into perfect prayers before the throne of God. The passage of time, the fact that Genie and I had lived long enough to see empty rooms, dust gathering on old toys and sports trophies, was the hollow victory of answered prayers. Our children *had* all grown up safe and well. I felt lonely.

Genie and I were about to find out if we were married or if we had only thought we were while our children bound us together. We had been raising our three children for the better part of thirty years. Genie and I grew from bewildered teenage parents into adults forced by our children into taking responsibility for making a home and a life. The parameters of our fights were circumscribed by the need to feed, house, and clothe our babies. Things were left unsaid or half said when the children were around. Anger was swallowed by the needs of the kids. Even sexual intensity was magnified by the children; weekends "without the children," brief erotic bliss sandwiched between breast-feeding and driving to soccer league, stolen moments made passionate by the scarcity of privacy.

We did not know what would happen now. We had never been alone. What were we to make of empty afternoons? What of uninterrupted evenings?

Should we get naked in the living room or go on locking the bedroom door? We were free but free to do what?

———————————

the only proof that I exist
is handed to me some days after evening chow
parents pouring motivation into envelopes
distributed by senior drill instructor staff sergeant George Marshal.
affirming my life when he says: "Schaeffer"
and I say: "HERE SIR!"

We moved into swim qualification week. The Corps wanted to make sure that we would not drown in the first thirty seconds of an amphibious assault. We put on cammies and boots, were issued a rubber rifle, a helmet, a flack jacket, a pack, and tested in different techniques of surviving in the water in full combat gear.

We trained in a vast indoor pool lit by arched windows and overhead vapor lights. The pool was made of blue tile with red tiles along the sides. Marine instructors watched over us, orange foam floats at the ready. We were taught to swim on our backs and use our full packs as a kind of float. We lay on our backs, the water gurgling in our Kevlar helmets, the weight of clothes, packs, and weapons tugging us down. "Swimming" in combat jungle boots and heavy sodden cammies is rather interesting. Some recruits panicked, took on water, and sank fast. They had to be rescued, coughing up water.

If a recruit was having obvious trouble, the first two days were spent making sure that the recruit could swim basic strokes. A recruit had one week to pass the basic swimming requirements known as Combat Water Survival Level 4 (CWS4). If the recruit failed, he was sent back in training. Eventually, after three weeks training (with a new platoon every week), if it became apparent that a recruit was a "swim rock" or an "iron duck," he would be sent home without the title. Failure to qualify in the water, like failure on the rifle range, was a sure way to get dropped.

By swim week some of us were having second thoughts about the Marine Corps. We were at the height of training intensity and bone weary.

We were hungry and numb, had been on PI long enough to hate it, but were still far away enough from graduation that it seemed like an impossible stretch to imagine actually ever getting out, let alone going home.

The DIs had, of course, seen it all before and made it clear that pretending you couldn't swim, and thus failing the swim test, was actually a much slower way to get off the Island than passing and graduating. They told us (truthfully) that those who failed were not allowed to go straight home but would be kept languishing on PI for months in a "processing platoon" before they were finally out.

Dear Family,

I've had a very busy week and today, Sun, is the first time I've had to write since, wow, I can't even remember.

On Thur. I qualified CWS1 (Combat Water Survival) for swimming which is as high as you can go on PI. (To graduate you only need CWS4) Only 11 recruits including me out of our whole series (about 250) got CWS1. So that makes me look a little better, on paper anyway.

This week we have BWT (Basic Warrior Training) so I'll be doing the gas chamber and rappel tower and all that stuff (camping and MRE's) for three days. Also tomorrow is knowledge testing, another grad requirement. Nothing all that tough, I've got it down pat, and Saturday is Company Drill.

Last week was a little bit rough. We failed an inspection by the Series Gunnery Sergeant, as did the other 2 PLTN's and we spent a couple days in the pit, but redeemed ourselves yesterday while practicing drill by doing something called a drive by on PLTN 1092. What happens is that a platoon marches up along side another PLTN and they face each other and do drill movements like right/left shoulder arms etc. As SDI SSgt Marshal told them, "You just got your chow taken by 1093." We marched off in triumph. So a relatively happy ending to a tiring week.

Anyway after this week is two weeks of the rifle range, then Team Week, where we work in the chow hall. I can't wait. Then A Line (night movements, day movements, night fire etc.) then the

Crucible, then when we come back from the Crucible, the Warriors Breakfast, then the next day, Sun, 4 hrs of Base Liberty, the grad practice, then Family Day, Thurs, then grad, then *food!* So, as you can tell I've got a lot of things to do in the next six weeks.

Wed is the exact halfway point for training days even though I'm a little bit more than half way through as far as time goes. Dad, congratulations on all your civic duty stuff in town. All my love,

John

P.S. Continue to pray I qualify on all my stuff and don't get hurt please.

To Recruit John Schaeffer
September 29, 1999
Dear John,
As we head into Oct you'll soon only be looking at a month to go! So hang in there the end is, if not in sight at least a lot closer by a long way.

There was another piece in the *Times* on how the Army, Navy and Air Force can't recruit enough people and how far below their goals they are. Only the Marines have the amount of people they need. They said that is because only the Marines have a definite "self-image and esprit." But you knew that already.

My bags of stucco arrive tomorrow so Sat I'll try and get Francis up to hold the ladder while I get scared out of my wits and try and work thirty feet up the ladder! You know the routine.

We have a new cause besides the power tower. Some casino wants to come to Salisbury beach. And there is a state senator who is lobbying the town hard to let them in and to change the laws in MA to accommodate them.

Guess what? I got a call from the local paper asking if I opposed it! I asked the reporter why she called me and she said she was calling various "grass roots organizers." *Me,* a "grass roots organizer!" And all because I went on cable TV once up in Amesbury to debate the Mass electric guys about the power tower!

We're forming a committee with my friend, a neighbor Jerry

Klima (the retired lawyer who bought Mrs. Woodard's home at the top of the street). We're going to try and stop them from ruining our town! If that casino gets built Salisbury will become little more than an exit ramp for the casino and our town will get screwed. They have big bucks though so it will be quite a fight!

Well time for the post run, so bye for now. Blessings on you.

Love,
Dad

What my father said about the other services having recruiting problems was true, and it was a great source of pride to us—yet another proof that we were a part of something great. Marine recruiting posters did not appeal to the potential recruit's individualism, let alone hold out promises of benefits. The Marines did not tell you to join so you could "Be all you can be," or so that you could be "An Army of one"; rather, "Maybe you can be one of us."

At the entrance to Parris Island was a sign stating that this was "Where the Difference Begins." The Corps let each recruit know that if you came from typical selfish "nasty" America it did not like you the way you were and would change you or break you. The Marines's honesty worked. At the time I joined, the Marines had more recruits than they needed.

We were better, we were the best, and we knew it. We pushed ourselves to widen the gap that we already felt growing between the "lesser services" and us. We felt that they had sold themselves short, become a part of something that did not raise them above anything, made them merely civilians in uniform. The other services' recruiting problems were merely another example to us of how worthy the prize was for which we worked every day: the title, United States Marine.

To Recruit John Schaeffer
September 30, 1999
Dear John,
Many congratulations on being CWS 1 in swimming! We got your

letter today with that and other news. Well done. The days in the pit sounded rough but I'm glad things worked out with the "drive by" and SDI SSgt Marshal telling 1092 they got their "chow taken" by you.

It sounds as if you are in the thick of things now, maybe even looking forward to one or two events (not including the gas chamber, of course). We're counting the days too. We very much enjoyed your letter and will pass the Waring letter on to Francis again.

Tonight I'll go with Genie to Boston to be with her after her design class. Before that I'll run out and buy you cough drops, more Gatorade, and Power Bars and get them off to you in a separate package tonight.

Genie is into all her homework projects for school. Between her projects, my work on the house and all the usual ROP stuff [the mail order company Genie runs] we've been busy. Up at 4–5, crash at 9. We must talk about you 10 times a day, no kidding.

We got two headlines in one day, one for our tower committee when we hired a *Boston* lawyer (that's a *big deal* hereabouts!) and another when Mass electric announced that they would consider an alternative to the towers, maybe go under the river with the cable the way we want them to.

I spent all afternoon yesterday in the basement of the old folks home over on Water Street, helping get out our mailing to the list we're building. I stuffed over a thousand envelopes. We are now called the "Committee for an Open River." Our anti-casino deal is called "The Salisbury Taxpayers Association."

Much love,
Dad

Genie and I settled into the routine of being alone. I felt guilty when I'd catch myself feeling relieved that all the children were gone. I experienced an utterly forgotten emotion: I felt relaxed once in a while!

Gradually it dawned on Genie and me that many of the tensions in our lives had been caused by the strain of being parents, parents who enjoyed their children immensely but who had never had a moment to catch their breath. We missed John horribly but were mighty glad the scramble that had begun when we were eighteen and nineteen was finally over. At first we did not dare to admit this even to each other: it was nice to be alone!

14

chow to chow, Sunday to Sunday
let it wash over and
feed me its secrets
about shining boots
and deadly weapons

As boot camp progressed, we began to receive papers on graduation. We were also fitted for uniforms we would need on that day. We were briefed by travel agencies that had won government contracts to handle recruit travel arrangements from boot camp home and from home to MCT (Marine combat training).

Graduation still seemed an eternity away, but the light at the end of the tunnel began to shine—a little. We were warned by our Senior not to think too far ahead: "You're not on the bus yet, you're just in line to buy your ticket!" On some days graduation was a more distant goal than on others, but the idea of an end to all the madness began to rest comfortably in the back of our heads. One day we might leave PI and move on to bigger and better things than the pit!

BWT (Basic Warrior Training) came after swim qualification week. We spent three days in the field, doing such things as going through the gas chamber and learning how to rappel down walls and fast-rope out of helicopters—the "exciting stuff" you see in videos on Marine combat training. What you don't see in the videos is the lines of recruits waiting their turn on the rappelling tower or all the standing around or marching from place to place between events. By this point in training, we recruits were impatient with anything that seemed to slow us down. When a recruit did anything to hold up the progress of the platoon, say, hesitated too long before jumping out of the helicopter platform into thin air, he might well get several recruits around him muttering, "Any day now," or "Take your sweet-ass time!" We were starting to think like DIs. We were beginning to demand of ourselves the level of accountability the DIs were looking for. That did not mean we were any less nervous about failure.

For me personally, the gas chamber was the single hardest part of training that I had to go through on PI. The chamber is a small, claustrophobic, concrete, bunkerlike shack about twenty-five by thirty feet. We had been given classes on how to put on our M40 FPM gas masks, create a seal, and evacuate poison gases in the mask. We had taken knowledge classes on the mask and put them on in drills. The class dealing with the problems we might encounter with the mask ended on a less than reassuring note. "If the mask continues to leak after completing the above [the checklist on troubleshooting a malfunctioning mask in the event of a gas attack], contact the NBC [nuclear, biological, and chemical] Defense Specialist for assistance."

We were herded into the chamber a squad at a time. We were lined up against the interior wall of the dingy, smoke-stained bunker. The floor was wet and dark with, what? It turned out to be vomit, as was soon made apparent by the reaction to the gas by several recruits.

Our masks were already on and our hearts were pounding. "If problems persist . . ." "Pull the head harness . . ." "Ensure mask is secure . . ." "There are four steps to this procedure once the chemical alarm has been sounded . . ." "Take two fingers and push in the center of the Outlet Valve Disk Cover and blow as hard as you can . . ." "If you are having problems check the seal . . ." "You may find a leak by . . ." "Step 1: Stop breathing . . ." "Inhale your breath and hold it . . ." "If problems persist . . ."

A tall masked DI, reminding me of Darth Vader and sounding like him while speaking through his mask, stood in the center of the room and lit the stick of CS. He then held it over us as some kind of threat while it billowed the noxious white fumes.

"If you try and get out of here we will drag your nasty ass back in here and you'll DO IT ALL AGAIN! Understood?"

"AYE, SIR!"

As soon as the chamber filled with the pall of CS, so thick that we could no longer see across the room, we were ordered to crack the seal on our masks.

We had been instructed to hold our breath, and if we were not confident of our ability to do so, we should take quick, shallow breaths.

The feel of the gas as it hit our skin did nothing to reassure me that "quick shallow breaths" would work very well! Cuts and nicks from dry shaving our faces in the field began to sting as the CS hit the little open wounds. I had elected to hold my breath, and did very well for the first test in spite of the fact my flesh was burning. Concentrated CS—"tear gas"—in a small closed space is rather different than a whiff in the open (e.g., "gassed" at some outdoor demonstration).

When we were ordered to put our masks back on, we flushed out the gas by exhaling and remade the seal. We were given about thirty seconds to rest and then were ordered to pull our masks off our faces but keep them on our heads.

The last test was to completely remove our masks and hold them directly out in front of us. The DIs had decided to test 1093 to the limit and made us stand like that, without masks, blinded by the gas and at attention, masks at our feet in the dark fog, for what seemed like five minutes. Some recruits began running out of air and tried to take shallow breaths. This failed. CS makes the body feel like it's suffocating; you cough, and with each cough you breathe the gas deeper into your lungs. I learned later that the other recruits and platoons (that I got a chance to talk to later) were instructed to breath shallow instead of holding their breath. Maybe our DIs were screwing with us again.

Several recruits tried to rush out of the chamber blinded, gasping, choking, vomiting. The DIs tackled them and forced the screaming and shaking recruits to the ground. Then the panicked recruits' masks were forced back over their faces, and they were held down in the chamber until they ceased to convulse. The DIs made any recruit who "lost it" go through the whole series of tests again until he got it right and could face the gas without panic.

During this testing I had been in terror waiting for the moment that I would run out of air and lose control while our masks were off. (My mask was working fine when on, except for the fact that there was enough CS residue in it to render me almost completely blind.)

At the moment I was about to panic I heard the order to don our masks and clear the gas. I did not realize it, but I had just passed the most personally trying moment in all of boot camp. Maybe the fact that I could hold my breath so long had something to do with swimming underwater when I went snorkeling with Dad.

———————

Dear John,

I'm quite happy because I heard that my novel "Saving Grandma" is coming out in German to be published there under the title of "Calvin" by Eichborn. That makes seven languages my novels are in now. Also I got word that a nice royalty check is on the way for "Portofino" and "Saving Grandma" from Berkley-Penguin. So they must still be selling. Hey, I'm not dead yet!

So now I've done my writing, and written to you. It's off to a special meeting with the local "sportsman's association."

Ironic after all the years I've tried to keep those duck hunters off my marsh that now we are on the same side about the casino since it would impact duck habitat.

Love,
Dad

———————

mission accomplishment
never forget that you do not matter
the only people that care about you are the ones right around you
they are the ones that will keep you safe
everywhere and to everyone else you are a number.

(From Recruit Schaeffer. Dad, please forward this to Jane Vizzi) 9/20/99
Dear Jane,

Hello from Recruit Training. I don't have long so I'll jump right into the advice on what you need to do to prepare to come down here.

Drink a *lot* of water, get used to it and get used to it being warm, there is *no* cold water on Parris Island. Eat meat [Jane was a vegetarian], eat it every day, you could theoretically be a vegetarian but put it this way, I've been eating the most fattening things I could find and I've still lost 11 pounds. You won't have time in chow after you get picked up to make a salad. You need to grab what you can.

Be ready to function while you're sick, everyone *will* get sick in the first month, cough, fever, flu, etc. So many diseases from so many parts of the country.

When someone starts screaming at you do NOT lose your bearing, stare straight ahead and *sound off* with *confidence*.

Bring a prayer book, church ain't worth much in the way of worship from the Orthodox POV. [Jane was also a Greek Orthodox.]

Don't get discouraged. It gets better after a couple of weeks of fear and boredom. Start doing everything faster, dressing, showering, eating, moving, just get faster.

That's about it

All the best,

John

The idea of someone following in my path, stepping onto those yellow footprints behind me, forced me to examine my thoughts. Marching around the Island, I saw recruits who were behind me in training doing *exactly* what I had been doing almost to the minute on *exactly* the same training day I had done it and having *exactly* the same things yelled at them by their DIs who made it all sound spontaneous.

The DIs made the hazing sound original, as if it was the first time they had ever shouted some particular line, inches from the face of a trembling recruit. It turned out each and every recruit was the "nastiest recruit to ever come to Parris Island." Every platoon was "the worst I've ever seen." Every aside, each instance of a DI "losing it" in "despair" over how "hopeless, nasty, and selfish" some recruit or the whole "fuckin' platoon" was had been said to every recruit at the same point of training on the same day and during the same activity a hundred times before.

I was beginning to look back on the lows of punishment, the emotional highs of another training day successfully completed. I felt pride when a junior recruit looked at me in awe for having come so far, for having survived the first impossible weeks. I knew full well that they would know exactly how I felt when they reached the same point in training. This realization was inspiring. I was looking forward to knowing that I would soon feel the pride of the senior recruits ahead of me by a few steps on the training path who had accomplished so much more than I had.

As long as I could remember it had always seemed to me that I was watching my life from a different perspective than that of my friends, even my best friends, "The Boys." At first this sense of distance from the world around me held true for me in boot camp. I withdrew into myself and watched as the training happened *to* me. Pain, stress, happiness, they all happened *to* me while I watched. Events never absorbed me fully (with the exception of a bad five minutes in the gas chamber) to the point where the experience was so total or intense that I forgot myself.

I changed my sense of being withdrawn from events by watching the recruits around me experience boot camp. Seeing them being broken down to nothing, then rebuilt as self-confident Marines was much more powerful than experiencing this transformation myself. I watched the Corps saving lives that had been going nowhere. We had boys who couldn't speak English and who, by the end of boot camp, only knew "Marine English" (commands and the proper responses), but who still could not carry on a conversation. We had a few married boys who left teenage sweethearts to become Marines, even some fathers who wanted to join so they could provide medical insurance for their child.

Most of us didn't know why we'd joined or what we were looking for. Nevertheless those of us who made it into the last weeks of training were all proud of our choice, proud of each other, and anxious to earn the title and graduate. I found that I was no longer only observing my life but that I was a part of something.

Dear Family,
Well, much has happened since I last had time to write. I've finished Basic Warrior Training and in a couple hours will be moving to the rifle range barracks for the next two weeks.

I got gassed, it wasn't fun, but I didn't breathe any of it. I was practically blind for about 20 min afterwards and my nose decided to empty itself *completely* of all the mucus that has *ever* existed (nasal spray x 100,000!). All exposed skin hurt like hell but I made it out and didn't die. I also jumped off a helicopter simulation tower with nothing to save me but a rope, twice. (It was 47 feet tall.) I was pretty scared but it's one of those graduation requirement type things and since I will do basically *anything* to get out of here on time, what the hell? Why not?

So anyway, there are 29 more training days to go, but since Team Week doesn't count for training add an extra week before graduation.

Oh, I almost forgot, we took second place in Company Drill so drill has officially ended. This week we also went and got fitted for uniforms that we'll wear on liberty, very motivating. Next week we get real haircuts. So we're closing in. The only big hurdle left is rifle qualification. Here we go.

All my love,
John

P.S. Still dreaming of food.

Dear Family,

Well, it's Sun. One less Sunday to go. On Tue we start the rifle range in earnest, shooting every day until Fri (Qualification Day) then we go to Team Week, where training stops altogether and we do work in the kitchen or do whatever else needs to be done (personal business etc.). Then into A-line then the week of the Crucible, then graduation week, then *relax* and *eat!*

I've found that homesickness really hasn't diminished at all since I got here, but has changed. I no longer really care about sleeping in or taking 15-minute showers or anything like that but want to do small things even more like take a walk, read, talk, watch a movie, eat. (I need junk food too!)

I would like to know when we'll be getting home from PI on Saturday. It's in the morning right?

Anyway I was just imagining the Fri afternoon after graduation. Can we go straight to eat (something quick) then go to Savannah (if that's where we're staying) and just spend the day (walk, eat, go see a movie?). Oh and we need to hit a supermarket, I will *need* snacks that night.

Oh well, enough daydreaming. Just counting Sundays there are 4 left after this one. Food as you can tell is still a big factor. If you can do it, I would love some ("some" being a figure of speech—"mounds of" would be better) pizza when you come down on Thurs.

The rifle range is the last big obstacle before graduation. A lot of people get tripped up here. What happens is that they screw up on Fri. If you fail on Fri. you go to MTP (Marksmanship Training Platoon) and every day that next week (Mon–Fri) you get a chance to qualify and rejoin your platoon. If you don't then you get recycled to another platoon back in training, *very* scary, especially this late in training. So pray for me please.

Lord willing I'll get through this and move on to graduation without a hitch.

All my love,
John

P.S. Mail food, cough drops, and Gatorade *please!* Especially food and *cough drops.* I know I've been beating this horse for a while but it weighs heavily on my mind.

To Recruit John Schaeffer
October 5, 1999
Dear John,
Great news that the gas chamber is done! That must be a relief. Well done. Also it's great you finished Basic Warrior Training. I think you will enjoy the rifle range so I hope that is going well. The jump sounded scary. Having been clinging to ladders while fixing the chimneys all week I have decided I still don't like heights!

The weather has turned cold, fifties dropping to thirties. Besides being outside I'm writing but this work around the house has taken a ton of time.

It feels like you've been away a long time now. Genie and I miss you. Keep dreaming of food big guy. This is one dream I have it in my power to fulfill!

My novel I'm working on (reworking) is going well at last. I'm reading Genie the chapters and she likes them, which she didn't before. So that's good.

We got a great break! It turns out that the gambling lobby in MA went too far. They snuck an eminent domain clause into the legislation to legalize casino gambling here and that meant we were able to break the story that the properties they wanted could just be taken by the state on behalf of the casino! Jerry, bless him sat down and read the whole piece of legislation and found out what they'd slipped in! The town went ape and called a meeting. The local state congressman is in the doghouse and may have to resign for going along with this crap.

Love,
Dad

15

black targets on a beaten white barrel
pick one
aim in, controlled breathing
loose the round at the bottom
of the exhale,
ready to fire on real targets
tired of snapping in for hours
in one position,
let's go, move on.

Life after drill flew. Each day seemed to pass more quickly. It was time to head for the rifle range for two weeks of training. Week one would be mostly theory and "snapping in" (learning to sight our rifles on a target and a little shooting to correct our sights). Week two would be spent on the range shooting. Friday of week two "Qual Day," we would have to pass the ultimate test for any Marine recruit: qualify with the M-16 rifle at two hundred, three hundred, and five hundred yards.

The range occupied its own isolated area of the island, "Weapons Battalion." Located behind thick pine and poplar woods, in a parklike corner of the island, Weapons Battalion had its own barracks, chow hall, chapel, officers, and way of doing things—strict—all centered around one activity: making sure that the Marine's claim that every Marine is a rifleman remained true.

The range was less than a mile west of our squadbay. (I learned this later.) We were bussed out with our heads down, and, by the time we got to the range, we felt as if we had been transported to some far distant place. This sense of distance from everything familiar served to heighten our nervousness at the fact that we were now entering the make-or-break phase of training. We settled into a smaller and unfamiliar squadbay, went to chow, and prepared our equipment for the next day.

Life on the range started with "Grass Week." We sat, stood, and lay on the grass for our first week near the range, adjusting our sights on the rifle and learning the correct positions for shooting, how to compensate for the wind, and how to gauge wind speeds by looking at our surroundings. The rest of the time was taken up with intensive instruction both in a class setting and, while on the grass, one-on-one with a PMI (primary marksmanship instructor).

Once in a while I glanced around and tried to figure out what this new place consisted of and where it was in relation to the rest of the island. There was the "tower" (a mobile white hut observation and command post, about the size of a small garden shed, about twenty feet high and on wheels) from which instructions were bellowed over a fuzzy loudspeaker. The range stretched five hundred yards into the distance to the grassy slopes of the berm that held the targets. The targets themselves were popping up from behind the berm and looking impossibly far away. For every two recruits shooting there was one coach. Supervising the whole show was the range instructor sitting in the tower.

As I settled into Grass Week, I observed the recruits ahead of us who were being marched past us to and from the range a few hundred feet away. Each platoon that had been firing underwent a "shakedown" where they had to report they had not carried any shell casings, let alone ammunition, off the range. In case any recruits had ideas about collecting a souvenir, each recruit coming off the range had to report, "This recruit has no brass, trash, or saved rounds to report at this time, SIR!" as they left the firing line and stood on line to be searched. They were then subjected to metal detector scans.

Lunch on the range was brought to us in bags. There was even less food than we got in the chow hall. Grass Week tested our discipline in a new way that went far beyond meager bagged lunches. The first week on the range was one of mind-numbing boredom. There were endless discussions and lectures on the theory of properly firing the M-16, as well as constant hands-on training about the correct way to hold, aim, and fire your weapon.

An instructor using a blackboard, set up in a two-sided open shed, carried out the lectures. We sat on wooden benches trying to remember a flood of important facts on which we would be tested and, more important, that would make the difference between learning to shoot well or failing and being sent home. Any time a recruit began to doze, the whole platoon was marched into the pit for a "wake-up call."

"Memory key—BRASS-F!"

"BRASS-F! *B*-Breathe, *R*-Relax, *A*-Aim, *S*-Stop, *S*-Squeeze, and *F*-Follow Through, SIR!"

"SECOND SAFTY RULE?"

"NEVER POINT A WEAPON AT ANYTHING YOU DO NOT INTEND TO SHOOT, SIR!"

"Remedial Action!"

"SPORTS! *S*-Seek cover! *P*-Pull the charging-handle to the rear and attempt to lock the bolt to the rear! *O*-Observe for a round to be ejected and take appropriate action to clear the stoppage! *R*-Release the bolt! *T*-Tap the forward assist! *S*-Sight and attempt to fire, SIR!"

"Sight alignment?"

"The tip of the front sight post centered both vertically and horizontally in the rear sight aperture, SIR!"

"Bone support?"

"The body's skeletal structure provides a stable foundation to support the rifle's weight, SIR!"

"Muscular relaxation?"

"Muscular relaxation helps to hold steady and increase the accuracy of aiming, SIR!"

"Natural point of aim?"

"Natural point of aim is the point at which the rifle sights settle when bone support and muscular relaxation are achieved, SIR!"

"Prone position?"

"Left wrist is straight. Magazine does not rest heavily on the arm. Sling pulls straight from the center of the arm, SIR!"

Dear Family,
Well, we've moved out to the rifle range and we're in the weapons

battalion barracks for 2 weeks, but mail should still go to the same address.

We've started eating the power bars on a regular basis. Can you send more of everything, especially *cough drops* (a lot) and power bars (a lot). Actually any kind of nutrition or bodybuilding bar is great. Things are going ok with the rifle. Final qualification day is next Fri. Prayers would be very much appreciated on that subject.

Anyway training progresses, as does the desire for real food. I've made a deal with a guy named Reyes, he's a Latino from Miami, that on liberty Sunday (we get 4 hours of liberty the day after the Crucible), we're going to make a tour of all the fast-food joints on base, which of course we are never allowed in as recruits and eat ourselves sick and then go to a convenience store, buy junk food.

Days are going really slowly now because all we have is classes all week, but today was Wed so we're half way through the week. The DIs are relaxing a little bit more now, it wouldn't seem relaxed to an outsider but it's a big difference from the first insane month, anyway, gotta go.

All my love,
John

P.S. Nutrition bars and cough drops in bulk please.

To the Waring High School (read at meeting).
Dear Waring,
Well it's a month and 2 days to graduation, and people are really counting down around here now. Training continues to get harder and we recruits continue to raise our level as a team to meet the challenges presented us.

This upcoming week is a big stumbling block for a lot of recruits. It's rifle qualifications week. This week Tue through Thurs we will shoot every day from the 200, 300 and 500 yard lines in prone, sitting, kneeling and standing positions. Fri will be qualification day. If you fail you get recycled, meaning you go back in training to another platoon to try again.

To give you a picture of how challenging this is last week out of

500 recruits 136 failed on the range. It's hard because first you have to make sure your sights are adjusted properly, taking into account wind speeds etc. and also the Marines have to qualify from further away than any other branch of the service.

Moving on to other matters. Thanks to Tony S. for sending the postcard [Tony's card was a "Go Army!" card. The DIs were not amused!]. That won me approximately half an hour in the pit! It's okay though for two reasons—1st they were looking for a reason to pit me and 2nd that half hour will give me the strength I need to pay Tony back properly when I return!

This week on the range is the last major obstacle to getting home on Nov. 13th. So next week I'll write and tell you whether or not to expect me a little later than I had hoped.

All the best,
John

P.S. How is soccer season going?

I don't know why I wrote my old school. Even at the distance of Parris Island, and with the growing sense of confidence I was getting with each passing day I still felt a need to try and explain myself to my peers, perhaps from a desire to be understood by people whom I liked and respected. Maybe I felt inferior to the kids going off to college and had something to prove. Mostly I wanted to explain myself to teachers whose good will I valued a great deal but who had never come in contact with military life, beyond what Jane Fonda had told them about Vietnam.

I had made some of my teachers and fellow students uncomfortable. I wanted my old teachers to know that the parts of me that they had valued were still present. I admired the headmaster, Peter Smick. I wanted to tell him that my attitude about life and maybe a little bit of my perception of reality had been altered but that I was not a baby killer nor did I yearn to destroy small Asian villages! It was very gratifying to me to have my dad write to me that the Waring community was following my progress through boot camp.

Sitting on the rifle range at Parris Island was a long way from that last summer at home and my poems about what I thought boot camp would be like. Now I knew. It was a way of being, not an idea. It was a way of being that was ignored by the parents of the children who went to Waring. Defending their country was definitely someone else's job, not *their* children's concern.

No one would have mistaken 1093 for the Waring graduating class. The "rich" recruits came from families with two cars, and a small home or apartment. The average Volvo or SUV driven by the average Waring parent cost more than most recruits would earn in the four years they had signed up for in the Corps.

This is not to say that I joined the Marines because of some desire to cross the divide between the "upper class" Waring world and the typical less privileged recruit. I joined because I was bored and sick of my lack of discipline; I didn't want to go right into college and wanted to do something different that didn't have all that much to do with my previous life.

The rifle range was "different" all right. During Grass Week, we would move a white fifty-gallon oil barrel out into a field behind the range and "sight" (point our rifles, learn how to use the iron sights, and get our bodies into stable firing positions) on the miniature targets that were painted on the barrels. About two hundred yards from us, the rifles of the recruits who were ahead of us in training could be heard cracking away like a distant roll on a snare drum as they sent 5.56 mm rounds flying downrange to targets so far away you could hardly see them, let alone the almost invisible bull's eye.

We were nervous about qualifying. Each crack of the nearby rifles was a reminder: your time is coming! Our nervousness manifested itself in the high degree of concentration we gave to our instructors and the tedious and tiring business at hand: endlessly pointing our empty rifles at the little black dots and head and shoulder silhouettes painted in rows on the barrels twenty or thirty feet away, hour after hour, day after day from the various firing positions; prone, sitting and standing, until we went numb and some heads began to nod.

The DIs would scare us awake by saying things like "Remember all those times I threw your rifle the length of the squad-bay? Well every time I do that it gets a little more broke! Those rifles are about twenty years old, just imagine how far the sights are off now!"

The DIs said that anyone can shoot if they follow instructions. Well, we wondered, what instructions could make the nearly invisible bull's-eye on some target five hundred yards away seem closer? We would be shooting with iron sights only; in other words, just the simple metal sights and no fancy scopes. Some bullet-riddled plastic flowerpots in the garden shed I'd plugged away at with my B-B gun years before represented my sum-total knowledge of shooting. Now making the cut all came down to this: qualifying with a rifle while shooting the length of five football fields.

We were beginning to sweat and obsess over how we would do, whether we would fail or pass as "Expert" (scoring 220–250), "Sharpshooter" (scoring 210–219), or "Marksman" (scoring 190–209), depending on the number of hits on the target at the various distances, up to the intimidating five hundred yard mark.

We looked with awe at the PMIs wearing their "Rifle Expert" medals (a silver pair of crossed rifles over a laurel cluster). We would have all gladly settled for the Rifle Sharpshooter cross with its eagle, globe, and anchor or even the lowly "pizza box" (a square target-shaped medal) for the lowest pass grade of "Marksman."

Dear Family,
Don't have much time, which is good in a sense, because it means that time is moving.
Feeling homesick, ready to come home, relax get kissed and hugged and *eat*.
Oh well, about 5 weeks to go, if I've done this much I can do more.

Love
John

The desire to graduate was overwhelming and led to an almost desperate determination to pass the rifle requirement, no matter what, and to keep quiet about our mounting injuries. By this time my foot was numb from the nerve damage caused by bone rubbing on bone after I'd worn out the cartilage between the joints of my big toe during long humps. Some of the other recruits were suffering from stress fractures, hernias, pneumonia, and other assorted injuries and sicknesses.

Memories almost made sense to me again as the larger outside world got tantalizingly within reach. I started to dare to remember what it felt like to lean against a wall in the sun and relax while staring at the tide running swift and blue in front of my house. My family became more real again too as I let myself daydream a little. News of my father working on the chimney brought back memories of other jobs that we'd done together around the house and barn: painting, clearing land, endless grass cutting while fighting off the greenhead flies and mosquitoes on a hot humid day.

All the community activity my dad was involved in really surprised me. I remembered that Dad had not even wanted to paint our house number on the gate. "Why let people know where we are?" he said. Now he was out in the town giving speeches about saving the beach from the casino up at town hall. What was going on? Had my joining the Corps changed the way he saw the world?

Erica also started to have a face once more. Her face, however, seemed different now, younger in comparison to the men her age I saw around me struggling to learn their marksmanship skills. She did not seem more distant from me; it was I who was more distant from her. Judging by her letters she had not changed. I had.

To Recruit John Schaeffer
October 10, 1999
Dear John,
Today at church the "old-boy" ex-Marines, Byron, Tim and Peter, *et al.,* were asking about you and pleased you're getting along. I heard Peter call Byron "Staff Sergeant." So I guess that their asking about you got their Marine juices flowing! Then Mary P came up to me joking about the fact that it looked like the casino was about to cave in and she called me, "a man of the people." That got a good laugh!

Francis is pleased because the JV soccer team he's coaching is 4 and 0. Having just beat Landmark, Francis is hoping for an undefeated season. Jane went to some pooley event on Friday and kicked butt, did 16!!! male pull-ups (not female hangs) and 86 sit-ups! They were calling her "GI Jane." (To me she'll remain the "bionic nun!") She'll be on the yellow footprints Wednesday 2 A.M. or thereabouts.

I don't think the women DIs will have ever seen someone quite like Jane: brains, motivation and kick-you-know-what in shape.

The gambling lobby are such sleazy bastards! They started conducting a "poll" where they had some company call everyone in town asking them such "questions" as, "Do you favor cutting your taxes in half and doubling your income if a casino gets built in your town?" This whole thing is taking tons of time! The only people who want them here are several of the selectmen and twelve or so landowners looking to clean up at the beach.

What was it Churchill said about democracy being the worst of all systems except for everything else? What is so great is that here in America we even have a shot of stopping these people. Imagine in Switzerland trying to go up against the banks if they wanted something? God bless America!

We pray for your safety and, God willing, a timely graduation. I lit a candle for you today in church as ever and never watch the Great Entrance or the Procession of the Gifts without thinking of you serving at the altar.

Love,
Dad

Dear Family,

Life is going pretty well (relatively) here on PI. The days are slow but they don't seem that way at the end of the week, it's Fri right now and next Tue we go out on the firing line for 3 days of shooting before qualification day (Fri).

Life on the rifle range day to day really oozes—we practice sitting in the shooting positions basically from chow to chow and lunch is a pitifully small bagged affair that gets delivered every day. But at dinner the SDI has really been letting us eat. This week, he took us in as the last PLTN twice (which would normally be bad because they would be out of a lot and you only get one scoop of food) but he let us go through the chow line *3* times and finish *everything* they had. I was almost *full*, something that hasn't happened once since I got here, and we're eating power bars etc. pretty much every day. So all those sorts of things in large quantities would be very much appreciated, as would be lots of cough drops.

Love,

John

P.S. I still dream of food obviously. Filling my belly is about the most comfortable feeling in the world.

The Monday after the end of Grass Week we moved onto the rifle range. The numb hours of "sighting" on miniature targets painted on barrels were done. We had often had to sit in one position, unmoving for so long that legs and joints would freeze up, and it would be impossible to stand for a while once we were ordered to.

We were to be issued live ammunition at last to fire in practice, not merely for "zeroing" (adjusting) our sights as we had the previous week. All our training not only with rifles but also in unflinching discipline and absolute concentration came down to this moment. It was make-or-break time.

The distances we were shooting from were 200 yards rapid fire, 200 yards slow fire, 300 yards rapid fire, 300 yards slow fire, and 500 yards slow fire. We took pride in the fact that as Marine recruits our lowest score—that is, the score a recruit could get and still pass—would qualify us as rifle "experts" in any other service. No other service made their basic recruits shoot at distances greater than 300 yards. Our worst Marine recruits were better with their rifles than the "best" the other services could offer in basic marksmanship.

Our men and women recruits all had to qualify at the same high standard. "Every Marine a rifleman" is not a hollow motto. A Marine cook or driver or general, male or female, can kill the enemy at 500 yards with a standard issue M-16 using only plain iron sights. All Marines must keep that skill through their career. In this sense there are no "desk jobs" in the Corps, any more than there are fat Marines.

The first two days on the range were devoted almost entirely to "sighting in," making sure that our sights were adjusted correctly for each distance and getting the knack of adjusting for wind. We shot every day and kept a written record of each shot, conditions it was fired under, wind adjustments, and the result. We were given constant and high-quality personal instruction all along as it was needed.

In the morning half of us in the platoon would shoot while the other half worked the targets at the end of the range, "pulling pits." When the first half finished, we would switch.

Pulling pits was a tough exercise. We would spend half the day in the concrete bunker behind the grassy berm, above which the targets popped up into view. We did this while the bullets whistled and cracked harmlessly a few feet above us.

The targets were mounted on wood frames that ran up overhead on ladderlike steel rails. We would reach up again and again, pull the target frame down after each shot tore through it, mark the hit with a sticker (white on black, black on white) so that the recruits downrange could see where their rounds had struck, then shove the target back up into position. Then we would raise a pointer stick and signal the score of the shot so the recruit shooting could see how he had done. (A month or two later my friend Jane got a hernia when she ripped her stomach muscles pulling down a target. Of course she told no one and graduated without being recycled. Later she had surgery.)

Life in the pit was presided over by a stocky, gravel-voiced, chain-smoking pit sergeant in his mid- to late-twenties. He had a thick southern drawl and a leathery tanned face and he delighted in telling us just how and why we were all going to fail on the range and get sent home. He tried to distract us, as if it was his personal mission to make us not only screw up but screw up some other recruit's shooting too.

The pit sergeant constantly reminded us that if we marked the shot wrong someone might not qualify or sight their rifle incorrectly and score lower. Then he'd rattle on about how important it was for "psychological reasons" to do our best for the nameless recruit aiming at our targets. (If the pit was not working fast enough or if there were awkward delays it made the recruit shooting nervous and could throw off the rest of his day, a day already over-whelmed by one thought: "If I fail to qualify I'll be recycled!")

Our pit sergeant would light up a butt off the one he'd just smoked, laugh, and begin to rag on us some more. I never did figure out if, like so much on PI, this harassment served some purpose, say to teach us to con-centrate under duress, or if the sergeant was just bitter at having pulled such shit duty.

16

To Recruit John Schaeffer
October 7, 1999
Dear John,
Erica called a while ago. She was at school and sounded fine. We talked for a good long time about this and that, mainly how you were doing. It was nice of her to call. She also mentioned that her parents miss you as well. Erica said her classes are going well and that she likes her new roommate better.

After I talked to Erica, I called Jane to say good-bye. She will be picked up Monday evening and sleep in a hotel that night and fly down Tuesday. You know the routine after that! Anyway she's nervous and anxious to get started and always very interested to hear every least thing about you. Maybe you'll see her. Let us know if you do.

We love you and are proud of what you are doing. We pray for your safety all the time.

Love,
Dad

P.S. By the time you get this there will only be 4 weeks to go! The tower deal is going well. I'm convinced Mass electric will cave. Not only will the cable go under the river, but now it looks like they may even take the old 1943 wood towers down too! Those things only got built during the war because of a shortage of materials so they went over the water.

I got old Sanders to come to a public meeting we called to testify about all the birds, including osprey and bald eagles that have gotten killed hitting the wires. They had some slick PR guy there but he was no match for Sanders. "You're a jackass sonny! I watched them towers built and they had so many birds hung up in the wires it looked like a laundry line!"

_____

To say the least it was surprising to me Erica got in touch with my parents. The fact that Erica got in touch with my Dad, of all people, was a sign to me that she truly missed me. I could not recall any occasion that she had ever made any effort to make contact with my parents or to be even polite to them. She had always hated my parents. While at boot camp I had thought about why she hated Dad and decided that it was because he did not fit into her image of what a serious father should be: a sort of soft, feel-good friend.

I did not know how to feel about Erica calling my father. It forced me to reconsider my evaluation of her. Was she ready to accept that I did, in fact, have a family I loved? Should I try and revive my feelings for her?

Ironically, I was about to stop writing to Erica altogether just as Dad wrote to tell me she had called him and had been friendly. So I continued to write to Erica. I decided I'd keep in touch until I had a chance to find out for myself if she had really changed in some way beyond what was coming through her letters. I decided to wait until the end of boot camp and see how things went while I was home for my days of leave. Meanwhile I was drawing closer to some of my fellow recruits than I had been to anyone outside of my immediate family and the "Boys."

Reyes became a good friend. (He was the Colombian recruit from Miami I mentioned before.) On the range, Reyes and I began to talk more than we had back in our old squadbay. I learned that his family was tight knit and loving. Reyes lived with both his parents and they were still married. This was always a big point. A lot of recruits came from broken homes.

Reyes was a stocky, strong little guy with a friendly light brown round face that made him look less tough than he was. He never complained about pain or hardship and smiled a lot when he talked about his family. He did his best to watch my back and help me get through each day, and I did the same for him.

Reyes had no idea why he joined the Corps, beyond wanting to do something "different." He didn't want to spend the rest of his life in Miami, he said. He didn't have the money to go to college. So he was going to learn data systems as his MOS and planned to have a good job someday.

Reyes was also a lot more serious as we got closer to graduation than when he came to PI. At first, early in training, he was always joking, somewhat of a smart ass. Big doses of being quarter-decked and pitted quickly made him a lot more sober. When he discovered that the DIs were quite prepared to "thrash his heart" and that they had no sense of humor, Reyes cut the crap and became a model recruit.

His family was big, friendly, and Roman Catholic. Reyes was not used to being away from home, let alone having people in his face yelling at him, and he worried a lot about his family and how they would do with him away. His parents did not speak any English and lived in a tough neighborhood. He had had friends that had been shot and killed.

Reyes and I were drawn together, not through common backgrounds or experiences, but because we worked well together and we survived better together than we did apart. After a while Reyes and I began to talk (when we could) and found that we got on very well. Both of us needed someone to confide in when our strength began to flag. We helped each other in many small ways, from squaring away gear to exchanging warning looks when a DI was on the warpath.

Each night (before the platoon hit the rack) there was "devotional time," in which we recruits could pray or not, as we chose. Reyes and I began to pray together for our families, for training that would go speedily, that we would not get injured, and that the platoon would have a good next day and for a chance to eat enough food. I would always go to his rack and we would both kneel on the concrete facing the footlockers and pray. One night I did the prayers from my Greek Orthodox prayer book, the next night it was his turn and we did the Roman Catholic prayers. I was Greek Orthodox and he was Roman Catholic but we were both Marine recruits and, when it came time to add our personal requests to our prayers, we both expressed identical concerns.

―――――――――――

To Recruit John Schaeffer
October 12, 1999
Dear John,
Well this was a big day. We got 2 letters from you! Reading between the

lines I'd say you are hungry, being the operative word seems to be "power bars!" So I sent a pile off priority mail and more cough drops too. You should have them by the end of this week, maybe before this letter. Be sure they will keep coming. (What's with the cough drops anyway?)

I'm glad you are finally out on the rifle range or rather the firing line. If you get this before Friday know I'll be praying for you especially for your qualifying. If it comes after know you were prayed for.

Good news on your SDI letting you eat more. I hope this trend continues and you gain some weight back. Let me know of any other food you can have and I'll send it pronto.

Keep an eye out for the Bionic Nun. She'll be there by the time you get this. She called every day for the last week before she went down. I think Genie and I are about the only people she's close to who understand what she's doing. Also she wanted to know every last thing you were doing we could pass on to her. She admires you a lot.

The leaves have started to turn bright reds and yellows. The nights are cool and the days crisp and sunny. The marsh has rust colors and reds beginning to creep across it. The starling flocks are huge and at night I hear the geese go over. The first frost did in the basil though some parsley remains.

The town referendum on the casino is on! And I think we have a shot. They will outspend us about a million to one literally.

I feel so proud driving up to town meetings with the Marine sticker on my car. Somehow with you doing what you're doing and me fighting these local tempests in a teapot at last I feel like I'm from someplace. My son is a Marine, I pay my taxes and form "local committees" to be a pain in the ass to corporate America!

Sorry if there was a gap of a day or two in the mail. Between the long weekend, Columbus Day, and me being stuck up a ladder for a week and the casino campaign a few less letters went out. Missing you as much as I do it's a big pleasure to write to you and feel close for a few minutes.

A *big* hug old boy!

Love,
Dad

To Recruit John Schaeffer
October 14, 1999
Dear John,
Tomorrow you'll be on the range doing your shooting to qualify. This will get to you after that but we are thinking of you and praying for a good result.

Last night at the parish council meeting we spent, among other things, about ten minutes discussing the late Mrs. Nicholson's cat. She left her house to our church and her lawyer now wants us to make a donation to the cat shelter in her name! But we have good information the cat, in fact, is *not* in the cat shelter but someplace else with some lady in a new home. So it was left that if we find the cat *is* in the cat shelter then we *will* make a contribution, the amount to be determined at the next council meeting. If the cat is with this lady then *no contribution* will be made despite the heartfelt appeal that ended, "I remind the members of the council that our Lord told us to be kind to small creatures." Well this reference drew a blank with me. I have no idea what Bible verse he means. So maybe this will need to be referred to Holy Cross Seminary for clarification! I'll keep you posted.

It is a rainy day. The leaves are flying around the garden driven by the big gusts. A little later in the month and this wind would strip the trees bare. But a lot of leaves are just now turning so they are still clinging on.

By the way bring me back an anti-personnel mine! (Just kidding Mr. DI!) There is a dog that pisses on my *NY Times* about every three days or so before I can get up the drive to retrieve it. I'm tired of urine-soaked news! In any case this dog seems to regard my *Times* as a kind of movable fire hydrant.

Less than 4 weeks to go! We pray for your safe and timely graduation. I hope you get to keep *all* the power bars I send now. Let me know how many you actually get.

We are proud of you old boy and miss you A LOT!

Love,
Dad

P.S. Speaking of morons at the selectman meeting one selectman proposed a motion to endorse the casino then forgot it was *his motion*, went to sleep, then woke up and voted against his own motion! The motion lost! Well, we'll take all the help we can get!

---

bye bye Marshal
just couldn't do it
stare at the flags
flying over the berm
see what they tell you
send rounds after them
into the south Carolina
marsh, bye, bye Marshal

"Qual Day" on the rifle range was the single most stressful day in all of boot camp. (The gas chamber was the most frightening moment but was not as stressful.) The night before qualification I had the only bad night of sleep during all of training. Up till that night I'd rested better at boot camp than I ever had before. On the night before going to the range to shoot my qualifying rounds, I tossed and turned and fell asleep only moments before being wakened by the usual DI barking.

We woke at 0430 and marched through the wet cold grass out to the rifle range before dawn. We needed to be on the range before sunrise, preparing to shoot in the windless conditions just after first light. The earth berms that hedged the range in, leaving it open only on one side, looked like distant hills, as if they were miles away rather than only a few hundred yards.

In the distance I could just see the numbers, painted on fifty signs about six feet high, marking the target positions. At the top of the target berm were the six-by-six targets. Two huge red flags lay limp in the still air. They indicated that the range was "hot." (Later those pennants would serve to help judge wind speed when the morning breezes began to stir.)

On Qual Day our Senior DI had put the worst shooters first to give them the best chances of qualifying when the air was still. The better shooters were marched to pit-duty to pull targets for the morning. I was among the better shooters so had to bide my time behind the target berm and pull pits until after lunch. We better shooters were thought more capable of making adjustments for the wind that always began to blow as the sun heated the ground, or so the DI said.

While pulling pits I noticed quite a brisk breeze was beginning to blow. I had all morning to obsess over wind velocity and determining correct "windage." Range X wind velocity (mph) = clicks for full value wind . . . forty-one clicks to center . . . three to five mph, wind can be felt lightly on the face . . . five to eight mph, wind keeps tree leaves in constant motion.

All the recruits out on the line would face the tower and scream the safety procedures at it in one voice. When the control tower range safety officer was satisfied, he would send the first group of shooters up the line. When your target slid up into view and you were in whatever firing position you were supposed to be in, you were allowed to start shooting.

"LOAD."

"LOAD!"

"MAKE READY."

"MAKE READY!"

"YOU MAY COMMENCE FIRING."

Out of eighty-seven recruits we had twenty-eight go "UNQ" (unqualified) that day. We were not the worst platoon on the range but our senior felt that we had taken way too many UNQs. (Twenty-eight UNQ was much higher than the average on PI.)

The recruits who went UNQ still had all of the next week in MTP (Marksmanship Training Platoon) to qualify and remain with the platoon while those who had qualified would be on Team Week working in the kitchens. If the UNQs did not qualify during Team Week, they would be dropped down two weeks in training to a new platoon. Then if they went UNQ again they'd have one more chance and be recycled again. Then if they *still* could not qualify, they would be on the bus home after sitting around in the processing platoon for another two months, having just sweated their guts out for nothing.

Our Senior had made all the recruits who were in danger of going UNQ that day write a letter home the day before saying that they would be graduating two weeks later than our grad date of November 12 if they failed to qualify. He mailed the letters that day. If a recruit qualified at any point in the next week, he was allowed a thirty-second phone call to his parents to tell them he would be graduating on schedule after all. The knowledge that families were being informed of a recruit's problems on the range was one more form of "motivation."

Marshal got dropped. Marshal was a twenty year old from Brooklyn. He was tall and thin and had a cheerful smile. He had tried hard to become a Marine, always sounded off well. Marshal had ebony-dark skin and high cheekbones. He was relatively wealthy, as Marine recruits go, and very intelligent. His parents were still married but horribly inattentive. Marshal received no letters in boot camp, not one. I'd see him staring straight ahead at mail call when most others got mail.

Marshal couldn't shoot no matter what. He got dropped back twice after he went UNQ on Qual Day and went through all four weeks of shooting training again. Then he got sent home. Somehow he couldn't translate the instructions to his hands, arms, posture, and breathing. I knew he was trying but the instructions did not compute into physical action; he just didn't "get" the connection between the sights, his posture and how to adjust for the variables of wind and distance. Unfortunately for Marshal the Corps could use all sorts of talents but in one thing everyone must excel: shooting. The gospel according to Parris Island is that shooting well is the bedrock of discipline. Other branches of the military might rely on fighting enemies from "over the horizon" (or outer space at the push of a button), but the Marines still needed to know how to kill people they could see.

At five hundred yards a twenty mile per hour gust of wind can affect a round traveling down-range and displace it more than six feet from the point of aim. A very slight problem, like a loose rear sight aperture with a rifle, can throw off a score. A bad night's rest, flu, a fever (a lot of us were sick) can drive scores down. For the recruits like Marshal who were teetering on the edge, by the time we got to Qual Day the variables, wind, tiredness, tension, or lapse in concentration were a huge concern.

One miss not only drastically affected our scores but also had a deep mental impact. The foremost rule of good shooting is to be relaxed, to use your bone structure as a steady "tripod," and to allow the rifle to rest easy in steady hands. A pounding heart, let alone being out of breath, as your confidence slips away after firing a bad round doesn't help. There are few things more disheartening than sending a round downrange and having the target raised up from the pit, with the scoring stick next to the white or black dot scoring your shot a "zero" or waving in front of the target signaling "no impact."

Strangely enough at noon, when I got my turn to shoot to qualify, it was not as nerve wracking as I had expected. It felt like every other day I had shot that week. I had my sight adjustments calibrated perfectly and was able to relax, somewhat. Shooting for me was not hard. I was not afraid of the rifle or the kick and rather enjoyed the idea of sending a piece of lead through a barely visible black outline 500 yards away. By Thursday, the day before Qual Day I was so relaxed that I took to trying to shoot the scoring stick that was held aloft between shots on the slow fire exercise. I'm pretty sure that I got it at least once. Some Marine may have a good story about getting his hands "stung wicked-bad by some fucker on the five hundred," as we would put it in Salisbury.

Late Friday afternoon, right after shooting at 500 yards I qualified "expert." I had shot near perfect rounds from 200 yards and 300 hundred yards, and by the time I got to the 500 yard range was told by my shooting coach that my score was high enough so that, "If you hit the target at five-hundred yards just once you qualify. So just relax, Schaeffer."

A moment after the DI told me that I'd shot expert, I realized that the only obstacles between me and graduation was the Crucible or an injury too severe to hide.

17

Dear Family,

Well it's Fri night and guess what, I qualified, and on top of that, I qualified "expert" which is the highest rating. I got 7 out of 10 bulls-eyes from the 500-yard line. I also was pretty damn lucky on the shooting coach I got. He was on the Marine Corps shooting team for 6 years and is an Olympic medal winner, so he broke things down pretty easily for me. Anyway it was simple. I didn't have any problems. So my saying for the day is—"Well . . . my work here is done!"

A couple of things though, first, yes Jessica I get all your letters and they are great, second, well I don't know what was second . . . so I'll move on.

Tomorrow we start "Team Week" and boy am I gonna eat myself sick!

Oh, yeah, the second thing was an answer to a question, cough drops are the closest thing to candy around here that we can get.

Go Ha Go!

Love
John

After we moved off the range Team Week began. The platoon was split up into working parties that were sent all over the Island doing different tasks. Some worked cutting grass, others cleaned offices. My working party was assigned the Weapons Battalion chow hall.

Reyes and I had found out that there was no Burger King on PI in the food court. Of course we had never been near the food court ourselves, but we had the facts from a newly graduated Marine. Via letter Reyes organized it so that his Mom would bring us each a BK Broiler on Family Day. This BK anticipation became a huge part of our motivation toward the end of training, driving us each day to try hard and bring the day to an end more quickly.

On the range, while wolfing a meager bag lunch each noon, we had encouraged each other with whispered, "BK soon!" "Don't give up, BK on the way!" My parents were going to bring pizza. With those two foods, all my small wishes would be fulfilled.

If someone had told me, twenty years before, that "the little shit from Switzerland"—as some friends in English boarding school were sometimes wont to call me—would have a son in the U.S. Marine Corps and that I'd be sitting in the Salisbury Town Hall staring up at the stained ceiling tiles and arguing a case against a casino being put smack-dab in our wetlands to five selectmen (rather, to three of them—one was asleep and one was on my side), I would have bet my house against it. As Jeeves might have said, "The contingency would be remote."

I had come a long way from the days when, like most cowed Europeans, I minded my own business lest worse befall me. After moving to the States, I even became optimistic enough to fight city hall. I even—and here I would have *never* been mistaken for a Swiss—believed our committee against the casino could win against both a state senator and well-funded private interests.

I never felt a personal stake in the United States until I came "home" as an adult. Besides a few treasured copies of *Mad* magazine, candy corn, and other "American treats" sent by distant relatives, as well as one trip to Pittsburgh Children's Hospital when I was seven for surgery on my "bad leg," all my youthful ideas about my country came from the American students visiting the mission and from my parents. (Weirdly, my parents taught me almost no American history.)

I had traveled in the States as an adult but stayed in hotels, and I never lived anywhere longer than a day or two. For Genie it was a homecoming when we moved to the States; for me it was an emigration partly driven by the fact that I wanted to direct movies. To me, America was just one big mine from which to extract a living.

I still believed much of my father's fundamentalist Calvinist critique and entered my country with some trepidation. He had made it seem dangerous and rather wicked. I knew nothing of day-to-day life in America and my father's (and other fundamentalists'), lurid descriptions of its "decline" seemed to be at odds with the reality I discovered. I was learning that America was a lot more than either a "declining culture" or a mere "heartless money machine." Neither of these descriptions fit the little town in New England where we settled, or New York where I worked on various writing and film projects. Or even Los Angeles, where we lived off and on for a number of years, home to "degenerate Hollywood."

I was amazed by the opportunities. In the early 1980s I worked on a series of documentaries. In 1985 I directed my first feature. Three more— none good, but that was my fault for being desperate enough to direct some very lousy scripts—followed over the next few years. In 1990 I became Greek Orthodox. In 1992 my first novel *Portofino* was published. Richard Eder gave it a glowing half-page review in the *Los Angeles Times*. Other reviews followed and the book began to sell well. In 1994 my second novel, *Saving Grandma,* was published and, thankfully, was also well received. From then on, when anyone asked what I did, I said I was a writer. When they asked where I was from, I answered, "New England." In America I could be what I wanted, change careers, even rethink my beliefs and change churches.

America was more than a mine from which to suck a living. America was a great idea, an idea that worked. The "godless Secular Humanists running Hollywood" turned out to be just grasping shallow narcissists bent on making a fast buck, no better or worse than the grasping shallow narcissists bent-on-making-a-fast-buck televangelists railing about them. My rich and generous country was not on the brink of ruin, fascism, satanism, communism, or one-world government and decline. Americans' worst complaints about their country looked downright petty when compared with life in Europe: the stifling powerlessness, the fatalism, the clunky top-heavy Eurosocialism, the entrenched ways, the ties to "blood and soil" (rather than to ideas and principles), the strata of elites blocking access to opportunity, the long waiting lists for nationalized health care, the racism. America was less racist than Europe, let alone the rest of the world. Tribalism and hatred of the "Other" was the norm, as I discovered while making documentaries, feature films, and working with local crews, traveling around Israel, Africa, France, Hungary, Canada, Mexico, and many points in between. In much of the world, to be from the wrong tribe—be it Tutsi, Basque, or Palestinian (or even Italian, trying to get a work permit in Switzerland!)—was to be excluded from meaningful opportunities, maybe hacked to death, or enslaved.

America compared well with other countries, not to mention to every other supreme power in world history. I thought about what the Romans would have done with our power post-1945 had they been in our shoes—killed every man, woman, and child in Germany and Japan, then sowed their fields with salt.

The world could thank its lucky stars that all they had to fear concerning American "hegemony" and "globalization" was an invasion of fast food, stupid movies, sneakers, and microchips. If the Saudi regime was the world's supreme power, they would be treating the rest of us to Shariah law, including the public beheading of homosexuals (not to mention the killing of Muslims who dared to convert to another faith), women banned from driving cars (and flogged for doing so), and every religion besides Islam persecuted and marginalized.

I discovered a great truth by simply living in America for twenty years, long enough to compare facts to "prophetic" doom-saying fantasies: The right, religious or otherwise, and the left, academic or otherwise, were wrong 90 percent of the time. All you had to do was wait, and, more important, remember what they had claimed was about to happen, as their worst predictions came to naught. It turned out that Ralph Nader and Pat Robertson were both full of shit!

African Americans were joining the middle class in unprecedented numbers. Teenagers could get summer jobs. Crime was down. The economy was productive beyond the wildest dreams of just about everyone else we were supposed to "learn" from. Women were treated better in America than any place else on earth. American minorities did better here than when they were the majorities in their native lands. Our universities were the envy—and our cities the cultural centers of—the world. Corruption of public officials was the exception, not the norm. Many races lived peaceably within our borders. If you needed a hip replacement, you could get it without waiting years. Our bombers were stealthy, our weapons "smart," and our military mighty. For the first time in a hundred years, there were salmon and sturgeon gliding back up the Merrimack River that ran in front of my house.

Proof of our good fortune could be seen at our border where huge swaths of humanity, of all colors and creeds, clamored for entrance. The nobility of the American experiment was reflected in the fact that the other nations looked to us for leadership and protection and, when anything went wrong, paid the ultimate compliment to our moral authority: they blamed us for not being true to ourselves.

When John joined the Marines, I realized something shocking: I loved America. I felt fortunate to be a small part of her. If any nation in history was a worthy cause, America was. If my son was called to defend her, I would be scared, sad, and proud.

---

down the home stretch
happy for once, riding
a wave of expert rifleman and
almost done, leaving
some behind but we
cannot carry them anymore
dead weight can be carried for
only so long.

Matt Snyder's family had been connected with mine long before I was born. Matt was a B-2 "stealth" bomber pilot, an Air Force captain with the 393d Bomber Squadron, "The Tigers." Matt's parents were once coworker missionaries with my grandparents. Matt left Switzerland and joined the U.S. Air Force when he was eighteen.

It was after bouncing my idea of joining the Marines off of Matt that I seriously began considering a life in the military. He visited my home after flying in an air show near us when I was a junior in high school. A life in the Air Force and a life in the Marines are very different but at the time, before I knew anything about the military, it seemed to me that one service was much the same as another. It was seeing how Matt made a life for himself in the service that helped set me on my path. Matt put an inspiring face on a life that was completely foreign to me.

Now that I was in boot camp I realized that Matt was "Captain Snyder" and that our relationship had permanently changed. From now on he would be "sir" to me, and, if I saw him while in uniform, he would receive the salute due any officer (with maybe a little sardonic smile behind the "*good morning sir!*"). Matt had told me that the military was a meritocracy and that you could measure yourself by tough standards.

The Friday night of Qual Week I was *actually happy!* It was the first time I'd thought of Matt and what he had once said, "You'll know how good you are." It was the first time that I was happy on the Island. I knew now that on my own merits I would graduate, that the only thing that could hold me back was an unforeseen injury.

The Crucible and the Battalion Commander's Inspection were the only two graduation requirements left. I knew that I could handle the two and a half days of sleepless conditions the Crucible offered. We had already overcome challenges in training that were more physically demanding, from humps with all our gear to the gas chamber. The Battalion Commander's Inspection was rumored to be something of a joke; as long as our uniforms and weapons were in the condition we always kept them in anyway, we would pass.

My platoon entered what is known as "Team Week." Every week a new platoon took over the maintenance of some vital area of the Island. We were grateful for the chance to rest. Best of all I was selected to work in a chow hall. (We were responsible for the weapons battalion chow hall.) We woke up at 0330 every morning. Our job was to prepare morning chow for all the other platoons that would be coming in to eat before going out to the range to continue their shooting. After we were finished serving the morning meal, we could eat as much as we wanted of whatever was left.

The Marine cooks let us relax; in other words, not have to sound off, stand at attention, and so forth as long as we got the work done. My job was to prepare food in vast vats, four to six feet across and five feet deep, scrub and clean the kitchens, cook and serve other recruits and EAT!

During meals I was head "deck recruit," cleaning tables and making sure the area was clean.

For the platoons on the range time was always at a premium. We prepared the food that would be brought out to them: One premade sandwich, one small bag of chips, one package of cookies, and one piece of fruit.

"Poor bastards! Shit I'm glad I'm not out there!"

"Yeah, and look how crappy this fucking lunch is!"

"Shit, man, who cares? On the range, ain't worrying about some goddamn motherfucking apple."

"You saying that 'cause you full now, motherfucker. Last week you was sucking that mayo packet same as everyone else."

After evening chow we could leave as soon as we were finished cleaning, usually around 2030. When we got back to the barracks we did a quick mail call and hit the rack the second after everyone had finished with hygiene time. Not only were we tired from the sixteen-hour workday of "rest" but also the cumulative fatigue of the last months was beginning to tell. The moment we let down after Qual Week, it felt as if we hadn't ever slept for our whole lives.

To Recruit John Schaeffer
October 19, 1999
Dear John,

Hey, hey, hey, "Expert!" Seven out of ten bulls-eyes from 500 yards! A big well done from all your fans here! Wow!

Thank you for writing Friday night ASAP after you shot your targets and qualified. We were anxious for you. How *great* you did so well and got the instructor you did. (Little note in the minor-mercies-of-God category: we never get mail, only junk mail, on Tuesdays so I was in despair at having to wait until Wed. *But* your letter arrived today, Tuesday! Great all around.)

I faxed it to Jessica right away only this time *as* the mail arrived she called up to see if we'd heard if you passed the shooting test yet. Good timing. Also, Matt was here visiting so there is the fact your news got shared with a B-2 captain, too, as soon as we got it.

Mom is baby-sitting Matt's little girl while they go out to lunch at Michael's for fish. I'm writing to you and have cut the grass, done my writing, and filled in a bio question sheet for the German publishers of "Saving Grandma."

We are so proud of you big guy! Mom and I were *thrilled* at the news. You are, as you may have heard once or twice before, a great son!

Love,
Dad

18

Dear Family,

Well it's Tues and I've been working since Sat at the mess hall. I stand for about 16 hours a day. There are 30 of us working there and at every meal we feed about 1,800 people. The one good part about all this crazy work (and I do work all 16 hours) is that during meals I get to eat whatever I want. At breakfast I ate 4 trays yesterday morning and didn't eat for the rest of the day.

Dad, you have no idea what you're missing in the way of cooking utensils. The galley in this place has the biggest ovens/pots/pans I've ever seen. I actually came up with an imaginary bumper sticker for Marine cooks—"Hey what's the big deal? I fed the five thousand too."

The only reason I have time to write this morning is because I'm skipping mess hall duty to go to my security clearance interview. I'm not really nervous about it because I know that there is absolutely nothing that I can do at this point to affect the outcome of a background check. This is just a big hassle in the end (the interview). I don't actually know what the point is.

Love
John

P.S. I have a little more time than I thought. Congratulations on the novels coming out in all those languages. I've been filling out forms for my security check like a madman.

With John in the Corps suddenly I wanted to know what John's—what our—military family history was. I started to press my mother and Genie and her sister Pam for facts. I wanted to know where this tall son who shot "expert" came from. Who was John? Who were we?

My mother's ancestors (Merritts and Sevilles), fought in both the American Revolution and the Civil War on the Union side. My grandfather on my father's side (a second-generation German emigrant) ran away to sea when he was twelve, joined the U.S. Navy, trained on the *Constellation*—"when the ships were made of wood and men were made of iron"—and fought in the Spanish-American war. Genie's great grandfather on her mother's side (King was the family name) was a deputy sheriff in the state of Arkansas and her mother's ancestors fought in the American Revolution.

As a pastor my father did not fight in the war but worked tirelessly in missionary relief efforts for young people in bombed-out cities right after the war. Genie's parents Stan and Betty Walsh were very definitely members of the "greatest generation." Stan was the son of an Irish emigrant family. His grandfather emigrated to America from Ireland, and his father and mother, as adults, came as homesteaders to western North Dakota in the early 1900s. Stan was raised in North Dakota. He grew up in the Great Depression and went to the University of North Dakota, after arriving with one pair of shoes and fifteen dollars in his pocket. He worked his way through college. He could not afford to live in the dorm and spent the first year living in a converted (and frigid) railroad caboose with five other students. At Georgetown Law, Stan was too poor to buy books; he completed his law studies using the Library of Congress books he was able to borrow because of the kindness of one of his state's senators. Stan served in the Coast Guard during the war, in spite of having had a very serious injury to his arm that should have kept him out of the service. He married Betty King, who first worked for the FBI, then the Coast Guard, assigned to the encoding unit. (She packed a forty-five almost as big as herself while carrying top-secret documents from one office to another in Norfolk, Virginia.) After the war Stan became a successful San Francisco lawyer, practiced and taught law, and raised a family of five. Genie's older brother, Tom, served in the Army during the Vietnam era.

Soon after John joined the Corps, Stan got John on the phone and pronounced a heartfelt, "We're all so goddam proud of you!" Coming from his much admired grandfather, those words meant a great deal. John's eyes lit up when he reported what "Grandpa Walsh just said." I later heard John mutter, "Goddamn proud" several times under his breath, rolling the words over his tongue. My mother called many times to commend John and to assure us she was praying for him.

To my surprise, through John we had grafted ourselves back into a strong American family tree. It turned out that from the perspective of who his family was, what John did when he joined the Corps was normal. It was only to me and to my "boomer" generation that it might appear strange to have a son serving his country when he was qualified to do other more "important" things.

At first, when John chose the Corps over college, I still had a need to justify John's choice to others. "John's joined the Marines," I'd say in answer to someone asking after my son. Then I'd add somewhat sheepishly, "Did you know that Art Buchwald says that the thing in life he's most proud of is his service in the Marines?"

As the letters from boot camp kept coming and as I read more and more about the United States Marine Corps's history, and learned more about our family's record of service, I got tired of my mealymouthed justifications.

After John started thinking about the Corps, I got some interesting reactions.

"Wow, your son sure is a hell of an athlete!" said the wealthy father of another player, as we stood on the sidelines of a Waring soccer match.

"Thank you."

"Where's he going to school next year?"

"He's thinking of going into the Marines."

"Is money an issue? Because you know what with those poems he read at the last school concert and his athletic ability he could get a scholarship."

"We can afford school."

"Then *why?*"

"He wants to."

"But he's so bright and talented and could do anything! What a *waste!*"

The father got very busy with his cell phone and scurried up the sideline. Moments later he cruised off in his behemoth, one-mile-to-the-gallon SUV, replete with a Stanford decal, front and center on the tinted rear window.

As I paced the sidelines I was seething. I was imagining the father of a

Marine serving in Vietnam and how he must have felt as he watched the legions of upper class males lining up for the student deferments. I was reading *Making the Corps* at the time, and one passage struck me in particular. According to statistics published by James Webb, secretary of the Navy, Ret., the number of Ivy Leaguers who died in Vietnam was tiny compared with the national average: Just twelve from the twelve thousand five-hundred who graduated from Harvard between 1962 and 1972, six from Princeton, and two from MIT. By contrast, the predominantly Irish working-class neighborhood of south Boston produced over two thousand draft-age men who served in that same time frame, twenty-five of whom died in Vietnam.

If the immorality of the Vietnam War was the only reason those lucky enough to go to college dodged the draft, why did we not volunteer to serve in the military later? Or why did we not encourage our children to volunteer at least in proportion to their numbers *vis-à-vis* the poor and uneducated once the war was done? Why was I so shocked when my son joined the military? Had we all become pacifists? Did our educated upper class cease to profit from American power? Did we no longer need a military? Was the world a safe place? Did America have no enemies or international responsibilities? Had God ordained that after say, 1968, only the middle and lower-middle classes and especially the poor should defend our country?

We were no longer in the Vietnam War, but the attitudes of many of my educated peers still seemed stuck in the late sixties. One impeccably dressed middle-aged lady in a movie theater—on the Upper West side in New York—expressed an attitude that I came to find infuriating. The theater was running prefeature commercials. One was for the Marine Corps. I heard the woman behind me groan loudly, then say to her companion that she didn't think it "should be allowed" since it was such a "disgusting display of jingoism." (She had not complained about the Pepsi commercial moments before.) "Look how *these people* trick the poor uneducated young men into thinking the military is such a great thing with all that *patriotic chauvinist bullshit!*" she said. "Trick them into what?" I wanted to yell, "into living on food stamps while they defend your rich moldy ass?"

Later, on the subway, I was still making up speeches of what I would have said, should have said, would say next time. "Does the Upper West side issue its own passports now? Last time I checked, New York was still in the USA, lady! Who the hell do you think is protecting you, the sanitation department?"

While working in the kitchens was less stressful than life on the rifle range, I started to get nervous because I had to go to a security clearance interview. I had signed on for an "MOS" (job) in military intelligence, involving cartography and map analysis (0231 Intel Specialist). It involved the reading and interpretation of satellite photos (or so a recruiter told me). I scored high enough on the ASVAB test (the general aptitude and intelligence test all military personnel take when they are initially recruited) to sign up for that particular job.

My chosen MOS required me to get a top-secret clearance. (Most jobs in the Marine Corps do not require any security clearance.) There would be various hurdles to be crossed. The first of these, after much paperwork, was to take place in an initial security interview on Parris Island. I was brought to the office where interviews were handled, and grilled by an official from one of the government agencies that processes military security clearance investigations. (Clearances were not handled by the Marine Corps.)

For an hour a stocky middle-aged white civilian threatened me with the consequences of fraudulent statements and tried to scare me stiff. What I noticed most about the man was how out of shape he was. I was not used to seeing flab in authority figures. Our DIs were taut, tough, hardened men. We recruits were thin and runner-wiry-to-weight-lifter strong. No one on the island (outside of new recruits in the pork chop platoon) was fat. This civilian Intel background checker was *pudgy!*

We sat in a small neon-lit office with no windows, devoid of all pictures and distractions. It reminded me of the interrogation rooms in a police station I had visited with my father when he was doing research for the novel he was working on the year before. (We had driven to Philadelphia together and spent three days touring the criminal justice system from prisons to police stations and the district attorney's office.)

I certainly felt like a suspect while being questioned. Another recruit from my platoon, Recruit Andrea, was there at the interview with me. We were brought into the office individually to be interviewed. My stubby interrogator fixed me with an intense stare that made me feel as if I was being accused of some heinous crime.

> fat civilian asking questions
> he already knows the answers
> but stares at me
> like I'm lying anyways
> beady eyeballs and sweaty
> forehead
> aging agent
> stuck intimidating the helpless.

"Are you now, or have you ever been, associated with a group dedicated to the violent overthrow of the United States government?"

"No, sir."

"Has any member of your family?"

"No, sir."

"Have you ever been addicted to drugs?"

"No, sir."

"If you are lying to me you will be prosecuted. Are you lying to me?"

"No, sir."

"Tell me about your criminal record."

"I've never been arrested, sir."

"Are you sure?"

"Yes, sir."

"What about your drug use."

"I do not use drugs, sir."

"Ever?"

"Only what I wrote down. I did smoke some pot in high school, sir."

"And what about all the other drugs you took."

"I did not take any, sir."

"Are you sure?"

"Yes, sir."

"Better tell me now and get it over with, 'cause if you did we're going to find out."

After the grilling was over I spent some more time entering the details of my life into a computer. Friends, relatives, employers, their names, teachers all went into the file. I was worried because I didn't know many of the answers to the questions, such as addresses or even street names of where my friends lived. I was told not to worry about it: "Just put the name and the town if you can't remember, we'll find 'em!" That, as you can imagine, did not exactly put my mind at rest on the whole Big Brother conspiracy theory front!

After the interview I went back out into the office and sat down to wait for my next set of orders or forms, whatever they might be. A staff sergeant came over and asked me a few factual questions about family and friends. (It was a relief to be back with a Marine and out from under the withering gaze of the fat civilian.) The sergeant asked me if I would think about changing my job over from Intel specialist to Signals Intel. He told me about Signals Intel—"It starts out with Morse code work but gets cool after that, real James Bond-type stuff!"—and informed me that the jobs for Intel specialists were filling up whereas Signals Intel was begging for people since it took passing a special aptitude for decoding signals in order to get into that MOS.

I agreed to do some of the preliminary testing for Signals Intel, not that I had any idea what this really was. (For that matter I had not understood my first MOS either.) I did quite well on the tests. The sergeant offered to let me switch my MOS and told me that this would add an extra year to my contract with the Corps, putting me in the Corps for five years rather than four.

I accepted his offer, along with Andrea and two other recruits from 1094, Snyder and Murfield. I returned to the squadbay feeling a little dizzy, and with a new MOS and an extra year's commitment to the Marines on my contract. Like so much that happened to me in joining the Corps, this decision, a big one that would add a year to my contract, was made before I thought about it.

Maybe it was foolish or maybe I was just used to obeying instructions. Maybe the truth is that I couldn't think of anything better to do with my time than some "really cool James Bond stuff," so why the hell not? Or maybe the whole point of joining the Corps was to serve the needs of the Corps. In any case, I'd bought myself an extra year in about thirty seconds, and changed my job for the next five years.

Both Dad and Mom had said several times, "Don't let the Marines talk you into anything without talking to us first." I could just hear Dad. " '*Cool James Bond stuff ?!*' You did what?"

To Recruit John Schaeffer
October 21, 1999
Dear John,
I called GNY Dubois this A.M. to tell him about you shooting "expert." He said to me, "Not many guys do that, you should be very proud of your son." Well he got *that* right! I, (we) *are* very proud. I e-mailed Rodman the news too. He told Prisca and John [my oldest sister and her husband] and they all send you their congratulations. Rodman said, "Not many make it. He can be really proud. Good man! For that is what he is now. The Marines build them." Prisca sent the message, "I'm happy you have done so well."

I wanted to say *I love you lots.* The best thing in the world is that we are friends. It is my greatest possession. I miss you very much and can't wait to see you! I am praying for you as you head into the Crucible.

Love,
Dad

Dear Family,
Well, life moves on here at PI, maturity increases as does excitement and calm (is that an oxymoron? Hold on I'll explain). Excitement increases for getting the HELL out of here, and calm increases in everyday life as things make more and more sense and the DIs begin to treat us as Marines and men.

Love,
John

As we moved into the last days of training, life on PI finally made sense to us. The seemingly petty discipline that had been forced down our throats so hard through everything that we did was no longer pointless busywork but an essential part of our daily boot camp lives. We began to understand why each individual task we were given, whether in the chow hall or the barracks, or even how we got dressed or were told to sit made sense. We saw how each detail of training contributed to being prepared for the larger challenges, how learning to think as a unit in the small things contributed to cohesiveness in the big ones. In the chow hall during Team Week, this was especially driven home. We could not relax or stop until every task was completed, from preparing vast amounts of food, to the last floor or surface that needed to be disinfected when you were bone weary late at night. Even in such a limited environment as the kitchen the adage "Mission accomplishment first, troop welfare second" was driven home by the chow hall duty variant, "Feed first, eat later."

With the completion of the rifle range, we began to imagine, in vivid detail, getting off the island and what it would be like. There was a recruit whose only desire was to go to a Wal-Mart, his logic being that a Wal-Mart "contains everything that is truly American, from merchandise to customers." (The fact that half the merchandise was made in China didn't faze him.) One recruit wanted to go turkey hunting, another dreamed of the taste of his first cigarette in three months. All these desires seem very minimal when considered from any perspective but that of a recruit. To us the small things we had given up had become life. They were not just symbols of our existence or a reward that we had won at the end of the race; they became something that reminded us that we were, in fact, alive in some way that had nothing to do with Parris Island. These small desires proved to us that we were not just the mindless tools of our DIs, that we could still do something beyond what we were ordered to do. Perhaps we started dreaming on such a small scale because we could not imagine doing anything more significant than eating a favorite food after such a long time of having no independent thought.

The end of Team Week came as a great relief to all of us for many reasons. It meant a return to slightly more regular hours of sleep. It meant we were one Sunday closer to graduation. It also meant a return to the routine of our daily lives.

We were not comfortable being left to our own devices for such long periods of time. (When I say such "long periods of time" I mean having twenty or thirty minutes to ourselves in the kitchens from time to time.) We *wanted* to be told what to do, where to go, what to say. The platoon was uncomfortable breaking apart, some working in the chow hall, others mowing grass, none of us together or under the supervision of our DIs. Having been of one mind for so long, we wanted to be back together, the body of the platoon with the head, the "brain" being our DIs.

"Individualism" was a word that was a curse to us. A platoon will not survive in boot camp if it is broken into eighty individuals. I had a rare moment of true happiness when I awoke on the first Monday after the end of Team Week to the routine yelling of a DI getting us out of the rack. I was truly content. We had returned to normalcy! Everything was right with the world.

By now all the recruits who had gone UNQ and had not managed to qualify during Team Week had been dropped to another platoon. When their name was called at mail call (they still received letters at their old address), if they were "shitbirds," in other words disliked as "turds" who didn't belong in the Corps, we shouted, "DEAD, SIR, DEAD! COULDN'T HACK IT, HAD TO PACK IT!" or "STRUGGLING WARRIOR!" if we thought they rated the title and we were rooting for them to make it. If they had been medically discharged, they received a "FALLEN WARRIOR!" (How we all knew who "rated" and who didn't I can't say but we did. By that time we knew who would be a "squared away" Marine and who was still a "nasty civilian" at heart. If it had been left up to the DIs they probably would have cut several more marginal recruits who we all sensed might well dishonor the Corps at some later point in time.)

Dear Family,

Well, its Sun. Team Week is over. I got 9 hours of sleep last night. I gained 12 pounds this week. I force-fed myself and snuck as much food as physically possible in 7 days, which was quite a bit.

Next comes A-Line which is sort of like a week of practice for the Crucible. It's very cold here. I went to church today, we're still living out at Weapons Battalion so I went to the chapel there. I'm not going back to main side until the Mon after A-Line so I probably won't see Jane until the Sun before graduation.

I'm very happy to get back into training and start moving forward to graduation again. We're so close! But the SDI said, "You ain't on the bus yet, you're only in line with your ticket."

All my love,
John

To Recruit John Schaeffer
October 23, 1999
Dear John,
What you have done is such a great accomplishment we are still glad you went down there even though being so out of touch is tough.

When I mentioned to Andre Dubus Jr. [author of *House of Sand and Fog*] you'd shot "Expert" on the range he was so pleased for you. Right away he said that his dad [Andre Dubus Sr., author of many short stories] had shot that too. The fact Andre Jr. knew that fact just goes to show what sort of accomplishment it is. Here is a famous writer telling his son about shooting expert years later and the memory sticks.

By the time you get this there will be not much more than 2 weeks to go! I love you very much.

Love,
Dad

19

From time to time I'd call my dear friend and screenwriting partner Frank Gruber and talk to him about John, boot camp, and the Marines. Sometimes I'd rail to him about my vicarious military zeal with the fervor of a new convert.

I was surprised that Frank—a subscriber to *The Nation*, a liberal living in "the People's Republic of Santa Monica," an entertainment lawyer and writer married to a professor of philosophy who sometimes called herself a "Stalinist" (a charming one at that)—was supportive of John's becoming a Marine. But Frank described himself as "of the nonpacifist, patriotic left." I'd vent to him nevertheless. (As old friends we tended to do that, all in good humor, though someone listening in might not know it.)

"The military chain of command ends with my son facedown in a sand pit. It begins with Clinton! What the *hell* is this draft-dodger doing as *my* son's Commander in Chief?" I said to Frank, while taking an impromptu break from working on a script with him over the phone.

"My basic response to you is 'fuck you, you weren't even living here during Vietnam and know nothing about it! Clinton opposed the war, so what?'"

"Clinton's the first of our generation's gaggle-fuck of boomers to make it to the presidency. Do you think he's worthy to be my son's commander?"

"Do you think the children of rich *Republicans* were grunts in Vietnam? By the way, have you ever tried beer can chicken?" asked Frank, having given up on talking any sense into me.

"What? WHAT?"

---

this is what some wanted, combat,
READY TO DIE BUT NEVER WILL.

> train, train
> lasers in the sky
> tracers flying north
> into the marsh

With the end of Team Week came A-line, a week of intense combat training where we went on night maneuvers, learned to fire at targets at unknown ranges during both day and nighttime, and to shoot with a gas mask on, something that was easier said than done.

A-Line involved many of the situations we would be confronted with in the field or in combat. We began by putting our rifle firing skills to the test on the twenty-five meter range where we learned the basics of sighting and firing from behind uneven obstacles, from platforms, and over the wall of bunkers and trenches. (After two weeks of firing at targets from two hundred yards and farther, these targets looked as big as a house.) Then we progressed to shooting at distances of seventy to three hundred yards at "pop-up" targets that appeared and disappeared. Finally we began to fire at "surprise" targets. The targets were "killable"—when hit, they would fall automatically. We fired from sandbag emplacements covered with camouflage netting, concrete bunkers, from behind piles of rocks, logs, and other barricades. Then we moved onto the Day and Night Movement Course.

We were taught the basics of surviving combat conditions. We learned how to negotiate difficult terrain while under fire. We had to race over walls, through pipes, crawl through trenches, negotiate barbed-wire barricades, practice aiming from behind cover, and learn to do all this both in daylight and in the dark. For those recruits on their way into the Infantry it was a first taste of things to come. For the rest of us it was a part of the hands-on combat training we would complete with three weeks of field training at MCT in SOI (School of Infantry) at Camp Lejeune a few days after boot camp ended.

A-Line was the kind of warfare training that most closely resembled what most recruits pictured they would be doing when they joined, taking cover from explosions and listening to the rattle of machine guns simulating combat conditions, the firing of weapons, inching on your back under barbed wire (while holding it off with your rifle), and marching silently through the night; crawling through mud illuminated only by the red glare of phosphorous flares and avoiding the flash-bang booby traps that the DIs had set up earlier to test our ability to move slowly and cautiously.

"If any of you nasties set off one of these in the dark, you won't be quiet and pretend it wasn't you. You're going to shout, 'Recruit so and so is *really* dead, SIR!' Good to go?"

"YES, SIR!"

"Same if you do it a second time. And if you do it a *third* time you're going to walk off the course screaming, 'Mama, where's my legs? Mama, where's my legs?' and while you're screaming that, you're going to make *sure* your brain bucket [helmet] is on tight and you're going to bang your head on a tree until I find you and tell you to stop. Good to go?"

"YES, SIR!"

The DI wasn't kidding. Later I saw a couple of recruits banging their heads on trees.

"What is your mission?"

"THE MISSION OF THE MARINE RIFLE TEAM IS TO LOCATE, CLOSE WITH, AND DESTROY THE ENEMY, SIR!"

There were moments of great discomfort. The Day Movement Course through simulated battle conditions was very difficult for all of us. After a week of doing "nothing" but working in the chow hall, and eating like pigs, we were all out of any shape to tackle the unbelievable amount of "low crawling" in full combat gear. However, these hardships had ceased to bother us. We were ebullient and unstoppable. The platoon was nearing graduation! Short of being beaten within an inch of our lives, there was nothing that could have slowed our steady progress toward our goal of earning the title United States Marine.

The end of A-line marked the last phase of our training. We had acquired the basic skills we needed to be Marines—in other words, disciplined riflemen with a rudimentary understanding of how to be warriors—though, of course, each Marine would then have to go on to specialized training in the skills required for his individual MOS. More important we had absorbed the real lesson of Marine boot camp: to learn to surrender our individual freedom for the common good of the Corps.

Now it was up to us to prove we had learned the hard lessons of the last three months. We were about to take the final "exam." The Crucible was that test.

We had three days to rest and prepare for the Crucible. Packs needed to be organized, weapons checked and cleaned, and the squadbay had to be cleaned and prepared for our departure.

During the Crucible we would be living at the Crucible Operations Center, dedicated to this last fifty-four-hour marathon of training in Corps values: honor, courage, and commitment. Selfishness would mean failure. Only teamwork could produce success. We would be living in a bivouac area in open plywood huts out of doors for a three-day period of combat simulation and team exercises to test the limits of our training, mental ability under stress, problem solving, and stamina.

Six major events requiring teamwork in simulated battle conditions, as well as specific exercises such as resupplying a small unit and evaluating and evacuating "injured" personnel, were designed to be both mentally and emotionally exhausting. Upon completion of this final three-day and mostly sleepless event, we would hump a final ten miles with full packs and combat gear to the Colors Ceremony and be awarded our eagle, globe, and anchor while we stood in front of the Iwo Jima memorial. From that moment on, even though official graduation had not yet taken place yet, we would be Marines.

There were no more classes. We spent our time between A-Line and the Crucible getting our gear ready and having our final fittings for all the uniforms that we had been issued over the course of training, from blue trousers to green "Alphas." We also learned we'd be buying these uniforms, as well as everything else we had used on the island. Money was even withdrawn out of our pay for our "haircuts." So instead of going home with $2,000, I would be returning with a little over $600 for three months' work. This struck me as a little stingy when I remembered that I made $600 a week painting houses when I was a kid.

Uniforms are a very big deal to Marines. They have changed little over time and are part of our heritage. Our buttons are emblazoned with the oldest American military insignia worn by any service: the eagle, globe, and anchor. The collar of the dress blue uniform dates back to the leather stock worn around the necks of American Revolution–era riflemen. The officer's sword (the Mamaluke Sword) is a replica of a sword given to Lt. Presley O'Bannon after a Marine victory on the "shores of Tripoli." The stripe worn down the blue trousers of officers and NCOs (noncommissioned officers) is, according to legend, the "blood-stripe" earned in the "halls of Montezuma" (the battle of Chepultapec) where officers and NCOs suffered 90 percent casualties.

We did not get much sleep in those last days. Imagining what the Crucible would be like and talking about it after lights out kept us awake far into the night. Pacts were made between friends. Reyes and I promised that we would each make it our personal responsibility to see that the other finished no matter what. We made a pact that if either of us was injured we would carry each other's load, and cover for one another so that the DI or corpsman would not see our injury. It was a solemn promise that many in the platoon had made and would keep.

The platoon was particularly concerned for Recruit Parks. Parks, a tiny and frail recruit from New York City, had developed double pneumonia and might not be allowed to go through the Crucible. It was rumored that he was close to being recycled. We all knew that he deserved to be with us on the parade deck when we graduated, as did our SDI. Senior Drill Instructor Staff Sergeant Marshal announced to the platoon: "Parks is going to finish with us if I have to carry him in my pack!"

The night before the Crucible, unbeknownst to our DIs (and to Parks, who would have refused), we picked out a few of the stronger recruits and divided the heavier items in Parks's pack among us to lighten his load. It was this type of camaraderie that made me believe that we had truly become a band of brothers, willing to carry the other's burdens. We were looking foreward to the final test of the Crucible to prove what we already knew, that we were United States Marines.

Dear Dad,
How goes the writing, well I expect, although I'm sure you don't feel that way. On Thurs when you wake up I'll be on the Crucible. Don't worry. I can do it. I want to pick some movies we can go see together. Unfortunately I can't sneak into movies with you anymore, with a security clearance search in progress even jaywalking would be a little risky for me! I'm waiting for Thanksgiving with baited breath.

All my love,
John

We were warned not to think ahead, to continue to take things one day at a time, chow-to-chow, as we had for all of training. All that we had left to concentrate on, we were admonished, was the Crucible and how we were going to get those of us who were injured or ill through it.

20

Dear Family,

Well I have big news! (Which you may or may not like) I have changed my contract and my job. I now have a 5-year contract as a Morse code interceptor/recorder in Signals Intel. The training will take place over the course of 9 months, 4 months in Arizona and 5 months in Pensacola FL. It was just something that I was a lot more interested in doing and also they had a massive shortage of recruits going into this field. So when I went to get my security interview I was tested and I passed so they asked me to change my MOS. I've enclosed a paper that explains (in very general terms what I'll be doing).

Sorry I gotta go, write later.

Love,
John

I knew that my parents would be upset with me for changing my job, especially because it added an extra year to my contract. I did not particularly care what they thought about it one way or the other. I was filled with zeal for the Corps. I knew my parents could not understand—from the civilian point of view—that it did not matter to me what job I was doing as long as I was doing it as a Marine. All I wanted was the title. At that point four years or five was not a big difference to me. I was not planning to turn the Marine Corps into a lifelong career. I had plans to go to college and I figured that while I was in I might as well do something that I was interested in, and that the Corps needed me for: end of story.

To Recruit John Schaeffer
October 26, 1999
Dear John,

We got your letter re changing your MOS. It was a bit of a surprise. However we are not in any position to judge one way or the other. The only thing we wondered about was you choosing something that seems to be so obsolete. Morse code is not used any longer in any commercial application at all. So we wondered why you would go into something that seems so limiting in terms of the future. Also we are sad you will be so far away. With your old MOS you would have been in the DC area for further training and that is driving distance from home. Where you say you'll be trained now will mean that you won't be home much and that we won't be able to see you during most of the next year.

I did mention before you went to PI that it might be an idea that you not change your MOS without talking it over with us or Marines like Rodman who have been around the block. In fact you told me you would not. Perhaps you forgot this. The reason I bring this up was that Max had warned me that the Marines will pressure recruits to go where they need them regardless of the consequences for the individual Marine, and that whatever you did to stick to your guns on this. I told you this too.

So much for all that. I hope things are in good shape otherwise.

Love,
Dad

John's decision to add a year to his contract with the Marines made me angry. I might yell at my friend Frank about all us "selfish boomers," but my knee-jerk response to my son, for increasing his commitment to the Corps, was not much better than that of the father on the sidelines who was so shocked John would "waste" so much time.

John's explanation answering my letter was scribbled on the back of the "Dear Marine Family" form letter from the commanding officer inviting family members to join in Family Day and graduation. (John had had crossed out the word "depart" in the letter and replaced it with the word "flee" as in,

"Following graduation, your Marine will pick up his personal belongings and is then free to depart—*flee*—Parris Island.)

Dear Mom and Dad,

The reason I changed my MOS is *not* just because they asked me to.

1st: my MOS is not what was originally presented to me. I would be posted with an infantry unit training and deploying to combat zones all over the world with them, not originally what I signed up for.

2nd: Who cares if Morse code is a dead-end field? I wasn't planning to make a career out of cartography or on-sight intelligence gathering either. (Remember I want to write and own a bookstore.)

3rd: I'm interested in Morse code.

4th: I joined the Marines for multiple reasons, one of which was the experience. Who else at the Waring School can say they went to boot camp and did signals intelligence?

I hope this helps a little bit, obviously we'll be able to talk in more depth when I call Sunday afternoon, but for now this will have to do. [The recruits were allowed one call home, the first in three months on the Sunday after the Crucible.] We're gearing up for the Crucible getting cold weather gear packed etc. Things are going well.

All my love
John

P.S. Do not throw this enclosed paperwork away; you need it to get on PI.

I have more time than I thought so as I said before, *do not* throw away the info packet; it's your ticket to graduation. I'd encourage you to do the whole thing, might as well get the full patriotic bullshit experience.

For the first time in my life I feel like I have an element of control/direction, and while I know that's a complete fallacy, it's a nice feeling to have. I also have a real sense of accomplishment. I think that's because in most other areas of life you can get through by faking or bullshitting, like at Waring or when writing. Even if you were working hard you could never be sure because there was the possibility that you might be bullshitting (self-doubt I guess). But here there's no room for bullshit. Either you got the job done or you didn't. Either you hit the target or you missed. It's nice to know I really did it.

I don't want you to be too sad about me changing my MOS. First of all, I'm only in Arizona for 4 months, a little longer than boot camp plus, we'll be in a lot closer contact when I'm at school as opposed to boot camp.

2nd: If I had stuck with my MOS I could have ended up anywhere in the world, Bosnia, Okinawa, Somalia. Marine infantry units never know where they will end up or when they'll die for some jackass who wants to make a foreign policy statement or improve his ratings in the polls. Finally I'll say again, it's only 4 months in Arizona and 5 in Florida (not that far), after that who knows? I might end up in New Hampshire. This will not be like boot camp. I can call, and write and travel and e-mail and take liberty and go on leave and all those good things. It isn't the total darkness of Parris Island.

All my love to everyone,

John

I knew John was lying for our benefit. John couldn't care less about danger. I did not like to see him trying to manipulate me through my parental fears. This was the first time that it came home to me that John had signed up to serve a machine, a heartless governmental machine, over which I had no control whatsoever.

"He's so weak! Why did he do this?" I asked Genie just before bed the night we read John's further explanations.

"Don't start," Genie said.

"I wasn't blaming you, only I wish you'd backed me up better with him!"

"There you go!" Genie swung her legs back over the side of our bed and stood up. "I *won't* put up with it! Do you know what I like least about the children?"

"Why don't you just get back in bed? I'm not fighting," I said.

"Do you know what I like least about the children?" asked Genie again.

"Okay, what?" I said, knowing exactly what she would say.

"When you put me in the *middle* between you and them! Why didn't you just talk to John yourself if you didn't like something?"

"You know I did! Only you never backed me up. You were too weak along with him, never made him clean his room!"

"You always overreact! Besides, you gave me that speech about leaving John alone! And you said it IN FRONT OF HIM and completely undermined my authority!"

"I don't know what you're talking about," I snapped.

"Yes, you do! You did it when he was twelve, gave me a speech about a boy being 'raised by his father' and that women should stay the hell out of the way! I tried to correct him about his schoolwork and you said he was a boy and didn't need a mother nagging at him and that from now on *you* were going to be the only person he answered to and to leave him alone! So I did!"

"And he turned out fine!"

"I never said he didn't! *You're* the one complaining."

"Well I'm going to write to him and tell him what I think."

"Don't you *dare* go after him while he's in boot camp! That's totally unfair! How is he supposed to defend himself?"

———————

I want to do this now
no need to explain
brotherhood, I am here and doing
no matter what I do
I am still a gear
in the machine

I did not care that Morse code had almost no civilian application. For one thing it was just an extra qualification, a-just-in-case. My real job I'd learn after I mastered Morse was something much more interesting (and classified). Anyway I had been raised in a home where we were taught that learning and experience should be gained regardless of monetary results or opportunities contained therein. I was taught by example from a freelance artist-movie director-writer who despised the career-oriented North Shore "yuppie scum," and yet now, when it came to me . . .

Dad did achieve one thing with his opposition to my adding a year to my contract; he made me think more about why I was in the Corps. One of the things that I had realized over the course of my time in boot camp was that no one I met had enlisted for patriotic reasons. It was not wartime. Then by the time graduation rolled around, and we were preparing for the Crucible, speaking for myself, I could hardly remember why I'd joined. In any case, what I imagined I was joining, and the reality of PI and the Corps were two different things.

If the recruiters had tried to explain the truth about the Corps to me before I signed up, I would not have understood them. I got the message about being "the proud, the few," but it hardly told the story. People enlisted in the Corps for selfish reasons: self-improvement; because they were broke; because they had nothing better to do; had something to prove to fathers, mothers, and girlfriends; or for training that would "pay off" later in the civilian world, such as aviation electronics. Some joined to follow in the footsteps of fathers and brothers. Some bought into the nice uniforms or just wanted to belong to something, anything, or to see the world. After we all got to Parris Island, our reasons for wanting to be Marines changed and deepened, or we got sent home.

By the end of boot camp, each of us believed that we might be sent to different parts of the world to die in causes that might seem utterly ridiculous. We knew that the Marine Corps is the only service that the president needs no congressional approval to deploy, and for that reason we are an all-purpose force: "land, sea, and air, first in, first to fight." We were aware that we would be involved in actions in which we had no say whatsoever. We knew we would do the job and do it well, not because we wanted to kill people or die, but because each Marine relies on another Marine watching his or her back.

That was the difference between the reasons most of us had for joining and the reality of what boot camp turned us into, and how it changed our thinking. For whatever half-assed reason we joined, by the time boot camp was done we were aware of our responsibility to the other Marines who depended on us. We were also aware of the tradition we were going to uphold.

We were constantly reminded of it by the simple white markers all over PI, reminders of Marine battles and sacrifices for country and Corps, from the Boxer Rebellion to World War II, Korea, Vietnam, and Beirut.

The issue was not one of patriotism. Speaking for myself I had no sense of the whole country. When I thought of defending something I thought of defending the people I loved, Mom, Dad, my brother and sister and our home, as well as my town and friends. "Patriotism" was too big a concept for me. To defend the things I loved I could grasp.

Most of all loyalty to the Corps was something boot camp made tangible. By the end of boot camp, we were trying to be good Marines out of loyalty to the Marine standing next to us and to those who would follow us onto the yellow footprints we had stood on three long months ago. On Parris Island I came to see and believe what I was told; each mission is dependent on another that came before. When it came down to it, as any recruit could tell you by the end of his or her training, the Marine next to you is more important than you are.

Dear Family,
Well it's Tues the 25th and (including today) there are 18 days left to graduation. I've become close to Rec. Reyes. In boot camp you sort of learn absolutely everything about everyone. Isn't it weird that the most personal question I could ask him was what his first name was? Very strange. His name is Juan. I only learned this yesterday.

Fr. Andrew sent me a prayer book and a little Icon of St. Basil the Great. It is very nice. There isn't much news other than that. Next Thur I go on the Crucible, finish on Sat and will call home on that Sun, because I'll be on liberty.

Oh! I forgot! My leave after boot camp has been extended until Nov. 30th—an extra 7 days—so I'll be able to be home for Thanksgiving.

Love
John

P.S. Pray about the Crucible.

I forgot that I had been given an extra seven days of leave to spend at home. Maybe I had a hard time imagining what a break could be like so that the news my break was to be extended did not compute. Maybe the idea of going home made me uncomfortable, as if I no longer belonged there. The word "break" no longer had very much meaning to a recruit. We had thought Team Week was a nice "holiday," and that consisted of at least sixteen hours a day of hard work.

The longest amount of time that a recruit ever gets to himself or herself is the three or four hours on Sunday morning, when he or she can organize personal effects and go to church. Even in those rest times, after about an hour I had no idea what to do with myself. I became phenomenally bored without orders to follow. The idea of taking undirected and "pointless" time off no longer made any sense. The only point of time to yourself was so that you could square away your gear to be better prepared for the moment when the orders started coming again. Once you had done that, what was there to do besides just standing by?

The thought of returning to the aimless civilian world was almost as frightening to me as the idea of being injured and remaining indefinitely in MRP. I knew that I was reaching the end of training, but the fact that I was almost at the goal of achieving the title of Marine was not sinking in. The prospect of using the first person to address a Marine or anyone else seemed unnatural; the very thought of it was repulsive. To think that soon I could refer to myself in the first person in front of a DI, without being punished, or that I would hear people address me by my name rather than as "recruit" hardly seemed possible.

A live John sighting! Jane was barely a month into boot camp when John was about to graduate. She wrote to us about seeing him. It meant a lot to us to hear from an independent witness that John was okay.

> . . . Something interesting happened today—call it serendipity—not only did I see John at the Catholic service today, but he was standing at the altar with me the entire service! (How appropriate the church setting is for us to run into each other where we had both been chosen to assist the priest.) Of all the places to stand he was right next to me! We got to speak a little (rare event on Parris Island turf) and

it was really a fantastic hour. John looks like a Marine. He looks very
healthy and well. He even scribbled a little note to me.

John's note to Jane was on a tiny scrap of paper torn from some photocopied
church program and stuck to her letter with a Band-Aid. She was kind enough
to send the original on to us. The torn scrap of paper, hasty scribble, and clan-
destine nature of the exchange gave John's note the dramatic feel of a POW
camp communication between prisoners.

Rec. Vizzi, I'm on Training Day 54, things are going well. We go to
the Crucible on Thur. Don't let things get to you. The DIs can't stop
time. Stay motivated. Rec. Schaeffer

To Recruit John Schaeffer
October 28, 1999
Dear John,
Hi boy. Just to clear something up: Whatever your MOS and wherever you are you know we'll make every effort to see you. DC would
have been nice but you've got to do what you've got to do if we like
it or not and Mom and I *will* find ways of coming to see you and also
bringing you home for holidays when possible, wherever you are. I
didn't want you to worry about that.

You're a good man, John, to plug away at all this. I am so proud
of you. I pray that the Crucible goes well and you are free from injury
till the big day.

Mom and I have been doing fine. The weather is cool, sunny, and
perfect New England in October. Jessica and the babies are fine. We
all love you very much and think of you constantly.

We have the Nevada lot on the run. I did an op-ed piece for the
paper exposing their phone-bank professional "push-polling" to our
town. Now they are threatening to bring in their spokesman Bill
Cosby (so much for Mr. Family entertainment!) to do a pro-casino on
the beach evening. What next?

Love,
Dad

My frustration at John changing his MOS was replaced by the excitement, however unreal it felt, at the fact that we'd soon see him. The anticipation of seeing John blocked out just about every other thought. Genie and I planned to make the pizzas he wanted on Family Day. I hung on to that thought.

John had written so confidently about his achievements and he sounded so much more self-assured than he had ever been before. I'd been asking myself all year, What does John want in joining the Marine Corps? I had my answer: "*For the first time in my life I feel like I have an element of control/direction, and while I know that's a complete fallacy it's a nice feeling to have. I also have a real sense of accomplishment . . . Either you got the job done or you didn't. Either you hit the target or you missed. It's nice to know I really did it . . .*"

I had inadvertently discovered a little about the "club" my son joined. With Marines stickers on my car and truck, I got a friendly wave from time to time from strangers with short haircuts. I even stumbled on a new garage just up the road from my house. One day, after John had been on PI about a month I stopped in for a minor problem with my brakes. The owner glanced at the Marines sticker, commented that he and his dad had been in the Corps, and nodded in approval when I told him my son had just joined.

The sticker was like some sort of password. I did not have to wait for service or repairs. Jobs on my two deteriorating Fords were done for less than the quotes. A mysterious transmission fluid leak that had baffled everyone got fixed at no charge.

I discovered that the waitress at Angie's, the diner where Genie and I went for breakfast, had two sons in the Corps. Our small talk over her open order pad cut to the heart of our lives faster than most talks with some of our oldest friends. I learned her name was Marie, that she was from Ireland, and that her oldest son was a sergeant in the Corps. Her youngest boy was just finishing boot camp a few weeks ahead of John. Marie, Genie, and I understood each other perfectly as we compared notes on what it was like to be so utterly cut off from our sons during boot camp. Marie shared cheering news on how well her son was doing who was already in the fleet and how "grand it's been for the boys" to become Marines.

The day after our chat with Marie as I drove up Route 1 to the post office, I noticed the monument to the war dead in Salisbury Square that I'd never paid the least attention to in twenty years of driving past almost every day. After dropping off the mail—and getting into a heated argument with one of the landowners who wanted to sell out to the casino—I crossed the street to the shady little park and read each name out loud. I thought of Marie and her two sons and of John, Asher, Max, and Jane and wondered how the mothers and fathers during Desert Storm, Somalia, Vietnam, Korea, World Wars I and II had been able to stand it when their children were "over there" beyond their help. I got a lump in my throat thinking about the boys like my son John who had come back from Vietnam to empty airports without so much as a welcome or thank you. The thought made me feel physically ill.

21

Dear John,

When you get this you'll be done with the Crucible. Well you are tired I bet. I can't wait to hear how it went.

I got back from NY yesterday. I had a good time. The rehearsals and the reading for the musical comedy version of *Portofino* were fun. There were great pros involved who earn their living on Broadway. The actors and director are terrific as only NY theater people are. (What a contrast to all those assholes in Hollywood!) Actually the show is quite good, needs a bit of cutting here and there but is fine. So who knows, hope springs eternal, maybe it'll even get produced someday!

Genie is well. We have been having a really good week. Marriages go up and down, as you know. But this is one of those times we are very close and happy. Maybe we are both content because you are doing so well. In any case, knowing how well you've done certainly contributes to our/my sense of well-being.

Well big guy on to the next! I'll see you about 5 or 6 days from when you get this!

Lots of love,
Dad

To hear that my family was doing well was a great source of relief to me, seeing as I always regarded myself as a sort of calming influence on my parents. (Other kids I knew said their parents had big fights. But in our house fights between Mom and Dad tended to run to the somewhat operatic.) I had worried about what would happen when I was finally out of the house and unable to diffuse situations before my parents really blew one of their arguments way the hell out of proportion. Judging by the letters, it seemed that my worries had been unfounded and that it may have been a good thing that I got out when I did, before my father and I had a chance to start knocking heads in a big way.

Dad's letters triggered a line of thought that forced me to realize that despite the fact that I have always considered my father to be a complete raving lunatic he often made good points inside statements that were wild exaggerations of the real situation. For instance he thought that Erica was a deliberately conniving and coldhearted person, which she wasn't. However, Dad's delusion sprang from a truth: Erica was an emotionally needy individual who required loads of attention. My changing views of Erica, and my discovery of the "one-day-at-a-time" principle Dad had always lived by gave me a new and interesting perspective on my father that I had never admitted to myself before boot camp: sometimes Dad was right!

As the platoon approached the Crucible tension started to build. It was our last substantial roadblock to graduating. None of us were particularly nervous about the events or obstacles of the Crucible itself. We had faced almost all of these challenges before, just never in combination. However, the growing fear of injury was now the shared nightmare of all recruits. We had everything to lose. To go through twelve weeks of training and to be injured on the Crucible and unable to graduate was a vision of hell.

To Recruit John Schaeffer
November 4, 1999

Dear John,
Today we got two letters from you including the information packet re graduation on PI. It was great to get all your news! Thank you so much for clarifying the MOS situation. In any case I understand

Morse code is a requirement for running a successful bookstore and being a poet! In fact last novel I had turned down they wrote, *"Dear Mr. Schaeffer, while we quite enjoyed your book we regret to inform you that it's not for us. We would have published it but for the fact that you do not know Morse code."*

As I write you are deep in the Crucible. *Mom and I are so proud of you!* I tell everyone I meet about your great achievement. Your point in your letter about knowing you did something minus any BS is instructive. It is a great thing to have done something hard and not been found wanting. You have been measured by a tough standard and have been found worthy of one of the great institutions in America: The USMC. Well done John. You make me proud to be your father.

I love you big guy,

Dad

P.S. Major pizza session soon underway here! We are on the way!

———————————

As the Crucible began, the platoon was broken down into squads, each led by a DI. We humped a total of fifty-four miles carrying all our equipment, ran obstacle courses, and undertook tests that forced the squads to work together to devise creative solutions to all sorts of physical and mental challenges, from walking together with our feet all strapped to the same log, to figuring out how to move heavy equipment over rope bridges while not touching any parts of the ropes that were painted red.

With only four hours of rest per night (eight in total over two and a half days), the course was physically exhausting. We were hungry and got only two MREs which had to last us the whole time. Six major events took place. These were centered on simulated battle conditions and involved such tasks as resupplying a small unit with ammunition, evacuation of an injured Marine, and "Warrior Station" obstacles. High towers simulating multistory structures had to be scaled, using teamwork to move bodies and equipment from floor to floor without the use of ladders or steps. The "battlefield" was crossed and "fought" through, including bayonet assault on the dummies, taking cover from machine gun fire, explosions, and other simulated battle conditions both by day and night. High rope bridges were crossed while ferrying dead weight barrels, bodies, or ammunition boxes. All this was done fast and well under the constant exhortation of the DIs.

The most difficult part of the Crucible was a giant mother-of-all-blisters that began to form on my left foot on the first six-mile hump out to Belleau Wood, an area of PI named for the French battlefield of World War I. By the last afternoon of the Crucible, the blister covered the whole of the bottom of my foot. It made walking a weird and painful experience. When I took off my boot it looked as if a large pink jellyfish was stuck to the bottom of my foot.

Many of the exercises in the Crucible involved designating a recruit as wounded and carrying him on a stretcher over, under, or through obstacles. Parks was not in my squad but he played the "wounded" recruit in one of our platoon's other squads. He was having trouble breathing and was running a high fever and still refusing to ask to see the doctors. Parks's squad carried him on a stretcher whenever any exercise demanded that one recruit be designated "injured." They carried Parks's pack and pulled him under the barbed wire through the mud. His squad carried him through the water and over the obstacle course. They steadied him as we inched along wood beams far above the ground and always put him in the middle of any group task, such as passing heavy barrels over high obstacles. Parks's team held the netting steady for him in the climbs and put a recruit on either side of him when they did the "Stairway to Heaven" scramble over the forty-foot structure.

Just before the final march to the Emblem Ceremony, the Inchon Individual Movement Course (an assault course made up of barriers, pipes, and bridges) had to be crossed in a resupplying maneuver while under battle conditions. As with every other area of PI, this particular course was dedicated to the memory of brave Marine deeds—in this case, the battle of Inchon. We paused briefly before the exercise to read the simple wood board notice.

INCHON
On September 15, 1950, the 1st and 5th Marines successfully accomplished an extremely daring amphibious assault far behind the North Korean enemy lines, relieving the pressure on the Pusan Perimeter and eventually routing the enemy to the north of the DMZ.

The rest of the Crucible took place in "Belleau Wood." We stopped and read the plaque.

BELLEAU WOOD
In honor of those MARINES . . . Fighting through supposedly impenetrable woods and capturing supposedly untakeable terrain, the persistent attacks, delivered with unbelievable courage earned them the nickname: "TEUFELHUNDEN" (DEVIL DOG) May 30–June 17, 1918.

On the last morning, the whole platoon, now thinking of ourselves as "Devil Dogs," humped ten miles back to the parade deck. The DIs made the hump a little longer just to have a little last "fun" with us recruits before we were proclaimed Marines. They also pretended not to notice that there was always one group of recruits bunched up around Parks, as we took turns propping him up as we marched.

crucible time
not really a terrible
challenge just one
more tedious trial
that we will be
pulled through by
the light at the
end of this tunnel
teufelhunden

As we stood at attention in the shadow of the Iwo Jima memorial and saluted the colors, while the flag was raised by the Color guard, and tears streamed down our cheeks, Parks stood pale and unaided on his own two feet with us. The moment was all the sweeter because we had finished as a platoon and had not left a man behind.

The men who had driven us for the last three months congratulated us and handed us the symbolic representation of what we had earned, a small black eagle globe and anchor emblem pin. Our DIs shook our hands, still filthy with grease camo paint and the grime of the last three days. It was the greatest moment of pride that I have ever experienced.

We received our eagle, globe, and anchor emblems and we were marched back to the barracks. No longer recruits, we marched as Marines. After all the buildup that it received, I found the Crucible to be a little easier than I'd expected. I was tired and hungry and my feet were starting to come apart, but I knew now that it was only a matter of time until it would be over. Nothing happened during the Crucible that was a greater challenge than the ones we had already overcome during training.

We dropped our sodden packs and formed back up outside the house. Then we marched to chow and stood in the chute waiting for the order to enter the chow hall.

Our SDI spoke to us: "You are now Marines and will conduct yourselves accordingly. You are an example to all the recruits who will be watching you." He then went on to explain to us that as Marines we were allowed to use more than one utensil to eat our chow, even to use *both hands!* From now on we could *speak* in the chow hall! We could even *lean against the backs of our chairs* and did not have to sit at the position of attention while eating!

All these ideas seemed ridiculously funny to me. I could not wait to try out these newfangled concepts while we partook in the "Warrior's Breakfast," something that we had dreamed about. Steak and eggs, all you could eat, was the reward for passing the final test of the Crucible.

The steaks were bad and the onions old and the eggs fake and powdered as usual. But the food tasted great to us. We new Marines could go through the chow line as many times as we wanted. In typical Marine fashion—always underfunded—the chow ran out after the third time through the line. This did not bother us either.

The realization that we had earned the right to eat in a relaxed position, to use more than one utensil, to speak to one another made me proud. We had earned the right to do things that every American takes for granted. We could eat at our leisure or at least for as long as the time constraints of our duties allowed.

It was funny to watch as new Marines sat and tried to relax, their backs against the back of their chairs and two hands up near their food. Slowly one hand would slide below the table, their backs would straighten, and before you knew it they would be at the POA (position of attention). Adjusting to new realities would take a while.

After the Warrior's Breakfast, our time was devoted to getting ready for our one last graduation requirement, the Battalion Commander's inspection, and taking care of the last few administrative details such as getting military ID cards. Two days after the Emblem Ceremony, I had my last security clearance interview with another man (not my first pudgy interviewer) from one of the civilian government agencies who needed to straighten out a few problems with my security form such as vague dates, and so on. (With a grandmother who had been born in China to missionary parents and a dad born in Switzerland, I never could keep anything straight.)

Only at the end of training, when we began to compare notes and to talk with our DIs as human beings, did we realize how many hours and days our DIs had put into us without eating or sleeping, so that we could become what we wanted to be. DI SSgt Perry had worked 160 hours our first week on the Island. (There are only 168 hours in a week!) He had had so little time to eat that he had lost forty pounds in our first month of training. (He was not fat to begin with.) It was this way with all our DIs. They broke themselves for us. They could have earned more flipping burgers. I felt grateful to them. They had led from the front, going step for step with us and for us.

Only at the end did we truly appreciate how much our DIs had given us. They regarded our transformation into Marines as a life mission worthy of many sacrifices and pains that we could hardly understand and were just beginning to appreciate. They had demanded a great deal of us and twice as much of themselves.

At the end of training, our SDI confessed to us that when he had taken the platoon "island hopping" (to every pit on the Island the day after we failed the inspection), he had been working so hard to torture us that he saw spots and almost passed out from the effort of our "heart popping."

"You bastards about killed me! Good to go?"

"Yes, sir!"

The last of the waiting was hard to bear. After the weeks and months of agonizing, my biggest concern was to get John's pizza right. How would we make a fresh pizza at four in the morning when we were set to drive to the airport? Should we make the pizza the night before?

Egg pizza is a Tuscan pizza wherein you make a plain pizza with the usual tomato sauce and mozzarella cheese and add chopped hardboiled egg and capers. If done right, not too much of anything, light on the tomato and oregano, and cooked fast in a very hot oven, the pizza is delicious, if, that is, you have Genie making your crust. I wanted it to be perfect. I had not invested so much care into the preparation of a single meal since Jessica's wedding reception, which we held on our front lawn. Then I'd filled our rowboat with ice, laden it with champagne, shrimp, strawberries, and cream and was up all night making a selection of veal-jelly-topped pâté canapés on Genie's best French bread.

I knew I was getting worked up into one of my fits, tightly wound, almost unable to stand the intensity of the reunion. I'd felt the same at Francis's graduation from the School of Foreign Service at Georgetown. When we'd been invited to the pregraduation awards ceremony the day before, and Francis had won the Foreign Service School's highest academic award, I was beside myself, barely able to remember how my camera worked to shoot pictures. Jessica's wedding was no better. I walked down the aisle with my beloved daughter in such a daze that the memory is right up there with coming out of anesthesia for utter confusion. I did not do well when unbearable love and once-in-a-life-time events collided.

The Sunday before we went down to PI for Family Day, we skipped church and sat in the living room all morning waiting for John's call. It was the first person-to-person contact in over three months with our son. John's voice was so hoarse I hardly recognized it. The call lasted about five minutes until John said he had to go because others were waiting in line at the pay phone in the food court. We told John we loved him and congratulated him on becoming a Marine, completing boot camp, and the Crucible. He sounded distant and happy but thoroughly disoriented, as if just awoken from a deep sleep. He would listen to our voices and then there would be a long pause before he answered. The call left me feeling terribly unsettled.

After John hung up, Genie and I talked over every word of the call, every nuance in John's voice, any indication of how he really was. We agreed he sounded older, older and very hoarse from sounding off for three months at the top of his lungs. Had his voice changed for good? Was he really okay or just saying so?

"I'll wait for you in front of the Iwo Jima Memorial. You can't miss it," John had answered.

"We'll be there," said Genie.

22

During our last days on the island, as Marines, we were no longer smoked or pitted. From our uniforms to our language and bearing, we were, however, held to a higher standard by ourselves and our DIs. You could not walk out of the squadbay without a DI hovering over you, tugging at your uniform, straightening it, looking over your boots, or upbraiding you for not living up to his expectations.

"Is that how you want to walk out of here, son?"

"Sir?"

"I just wasted three months of my life!"

"Sir?"

"Look at your gig line! Blouse *aligned* to belt buckle, buckle *to* trousers!"

"Yes, sir!"

This harassment did not pose a problem for us. We had already settled into Marine habits, and one of those habits is grooming. We Marines wear shirt stays in our dress uniforms (long elastic garters that fasten onto our socks, run under our trousers and clip onto our shirt tails) to keep our perfectly pressed Bravo and Charlie (khaki) shirts taut. We starch and press our cammies. The dress blue uniform has many features that stopped making sense to other services in the eighteenth century and has earned the Marines plenty of mockery from the Army, Navy, and Air Force in the form of epithets, "seagoing bellhops," and the like.

Everything in the Corps related to our uniforms is regulated from the number of creases up the back of our blouse (three) to the required distance between the buckle of our trousers to the bottom of our tie (one inch). A Marine standing tall in his or her dress blues is the product of a group effort. Each Marine acts as other Marines's full-length mirror. This grooming goes on among Marines of all ranks, as well as between Marines and their officers and NCOs. It makes perfect sense to us. Discipline starts in the small things.

last days on the island
end of a life
whatever you want to call it
tour Leatherneck Square?
why would you want to see
the dust I sat in?

The morning of the last Thursday on the Island, Family Day, the whole of Bravo Company went on the Mot Run (motivation run). The four hundred graduating Marines of Bravo Company ran past all the other battalions and rang the big brass bells that hang in front of each battalion office. (There are four training battalions on PI.) The run was about four miles or so at a very fast pace. It was another cool windy day with light rain. No one got tired or was short of breath. We were too happy to be running in what amounted to our victory lap to feel anything but joy.

We had seen others do the Mot Run every week and yet had never believed it would be a reality for us until the day it happened. This was not training but celebration. It was one of the events that we had been looking forward to through all of boot camp.

After the run we changed into "Charlies" (green trousers and short sleeve khaki shirt), and prepared to meet our families. Parents, friends, and relatives were allowed to spend six hours with their new Marine on Parris Island Depot and see a little bit of what their sons have gone through. On the Thursday of Family Day, families were given more or less free rein.

Having my parents on the island was one of the most uncomfortable and surreal experiences of my life. They were from a different world that had nothing to do with the Marine Corps. I had gone through boot camp picturing them where they belonged, in the garden, at the kitchen table, at their beloved Metropolitan Museum of Art in New York, walking under the oaks and hickory trees on their favorite path to the nearby bird reserve. *Never*, in my wildest imaginings, did I picture them strolling the sandy paths of Parris Island.

I did not want to return to their world. I had truly adapted to boot camp life and was afraid of leaving. I had a hard time not calling Dad, "Sir," and Mom, "Ma'am." I did not introduce them to my DIs. I tried to prevent our worlds mixing as much as possible. I feared what would happen when I would graduate and return to the civilian world.

The high point of our reunion was when we met up with Reyes on the rifle range. Seeing Reyes with his mother and sisters somehow made the weirdness of seeing my parents become a little more normal. He looked as if he was having as strange a time as I was. His family was standing in a silent knot around him, as my parents were around me.

Reyes's mom handed me my promised BK Broiler, and my parents gave Reyes his slice of pizza. Then we all stood around looking awkwardly at each other and smiling. Reyes and I were almost too shy to speak to each other in front of our families. We were still Recruit Reyes and Recruit Schaeffer to each other and here we were with people who thought of us as Juan and John. His family congratulated me, and my parents congratulated Reyes. Then we all stood smiling.

"They good boys," said Reyes's mom.

"Yes," said my mother.

"We are proud of them," mumbled Dad.

"*Si*," said Reyes's mom and smiled.

"Now they can eat," said my Mother.

Reyes's mother looked confused. My Mother pointed to her mouth and smiled. Reyes's mom nodded and grinned and patted Reyes's flat stomach. In the distance the rifles on the range began to pop. A platoon of recruits marched past to their outdoor hut where they were about to undergo their Grass Week instruction on sighting their weapons.

Reyes's mother hardly spoke any English, and his little sisters were shy and wide eyed and dressed in bright pale pink and blue dresses as if they were going to a birthday party. (Reyes's father was unable to get a day off work.) I was waiting for someone to yell at me for just standing around. It would have almost been a relief to have a DI run over and get in my face.

Now that Reyes and I had the food we'd longed for, we felt silly. Reyes had never had this strange egg pizza. My parents and his were from the opposite ends of the earth and life. Reyes and I weren't even hungry. We'd gorged ourselves silly since the Crucible. We ate our food together self-consciously while our parents watched each bite go down.

I returned to the squadbay that night and crawled into my rack for the last time. All our "trash" (uniforms and personal belongings) was packed and the squadbay was stripped and bare of everything but our seabags, hanging bags, and the uniforms we'd be wearing at the graduation. As I closed my eyes I realized that the platoon had not prayed together that night. Now for the first time, just as I was about to leave, I understood that the squadbay and Parris Island was my sanctuary and the only place I was truly comfortable. I felt frightened and sad.

Genie and I arrived on Parris Island laden with egg pizza, a cake, and other assorted treats. The whole way to the Island I was in the grip of an ecstasy of anticipation and nervousness. It was my first time on a Marine base, and I felt every inch the ragged "nasty civilian." None of my clothes seemed to fit. My hair felt too long even though I'd just gotten it cut. The polish on my shoes was dull. I hoped my limp would be mistaken for a war wound.

When at last we were on the long causeway that leads onto the Island, I was struck that, for a place that loomed so large, formidable, and complex in my imagination, the geography was simple and beautiful. Gray choppy water, marsh (much like our own north of Boston), patches of close-cropped lawn, graceful Cyprus trees bearded with Spanish moss, and a picnic area flashed by as our car, windows down, filled with the sweet tangy scent of sap.

At the guard post I fumbled—sweaty hands—for the papers John had sent us. The young Marine guard never asked for them and merely waved us through, along with hundreds of other cars arriving for the Thursday ritual of Family Day.

After passing several one-story brick buildings we were directed into a large parking lot just beyond the sparse hard-topped parade deck and Iwo Jima memorial. Following the instructions John forwarded to us, we went to the visitor center and signed in. It was a thrill to find John's name on the 1st RTBN roster under Platoon 1093. My ears were ringing and I was a little out of breath.

Suddenly John was there. He was in uniform walking toward us over the parade deck. It was the first time I'd seen him wearing anything but civilian clothes. It was the first time I'd seen him in three months. It seemed as if it had been a year.

John appeared nervous and tongue-tied. Genie and I hugged his gaunt body and he hugged us. In the next ten minutes, as we slowly walked up the sidewalk back toward the visitor center, we must have reached out and touched John a hundred times. He was so thin.

"Congratulations, John. You're a Marine!" I said.

Genie nodded and her eyes filled with tears as she hugged him.

"Yes," said John.

"We're so proud of you!" I said.

"Thanks."

"What would you like to do? We have pizza," said Genie.

"Great."

"Do you get to show us around?" I asked.

"We have six hours of liberty but we can't leave the island until after graduation tomorrow. Do you want to see my squadbay?"

To see John in uniform was a shock. To sense that he was at home in this strange place and nervous at our presence was a surprise. How had we become unfamiliar to our son? To feel this new thing, this layer, this uniform that had come between us was unsettling. The fact that John was subject to rules that separated him from us, "We have six hours of liberty but can't leave PI" made me feel queasy, as if I was glimpsing John through some thick glass wall that let me see him but cut me off.

As John glanced over our heads at other Marines (also awkwardly accompanying their parents), nodded, called out a name now and then, saluted officers, received the greetings of other uniformed stern young men or barked out an authoritative, "Stay motivated, recruit!" I felt as if my son was suddenly beyond my reach. Certainly John had been governed by the rules of others before, at schools, on teams and such. Those rules were ones I could countermand. If a school did something I did not like, I could take my children out. Now my authority had been usurped by something bigger and much more frightening than schoolteachers.

John kept trying to walk in step with us as he glanced unhappily at our undisciplined feet treading every which way on the sandy cracked concrete pavement. Finally John asked Genie and me to *please* walk in step, that he was feeling strange. Could we please keep step with him? He asked this with a laugh and joked that he felt that if he walked out of step, someone would yell at him. We all laughed but I could see from John's nervous glance at our free-form feet that he was sincerely perturbed by the whiff of anarchy we'd brought with us.

I could not help but study John's face. He looked toughened and more vulnerable all at once. The grime of the hard nights and days of the Crucible were still worked deeply into the skin of his large hands (so deeply that for weeks after no amount of washing would make him clean).

"It's the dirt we've been crawling in and the camo paint. The Crucible finished off my hands. I tried to bleach them but nothing works."

John smiled. His close-cropped "high and tight" haircut left pale skin exposed above the tan line where his cover had protected his scalp for three months of sun-baked, outdoor marching, drilling, and exercises. His "high and tight" made his angular face appear practically hawklike.

As he tried to guide us, John got lost several times. After about the fifth wrong turn, he explained that he had never seen PI from the inside of a car. There were whole parts of the Island he'd never visited. Moreover he had never been allowed to look away from whatever path he was on. Other than the trails and roads he had marched down, John really did not know the Island or how to get anywhere. In the end we gave up driving and walked.

"I don't know how to get to the chapel from here. We'll have to go back to the squadbay. I know how to march there from my squadbay . . ."

The scale seemed wrong to John. PI is really a small place but the DIs made PI as big as they wanted by taking the circuitous path or marching in circles through the woods. John constantly expressed surprise at how close each location we visited was to the next. He overestimated distances from one area to another and thought some places we asked to see, like the rifle range, were miles away when they were really only a few hundred yards from where we were standing. It was as if he had been lost inside a maze for months and had just stepped into the daylight to learn that the "endless" twists and turns he had been wandering were actually all in a space the size of his yard.

John kept muttering, "I didn't know *this* was here!" or "You mean you can get to the food court by just walking across *this* street? Wow!"

I knew John had suffered. I could see hardship stamped in his drawn face, skin tight over bone. I knew that tens of thousands of young men and women like him had passed through PI. Yet here it was, a small sandy place, barely more than a gritty little bump above the wetlands with a few palm trees and cypresses, so simple, stark, and worn around the edges that it looked shabby as an overused baseball diamond. Even the neat rows of yellow footprints on the pavement outside the receiving center were small looking.

John showed me the actual set of footprints he'd stood on the night he arrived on the Island. Somehow he remembered which ones they were. There was a tense smile on his face as he pointed them out. Moments later we took pictures of him standing under the inscription over the receiving center doors, "Through These Portals Pass Prospects for America's Finest Fighting Force."

All the memorials to the battles and fallen heroes were so small, nothing more than humble painted boards or simple white waist-high concrete posts with the names of battles in plain black letters painted onto them. I caught glimpses of platoons of new recruits as they were beginning the long journey my son had just completed. They were scared and pale looking and being marched from place to place, DIs hovering over them, badgering, yelling, hounding, running up and down the line, advising, correcting, screaming like a bunch of unhinged, overprotective, and bizarrely severe mothers. "They're going easy on them because you're watching. You ought to see them when there are no parents around," said John.

John's experience of the island had not included such areas as the PX or the food court, both locations he wanted to visit in the worst way, as if they were longed-for mythical destinations of surpassing beauty. Once we got to the store, a seedy PX-supermarket loaded with all the crap, the glitzy boom boxes, shit jewelry, and other nonnecessities the military pushes on under-paid Marines, John touched everything he saw. It was as if he'd just stepped off a boat from the old Soviet Union and had never seen the consumer wonders of an American store before. He was so disoriented that for the first time an inkling of the truth of just how intense his training must have been dawned on me.

John could not have been suffering more thoroughly from sensory depri-vation if he'd just been released from a cell in the gulag. As for Genie and me, we were happy enough to load up on Marine T-shirts and other kitsch memorabilia. My favorite was a shirt John bought me. It featured a drawing of a big heron swallowing a little frog. The frog was already halfway down the huge bird's throat. He was desperately reaching back out of the bird's beak and grasping the bird's neck. The tiny frog was choking the huge bird while being swallowed. Stenciled on the frog's ass were the initials, "USMC." The slogan on the T-shirt read, *"Never give up!"*

In his squadbay, John showed us his rack, the punishment quarterdeck where he'd done push-ups until muscle failure dropped him face down into a pool of sweat, and the sandpit where he'd had his "heart thrashed" until he vomited. He showed us the showers—"thirty second showers during the first weeks we kind of had to run through without stopping"—the gear locker, the nooks, and crannies of his Spartan world. He showed us the brass drain he'd adopted as his cleaning project, how it was shined up, how he could look over the marsh to the water, ships, and lights of the town beyond.

By the end of the afternoon John started to talk in sentences of more than a few words. When he did begin to speak, it was like listening to the slightly garbled playback from some faulty electronic device. We got bits and pieces, descriptions in the past tense mixed in with the present tense. When I happened to walk on a certain painted area on the quarterdeck in front of the DIs door, John hurried forward and urgently whispered, "Dad! You *can't* step there!" Then he looked bewildered for a moment, smiled, and said, "Oh, I guess *you're* allowed. I guess they can't smoke parents. Boy, if I ever did that I'd be pitted for hours."

"But, John," I said, "Now you're a Marine you can stand here too."

"Are you nuts? The DI is just over there!" hissed John.

I didn't argue. There were still teachers who would have given me sweaty palms if I'd seen them thirty-five years later. I understood.

We drove down to a picnic area near the entrance to the island from the causeway and sat under the cypresses. John ate more of his pizza. He ate with less gusto than I'd expected. He explained that his stomach had shrunk again during the Crucible.

When I said that I hoped there was not too much pepper, John laughed, *"Pepper?* I eat anything now! Remember how I didn't like cheese, except on pizza? Well, I eat it now. I was licking plates during the first weeks and sucking the last drops of catsup out of packets and asking for other recruits' apple cores. The pepper's no problem . . ."

As we strolled the Island after our picnic we saw raw recruits being issued equipment and confident recruits, halfway through training, marching up to weapons battalion to vibrant cadences that sounded like the offstage chorus of an opera punctuated by the rasping shouts of the gravel-voiced DIs. My favorite moments were when the recruits shouted their responses in unison, "Sir, yes SIR!" as they marched past.

Knowing that my son was one of them, knowing what they were enduring as mirrored in his gaunt face, seeing the furious dedication of the DIs was a deeply moving experience. I watched several platoons march past through the glimmer of tears.

I felt small, an alien to all the selflessness around me. I knew I was unworthy to be standing so effortlessly, so casually, on ground into which so many millions of gallons of sweat had soaked.

What had I ever done for my country that made me worthy to be defended by these young men and women and these selfless DIs? I was standing on the footprints of forgotten men who went forth from this place and laid down their lives so that I could go to my town hall without fear, speak my piece. They had gone forth to protect my right to take Genie for a wife, because we freely chose each other, to have Frank for a friend, to defend a way of life where Frank and I could disagree and still work together, even be best friends . . .

The ascetic spirit radiating from the DIs reminded me of the monks I'd met on the Holy Mountain of Athos in Greece when I traveled in pilgrimage to the fantastical cliff-dwelling monastery of Simonopetra. (The DIs and monks would have been mightily surprised to hear this!) Perched high above the Aegean Sea in that grim and beautiful eleventh-century stone fortress, I briefly lived with monks who, now, seemed to me to be somehow related to the DIs I was watching.

The monks and DIs seemed to both be searching for the same thing: the will to overcome the flesh for a higher purpose. One thing was certain, they were motivated not by greed but by love.

23

the night before graduation
I have one fire watch to go
Marines are ironing uniforms
in the shining lights from the head to be ready,
squared away
to leave this place,
get the hell off the island,
homesick once they leave

Many did not make it. Fifty or more recruits who had started with Bravo Company were dropped, hurt, sent home, or recycled. Twelve were dropped from our platoon alone.

I did not sleep well the night before graduation. We woke at 0430 to move out of the barracks and prepare it for the next platoon. We started by breaking down all the racks, sweeping and swabbing the decks, cleaning everything that we could think of and reach. Our uniforms had been ready since the night before.

As we moved all of our belongings onto the grass outside of the barracks—so that we could leave as soon as possible after graduation—one of our DIs said, "We don't want to see any of your ugly faces ever again, and if I see any of you in the fleet I'm gonna beat your ass!" In DI speak this was an affectionate farewell. (However, there were a few members of the platoon—"turds"—he really might beat if he ran across them.)

We formed up in front of the barracks before the beginning of the graduation ceremony, then marched to the road that led onto the wide concrete parade deck the size of a very large parking lot. We stood at attention off to one side on an access road platoon by platoon. Six platoons (one company) were graduating that day. In the distance we could see the parents already beginning to file into the stands—a sea of red T-shirts, red caps, and sweats. (Red was Bravo Company's color.) The stands held about two thousand people. It seemed a long wait before we received the order to march the few hundred yards onto the parade deck.

We had seen so many other platoons cross this place every Friday. We had never imagined crossing it ourselves. Our mantra had been chow-to-chow, Sunday-to-Sunday. Finally the last minutes on the island were ticking away.

It was freezing, and we were in our blue "Deltas" (khaki short sleeve shirts, blue trousers, and cover). We were cold, but none of us shivered. We marched. Four hundred pairs of "corframs" (shiny patent leather dress shoes) struck the deck together. Our bodies were solid feeling and warmed with pride and the discipline instilled through countless hours of what had once seemed like "pointless exercises" and painful punishments.

We felt the pride shining down on us from the beaming faces of our families. We had a sense of true accomplishment. We were United States Marines on the parade deck of Parris Island.

———————————

The sky was slate-gray. It was cold. I left Genie sitting alone on the stands overlooking the parade deck. We were among the first parents to arrive, and I went to get her a coffee. We had been fighting. We had almost lost our way to PI in the dark that morning and had argued about who had missed the way. Once I got back from the food court, we huddled together against the stiff breeze.

For a long time nothing happened as other parents began to arrive. Then we heard the platoons singing cadence as they began to form up outside their squadbays in the distance. Before we could see them, their voices floated to us on the chill wind. I squeezed Genie's hand.

I took a deep breath. I was happy. John was graduating! He had made it through boot camp!

Then came the parade and the saccharine upbeat canned speech sounding like something the Disney writers might have come up with for a new USMC ride about "your Marines." But nothing could cheapen the fact that there, on the parade deck, was the small red guidon snapping in the wind displaying the number 1093. Third man marching from the front, top of the row, was a tall Marine, my son, in step with the rest.

I wiped my eyes and looked around. It occurred to me that this was the first time I'd ever been in an integrated crowd of this size dedicated to one purpose and of one mind. I had lived and worked in Africa for a year with a mixed-race movie crew. I'd been in plenty of ball parks, concerts, and mixed-race events. I had black, Hispanic, and Asian friends. This was different. The parents and Marines on PI that morning were not only of many races but were representative of many economic classes as well, from the very poorest who had arrived by bus or crammed onto the back of pickups to one or two parents who wore expensive suits and cashmere overcoats.

A toothless Mexican grandfather stood across from me, so drunk his embarrassed family was doing their best to prop him up. We were white and Native American. We were Hispanic and African American and Asian. We were old ex-Marines wearing the scars of battle, or at least baseball caps emblazoned with battles' names. We were southern white crackers from Nashville and pierced skinheads from New Jersey and black kids from Cleveland wearing ghetto rags and big white ex-cons of no fixed address with ham-hock forearms defaced by jailhouse tattoos. We were fat mothers poured into bulging sweats and we were thin twelve-year old little sisters with big hair in minuscule skirts and skimpy tank tops, coatless and shivering in the steady cold wind.

I heard many languages. Families full of brown babies, squat wide mothers, and dark-skinned weather-beaten grandfathers were speaking Spanish. The aluminum stands groaned under the weight of large southern white tribes, their video camera–toting women painted gaudy, hair exploding in haloes of blond above huge bosoms, the guts of their men hanging over American eagle belt buckles.

A Native American with turquoise and silver braided into his long white ponytail was sitting silent behind Genie next to a stocky Romanian family, none of whom spoke English and who, even in the frigid morning breeze, exuded a miasma of garlic as they yelled and waved small American flags at their Marine, and blocked the view so that the pale, quiet, well-dressed family from Maine, sitting behind them, had to step out onto the stairs to see their Marine out on the deck.

None of the Marines looked our way no matter how much we waved or hollered their names. "Eyes front," they stood at attention, trouser legs flapping in the steady cold wind. I fell into a reverie.

The platitudes my educated North Shore friends mouthed about "racial harmony" and economic and "gender diversity" were nothing compared with the common purpose uniting the parents gathered in the stands to honor our Marines. In Georgetown, when I had visited Francis I always noticed that the African American students seemed to sit in their own corner of the dining hall, roomed with each other, and kept to themselves, as did the whites and other "ethnic groupings." I glanced around at the other civilians on the stands. We were strangers but our Marine sons were brothers.

In the fleet our Marines would room together as they had in boot camp, drink together, work together; southern crackers, wasps, blacks, whites, Arabs, and Asians, united by a high purpose: the defense of our country and loyalty to the Corps. (Somehow I doubted that anyone from Georgetown or NYU would be coming down to Parris Island any time soon to learn what an authentic multiracial, economically diverse culture looked like!)

We were cheering and rushing out of the packed stands and embracing our sons, brothers, sisters, cousins and each other. (Two months later when I attended Jane's graduation the same scene was repeated with two hundred female graduating Marines and their proud and joyful and mostly poor and lower middle-class families.) Then we were packing up and hauling John's seabag and his canvas hanging bag to the rented car. John's last words on Parris Island were, "Stay motivated!" spoken out the car window to three new and frightened looking recruits who glanced at him in awe, said, "Yes, sir!" and hurried on.

We took John back to the hotel where we would spend the night. The first thing John did was change into the civilian clothes we'd brought with us. When he stripped off his socks I was horrified at the state of his feet. They stank of putrid cheese and were raw with huge filthy blisters. Strips of flesh were hanging off them. John explained, "There's been no time since the Crucible to go to a doctor."

I washed out John's socks. I reeled from the stench of the infection and marveled at the willpower it must have taken to stay with his platoon and graduate. The big toe of his left foot was a swollen, twisted lump three times its normal size and bent to the side. I rubbed his feet with antibiotic cream and bandaged them. John seemed oblivious to the pain and muttered to me to stop making such a "fuss" and that, "A lot of the guys' feet are in the same shape. It's no big deal."

"They let you march on *this?*" I exclaimed, pointing to his misshapen toe.

"Are you crazy?" asked John. "I didn't tell them. I might have been recycled! You should have seen Yates. He had such bad stress fractures we had to carry him the last day of the Crucible so he could finish with us. But he made it. He's a Marine."

John's socks and underwear could not have been more grubby if he'd been living in a coal mine. John protested that he'd done all his laundry the day before, but that "after a while the sweat and dirt never really washes out."

An hour later Genie, John, and I strolled through the lovely streets and shady flagstone squares of Savannah. We spent a glorious day as John, having gone from tongue-tied silence to torrential loquaciousness, regaled us with boot camp stories. "It's just so strange, it's just *soooo* strange to be out here!" John kept saying.

24

this place makes
no sense, people slouch,
doors close in front of
old women, people are fat!
I hate the rudeness, the chaos,
sleeping in is heaven, watching
the sunrise every day
can get tedious
sunrise will forever have
a touch of violence now.

The return home from boot camp was like going to a place that you have known your whole life and suddenly realizing that it is the moon in disguise, and that you just had never noticed this before. People, places, all were strange. Nobody held doors open for other people.

I began to see why it is that so many Marines (especially new ones) feel isolated from the civilian world. Civilians did not follow basic principles, such as a level of politeness to always be maintained with one's elders or superiors. From the fat people I saw (with the exception of the civilian who interviewed me for security clearance I had not seen fat people for three months), to the drugs so many of my friends were taking at college, many civilians seemed to me to be in need of about ten years in the pit.

I went to visit two of my closest friends who were going to college in Boston. One of them was smoking so much weed that I was surprised he knew his own name or could feed himself. In the space of forty-eight hours, I watched him smoke the equivalent of roughly one month of my salary (about $1,100 before taxes).

Because of the undisciplined way that many civilians carry themselves, slouching, untidy, selfish, rude to their elders and superiors, many Marines (especially new, highly motivated ones just emerging from boot camp) are disgusted to the point of anger with the society they reenter. This disconnect was a factor that played a key role in my final alienation from Erica. I went to visit her the day I got back at her college up in New Hampshire.

In comparison to the dedicated Marines I had just been with, who disciplined themselves whether a DI was present or not, Erica seemed lost. She appeared to be waiting for someone to drop a life into her lap, anything that would tell her what to do, where to go.

I had chosen my path. The Marines gave me a purpose in my life. For the time being that purpose was to serve the needs of the Corps hour-by-hour. These ideals seemed like a joke to Erica and her friends, as they made clear by the looks and smart-ass comments I got. But they were ideals I had seen work to bring the recruits together to make us into a selfless unit, ready to put the people we were responsible for first.

After my visit to her college, I wrote Erica a letter telling her I did not want to see her again. It seemed much better at that time to just get it done. There had been soft landings on PI. It was tough to remember how people in the civilian world expected to have everything explained. I now realize this was callous.

I graduated boot camp two weeks before Thanksgiving, and, as there were no MCT classes starting at that particular holiday, I was given "recruiters' assistance." My job, between the holiday and MCT, was to live at home and report to the local recruiting station and do whatever I could to help them present the Corps to prospective recruits. I would be home until December 7, an extra two weeks on top of my ten days of leave after boot camp.

After Erica called six times in one day, even Genie got tired of "the Erica soap opera." She gently told Erica to please leave John alone, that John did not want to talk to her, and besides he was at a recruiting station working.

After two weeks of daily calls and messages, John relented and talked to Erica. They agreed to meet for coffee. When John came back he said they were now going to be "just friends." I told John this new arrangement seemed to me like a prescription for trouble given how Erica seemed to feel about him.

I hated almost every second of MCT (Marine combat training). MCT took place at Camp Geiger, North Carolina. The purpose of MCT was to teach all Marines except Infantry, who had their own school, basic combat skills beyond those learned at boot camp, from how to fire a machine gun, to the correct placement of shaped charge explosives and grenade throwing.

MCT was exhausting. I happened to be there during a bitter cold snap that kept the ground frozen and made living in the field an exercise in winter camping, both on the ground and in a fighting hole. (Other services may have "fox holes" but, as our instructor said to us, "Fox holes are to hide and die in. Marines use them to fight from. They are 'fighting holes' to us, not fucking 'fox holes!' WE *don't* hide!")

Several Marines were hospitalized with pneumonia and other exposure-related problems. The stress level was high and exacerbated by the fact that we were taking part in live-fire and other dangerous exercises while our fingers were too numb to feel the triggers of our weapons. Parks (the same Marine we'd helped through the Crucible) got his face smashed at ITB (Infantry Training Battalion) when he tried to break up a fight between two Marines. He was the "guide" (the Marine in charge of the platoon) and got between them, and was hit in the face with a Kevlar helmet. After getting his broken jaw and a cheek-bone wired back together he came back to complete training.

I saw Parks one night toward the end of training when he was getting ready to go back to ITB, just as I was about to graduate. Weirdly, the accident improved his looks and the sound of his voice. He went from a squeaky falsetto to a baritone. The surgeon did him the favor of straightening his nose while he set it.

We got anywhere from four hours to forty-five minutes of sleep a night for the three weeks of MCT. The only moments I wasn't miserable was when we were shooting. I enjoyed the live fire exercises, in an adrenaline-pumping way. We had to run along and shoot at pop-up targets with other Marines around, in front and *behind* us shooting past us in their lanes of fire. My back ached at the end of that day from muscles tensed as, minute-to-minute, I expected to feel a 5.56 mm ball round hit me in the spine.

For three days, we were involved in a FEX (field exercise) and we spent the majority of those days sitting in frozen fighting holes, vigilantly looking out for the "enemy" (other platoons) who only bothered to show up once or twice. We humped everywhere with full packs and combat gear, and had only one change of cammies. We were wet, filthy, and smelly, and my feet were falling apart again.

Genie and my bedroom had not changed since John was a baby, nor had our early morning Christmas tradition of opening stocking presents. We all knew our places. Genie and I sat side-by-side on our old four-poster. Francis, who drove up from Beverly the day before, leaned against the right post at our feet, and John sat against the left with his big feet wedged between us.

Our bedroom had once been the attic. We remodeled it into a master bedroom. It had a sloping beamed ceiling of rough white plaster, low wood-paneled closets running along under the eves and was filled with soft daylight coming from two skylights and the glass door that opened onto a small balcony. The door revealed the view of the Merrimack River.

A winter mist covered the garden and marsh that lay between the house and the water. The smell of the turkey roasting in the kitchen was beginning to fill the house. I wanted the day to be perfect and was almost vibrating with the intensity of trying to enjoy the moment and yet anticipate every step in our ritual from the big logs ready for the fireplace to the smoked salmon mousse Genie had made the night before chilling in the refrigerator.

Every time I looked at John it was with a sinking feeling of foreboding that all the roasting turkey smell and tangerines in the world could not mask. I missed my daughter Jessica horribly at Christmas and she was safe and sound in Finland. What would some future Christmas be like if John was overseas and in harm's way and my view of the river was unobstructed by his shoulders, and there was nothing but air and sick worry where his big frame had always been?

I felt I was tumbling toward some as yet unnamed trouble.

After stockings we went downstairs and had a breakfast of my mother's great orange rolls and hot chocolate, got dressed, gathered around the fire-place, and started slowly opening the gifts that were laid out under the tree. From time-to-time Dad would get up to check on the turkey. He seemed tense.

Around noon, we were about halfway through opening the gifts and listening to new jazz CDs, stopping to read parts out of the books we had given each other, when there was a knock at the door. It was Erica. She didn't bother to come in and say hello, let alone wish a merry Christmas to my brother and parents or even to me. She marched directly up the stairs to my room uninvited, bypassing the living room, as if the fact that it was Christmas, that she was interrupting a family gathering, that my parents and brother were sitting there ten feet away was of no concern to her. Clearly I was expected to follow her when she said commandingly over her shoulder, "We *need* to talk!" as she stamped up to my room.

Mostly Erica did the talking, about how she was furious with me for not calling her on Christmas morning or giving her a present, about how it was "so terrible" that our "relationship" had "gone wrong." Then Erica gave me a tearful and irate speech about what a bad guy I was for not "working harder" at "our relationship since you did that stupid Marine thing" and how she blamed the Marines for changing me. Then she stormed out.

When Erica left I returned to the rest of my family to find that my father was gone. I'd been upstairs with Erica for about half an hour. Mom, Francis, and I sat around waiting for Dad to come back. At first we assumed he was in the kitchen working on our Christmas dinner. He had left so silently that Mom did not realize he wasn't in the house.

Finally, about an hour later, Dad called. He'd driven a mile up the road and was brooding in a motel lobby while our Christmas dinner got cold. He told Mom to put me on the phone.

"You said you'd broken up with her!" I bellowed.

"I did," John answered.

"Then why has she been calling us every day you were in MCT? 'Just friends' my ass! Why did that girl come over?"

"She just did."

"You sent mixed signals."

"The only reason I kept writing from boot camp was because *you* wrote and said she'd called you!" John yelled.

"*Don't bullshit me!*" I screamed. "Why did you let her in the house? I was right about her! She wasted your last summer at home, and now you don't even like her and we can't get last summer back!"

"What the *fuck* was I supposed to do, make funny faces through the window at her until she went away?" John shouted.

"Tell her to fuck off!"

"Right. On Christmas?"

I felt so ashamed of my irrational outburst, so stupid. And yet before I could stop myself I yelled, "You just get the hell out until you clean this mess up!"

All my tension, fears and worry stretching back to the "Last Summer" and boot camp came to a sharp, nasty point in that moment. I felt as if I was suffocating.

I began to pack immediately with the full intention of going to my friend James's house for the remainder of my vacation. I figured I'd call Dad's bluff. He wanted me out? Fine!

I was packing when, about three minutes after the call, Dad ran in. With one glance at his face I knew he was sorry as hell but I still wanted to go to James's house at least for a few days. I was livid.

I kept packing as Dad followed me into the head. (There is no lock on the door, it broke and we never bothered to fix it, so I couldn't keep him out.) He sat on the toilet seat cover pleading with me as I shaved and got ready to leave. He must have called himself an idiot ten times as he begged me to stay.

After a few minutes I swallowed my pride and agreed. Dad hugged me. We even started to laugh as he helped me bandage my foot. It was a mess again after MCT.

my father flickers
near tree and fire.

he reads of treasure and rings.
I eat clementines and build
peel castles,
tottering columns of fire.
I can tell you what will happen next;
the dragon will fall, and so will my castle,
tumbling years as they scatter.
my father burns
blue and red and green
and I am burning ages.
four years, ten years, twenty years
flickering.

25

Five days after the second "Christmas breakup" with Erica, I met Mollie. I liked her instantly. My best friend James introduced us. They had gone to high school together, and Mollie was Lauren's (James's girlfriend) best friend. Mollie was from Dover, New Hampshire. She was home on holiday from her college in upstate New York. Her father was a bohemian Harvard grad and rare books dealer. He was divorced from Mollie's mother. Mollie and I spent most of the last six days I was home together. I wish I'd met sweet, sensible, kind Mollie years before.

Mollie was about as far from anybody's idea of a Marine's girlfriend as you could get. She was a vegetarian who had inherited her family's sixties countercultural lifestyle and politics. To her the very idea of the Marines seemed weird. We hit it off instantly.

When Genie and I met Mollie we took to her. (John brought her home about three days after they met.) Later John told me Mollie liked us and enjoyed my sense of humor. (It didn't hurt any that she had read one of my novels.) I made sure to cook her some great vegetarian dishes.

John was about to leave again, this time to his MOS school in Ft. Huachuca Arizona. He'd be gone at least four months.

The trip to Ft. Huachuca was lonely. I had just met a girl I liked a lot and here I was on my way, literally, to some desert about as far from her as I could have been sent inside the continental US. I awoke at 0400 on the fifth of January 2000, to begin my journey. The government purchased me a ticket for a flight leaving from Portland, Maine, a two hour drive from our house.

Dad drove. I slept most of the way, having turned night into day while with Mollie, unwilling to miss a moment with her. Dad and I shared a breakfast of microwaved eggs at one of those airport food stands.

We talked about the crazy Christmas, the fact I'd just met Mollie, my frustration at leaving her so soon, the Corps, and some further reminisces from boot camp. I told Dad that Mollie and I knew that we liked each other a lot and that we would like to be together. How exactly was I supposed to ask a girl that I had known for six days to jump into a long distance relationship with a guy she barely knew, beyond the stories that my friend James had told her about growing up with me and the nutty things we'd done in eighth grade? Dad said that if it was meant to be it would work out and that he'd do anything he could to help us stay in touch. It was like old times after a soccer game when Dad and I would stop at some diner on the way home and he'd feed me and we'd talk.

Walking into a Marine detachment for the first time was nerve-wracking. I wanted to make a good impression and had had eighteen hours of travel to worry. I was greeted by the DNCO (duty noncommissioned officer), PFC (private first class) Tawata, a Japanese American, whom I would later become great friends with but who seemed severe and cold that night. (I learned later that it was perfectly natural to take a cold-wait-and-see attitude toward a NUG—New Useless Guy.)

Tawata signed me in with barely a nod, issued some linen, and told me to be in the TV room in my "Alphas" (green jacket, shirt, and tie) at 0730 the next day. The big entrance to my first military post was a huge letdown. Tawata wasn't even an officer, just a private first class who happened to be the "duty." (The Marine at the duty desk.) He barely glanced at my uniform. It turned out that my official reporting in would not happen till the next morning, and I could have arrived in jeans for all anyone cared.

I went to my room, a small college-dorm type cubicle for two, made my rack, and fell asleep feeling lonely and scared. Checking into a duty station would have been normal for any Marine but a terrified new private—*me*—with no experience beyond boot camp.

As I fell asleep I told myself that next time I traveled to a base I'd travel in my civilian clothes and change in the airport after I arrived. My back was sore from sitting bolt upright for eighteen hours while trying to not wrinkle my uniform. (Normally it would have been a six-hour trip. Beware government travel offices!)

Ft. Huachuca is one of the training centers for Army Signals Intelligence where Army, Navy, Air Force, and Marines are taught various aspects of military intelligence work. My Morse code school was a small part of the larger base. Life on the base revolved around training and whatever was going on (not much) in Sierra Vista.

Sierra Vista, home of Ft. Huachuca, was a small town (population thirty-nine thousand, including the personnel on the base). It sat at an elevation of 4,623 feet, enough altitude to wind you while doing PT. The base was a mile from town. The desert began six inches from the reach of the last lawn sprinkler. Daisy-Mae's, the local steak joint located in a former whore house (the steaks were really good), and INS trucks, filled with dusty and thirsty Mexicans the Border Patrol stopped—being forcibly returned home, completes the picture of "life" in this military border town.

I was assigned a roommate by the name of Clevenger (we called him "Cleavage"). He was a stocky Marine, mostly raised in a foster home near Phoenix. Half the guys he grew up with were doing a lot of drugs and only had minimal jobs. Some were dead, some in jail. He was smart, had made it into Intel and was doing well. We were to become friends.

We Marines accounted for only about eighty out of the eleven thousand seven hundred military personnel on base. (There were about five thousand Army soldiers and the rest were Army recruits still in training and Air Force and Navy personnel.) We lived in our own barracks with some Navy personnel. Basically we took the view that we were living in an enemy camp and that the biggest challenge on base was to maintain our Marine discipline without being polluted by the slovenly indiscipline of the other services, most especially by the Army which, to us, was the lowest form of life incapable of even staying minimally fit. There were even a lot of *fat* "soldiers."

"How do you starve a soldier?"

"How?"

"Hide his meal card under his iron."

We went to code school with the other services. It became readily apparent to me that there was a hierarchy in BMS (Basic Morse School). The Army was at the bottom, they were too undisciplined to even realize that the rest of us were disgusted and considered them a joke. The Navy was next. We got along well enough with them. They were okay, if you didn't judge them by Marine standards of discipline. The Air Force was next. Though we considered them by far the least disciplined of the services, at least their uniforms were usually pressed and they had the prettiest girls.

The Army, I soon discovered, was the most disappointing service in the military. The soldiers were dirty, disorganized, and lacked any semblance of discipline that anyone who had been trained properly would have had. They were in worse shape than any Marine recruit who had gotten past the first six weeks of training on Parris Island. Their uniforms looked atrocious, and they would act, as our DIs would have said, "like they were back on the block."

Of course I knew that some of the more elite Army units, the Rangers and Tenth Mountain Division and the like, had to be better. However, judging by what I saw in Ft. Huachuca the Army was a mess. Soon after I arrived on base I saw three Marines chase twenty Army personnel up the sidewalk and threaten to take on their whole barracks.

A few days after my arrival, our CO (Commanding Officer) was instructed to call all the Marines on base together and lecture us on not harassing gay people. There had been no such harassment on our base. This lecture took place a few weeks after a gay Army soldier's roommate on another base beat him to death with a baseball bat. The pentagon, according to our "Lance Corporal Mafia" (what we called our rumor mill), sent all commanders a lecture he or she was supposed to read to the troops.

Our Marine CO did it his way. He marched all the Marines on base into a small classroom and paced around staring at us. He did not look too pleased to be there, and his jutting jaw kept flexing. He never glanced at the official document.

"The Pentagon wants me to tell you that you are not to beat anybody to death in their rack with a ball bat!"

"Yes, sir!"

"All such activities are to cease as of now! All you need to know about the Marine next to you is that he or she went to boot camp same as you and earned the title!"

"Yes, sir!"

"All you need to know is that you are *all* United States Marines! That goes for the male and female Marines and whatever else the fuck you call yourself on your own time! We *all* earned the same title! If there is a Marine standing next to you, he or she got handed the eagle, globe, and anchor same as you after completing the Crucible! Good to go?"

"Yes, sir!"

"Did he, she, it, whatever, earn the title?"

"Yes, sir!"

"Are all Marines brothers?"

"Yes, sir!"

"That's all you need to know about *that!*"

"Yes, SIR!"

I graduated Basic Morse School on May 17, 2000, exactly sixty-eight academic days after I started, which happened to be the "course expectancy." Then I proceeded to wait, and wait, and *wait* some more.

Days passed into weeks, weeks into months. I could not go forward in my training without at least an interim top-secret clearance. I was stuck in a holding pattern along with half of my platoon.

I hate Arizona
the flowing mountains
the dry valleys
the never-ending cities
the tin towns
all of it
this dead place, Ft. Huachuca Arizona
it taints everything,
now I hate it all.

On PI, while being asked to change my MOS I was told I was to be in Ft. Huachuca "for around four months." Then I was to be sent to Pensacola to complete my training. Training at Ft. Huachuca was to be in two parts. The first job was to learn Morse code at BMS. This could take several months. Then the next course of study was to do advanced code studies at AMS (Advanced Morse School). To move onto this second phase required that you get a top-secret clearance. Rather, it required that your provisional clearance had come through. (Obviously Morse code is not a government secret, but nevertheless we needed the clearance for certain aspects of the training.) After that I was to be sent to Pensacola, Florida, to do more training in signals intelligence work unrelated to code.

The training in Morse code was just an extra, just in case someone somewhere used Morse and we needed to be able to understand what was being said. But I could not even complete that training at Ft. Huachuca until I got my clearance, let alone proceed to Pensacola. And the word was that all our security clearances were "backed way the hell up some pencil-pusher's ass in DC."

What the sergeant on PI, the one who got me to change my MOS and add a year to my contract, had failed to say was, "Your new MOS is one where you'll do the little training you are allowed to do before you get a clearance. Then you'll wait indefinitely for some government agency in DC to take their thumb out of their ass. But they're not going to because what most civilians don't realize is that when they say, 'Oh yeah, bread, not bombs; cut military spending, cause that'll make us feel good about ourselves'—what's actually getting cut is not the weapons budget but the people needed to process your clearance! What else gets cut is benefits for single military parents who have to pay for day care on a paycheck that *already* qualifies them for food stamps! *See?* And *that* is why suckers like you are gonna get stuck in Arizona and will be weeding the barracks grounds instead of doing any training! Good to go? How does *that* make you feel about yourself? You won't even be allowed to wait in a reading room or study. You'll watch TV or pick weeds or move furniture from one room to another and back again six hours later because someone changed their mind. In fact you'll wish you were back at boot camp! Some guys get hung out to dry for *two years!* Welcome to the first day of the rest of your life! How do you like *them* apples? You'll just sit doing *nothing!* That, son, is *your* new MOS, *doooooooing nothin'!*"

What I was allowed to do (in other words ordered to do), after completing my initial training and while waiting for my clearance, was to watch CNN from eight in the morning to four in the afternoon in the TV room five days a week. No kidding! Then I was also allowed to sit in my room, stare at the desert, climb the walls, drink on the weekends, try and not become a drunk, and pine for Mollie.

It came as a relief to be given any task outside the TV room, from driving up to the airport to pick up some Marine—windows down, in my boxers, AC off to save on gas in the 110° heat—to weeding the piece stone around the barracks. We soon ran out of even bullshit "make work," and most of the time sat. The only good part of the day was our PT in the mornings when for a few hours we felt like Marines again.

With the inactivity and crushing boredom came the depression and the nightmares. In boot camp I had slept content. In Ft. Huachuca I had horrible dreams.

fire ants swarm
eyes and mouth
cramming between my toes
they are the notes in my symphony of pain
there is no running now
I am clean picked, shiny ivory
I am writhing red.

My second roommate in Ft. Huachuca was Moffit. Moffit was an alcoholic from Alabama. He was skinny, tall, blond and blue-eyed with an angular, friendly face. He had a thick accent and a serious fighting streak. He would gladly fight anybody who was not a Marine. Moffit was a wiry, tough redneck. He was fiercely loyal to all Marines.

From our barracks window I saw Moffit knock out a female Army soldier because she got in front of her boyfriend to protect him. Moffit and the male soldier were in an argument over the soldier having walked on "our" barracks grass. The female soldier, apparently counting on being a woman to protect her, jumped in front of Moffit and got in his face.

Moffit looked at her and said, "Don't stand at me like a man unless you fight like one cause I *will* knock the shit out of you!"

The Army female raised her fists and took a swing at Moffit. I blinked and by the time my eyes opened her body was midway in its first bounce off the pavement.

Moffit calmly looked at her boyfriend and said, "I told her not to stand at me like that, now get the fuck off my sidewalk." The boyfriend took off down the street. Moffit walked inside, came up to our room and went to sleep about two minutes later.

just below the surface
bile builds
like water sloshing into a bucket.
pour it elsewhere into something more solid than me
keep it in until the time comes
and I will show the night what anger truly is.

The crushing boredom of being stuck waiting for clearances (most of us were) led to a lot more fighting and drinking than there would have been otherwise. Many Marines had been waiting for their clearance for over a year.

Most of us tried to stay out of trouble. Not Moffit. If there was a fight, Moffit was in it, even if it had nothing to do with him. He did not care what the odds were or how badly beaten he got. He would take on anyone—including women in uniform—and any number of people, from huge hairy bikers in bars to ten soldiers at a time, though never Marines.

This was new to me. I had seen people take pretty good beatings before, myself included, but I had never been good friends with someone who would fight just to fight. The other Marines might have been in fights once in a while, but they were not fighters, in the sense that this is what they did as a vocation.

Moffit fascinated me. He had scars on the backs of his hands where his bones popped through the flesh after he'd broken them hitting people and objects. When the bones broke, Moffit would just keep hitting. He was, needless to say, the kind of guy you just did not fuck with, ever. We got on very well.

Boot camp seemed like a golden place of meaningful activity in comparison to the slow, motivation-draining purgatory of doing nothing. In Ft. Huachuca I learned that Marine recruiters pitch the challenge of boot camp to potential recruits. Nobody thinks past boot camp.

I looked forward to two things in life: first, talking to Mollie on the phone at night. She became an anchor for me, something that tied me to my life. Second was having someone come to visit me, pulling me out of my numbing nonexistence. I also started to work on this book with Dad and began trading sections by e-mail and writing poems. (He edited my writings into chapters.) I jotted down a lot of poems about my current life or lack of it, mostly bitter poems. I also got ready for surgery on my foot.

The doctor said he was going to put a pin into my big toe of my left foot to fuse the bones, remove bone fragments, and repair the other damage done during boot camp and made worse at MCT. Because of the surgery, I would be off PT for a long time. This was terrible news. PT was the only part of the day when I didn't feel like someone stranded in an airport.

26

Day 1

I'm sitting in a $29 a night motel room in the desert a mile from my son. I saw John tonight for the first time in six months. His foot is healed enough so that the bandages are off and he can walk without crutches. I will be here for two weeks.

John sits in Arizona waiting for his security clearance. He is still off PT, which means that his one pleasure here is denied him. This is a trial of waiting. This is the trial of stupid TV. Is the best "duty" the Marines can come up with, TV?! And this is "*Intel?*"

Did anything on Parris Island prepare these young men and women for this crap? On PI there are monuments to the men who fell on grenades but none to the men and women who watch their youth trickle out into wasted hours. Couldn't they be learning a foreign language that might come in handy for Intel work? Couldn't there be classes in military history?

Day 2

The young Marines know the difference between real work and make-work, "motivational bullshit." Yet they are still proud to be Marines. Whatever it is that their drill instructors taught them on PI was powerful enough to help them survive even this insane limbo. Today when I asked John if he regrets becoming a Marine he answered NO and looked at me like I was nuts. He is *proud* to be a Marine, even a sidetracked Marine-in-waiting. He quickly points out that the *nasty civilian* government agency in charge of security clearances is *not* part of the Corps. He blames the Corps for nothing.

Day 3
John works out in the weight room to fill the time after he is released from the TV room every evening. (He can't run because of his surgery, but he can lift the free weights in the weight room in the barracks. He works out with his buddy Roth for two hours or more each night.) John's tall, thin runner's frame has added new layers of granite-hard muscle from all the lifting. John's back is broad as the door to the garden shed. His laterals look like ship hawsers, his chest and stomach copied from a bronze statue of a Greek warrior. This is in spite of the fact he is recovering from surgery and has been off PT for five weeks now.

John and Roth jokingly worry that after their intense nightly workouts they might be unable to defend themselves if they happened to get into a fight with the Army guys. They stagger out of the weight room sweat drenched, arms heavy and sore, temporarily weak as babies. John said they would be unable to "punch effectively." He said he's already thought out a "strategy" if need arises: get behind an adversary and "get them in a blood-choke until they pass out." I wonder if his old friends from school are making similar plans at Berkeley, Bard and Brown?

Day 4
John spends the night sleeping soundly next to me here at the motel. I take as much pleasure from seeing his six-four frame stretched out next to me as I used to when I'd pat him to sleep in his crib when he was two.

He's nineteen and a Marine. I still want him to sleep well, eat well, and, above all, to be safe. Marine or not, John is my little son. His growing up has not made me worry less about him than I did when he was a small child. I just worry at a helpless distance.

This night in Arizona in this shabby motel I am glad to have him with me safe and sound. I'm relieved to have him back within reach, however briefly. I watch him sleep awash in a flood of cool air and white noise from the old air conditioner as it roars and rattles in the cinderblock wall across from me.

I discover again (as I did with Jessica and Francis), that children don't grow up in the sense of growing out of your worries and dreams. When John was at boot camp, I fretted he'd get hurt or fail. Now I worry that he'll be bored to death (maybe literally) waiting for his security clearance. The reality was summed up by what John said over dinner tonight: "The military is a big machine and I guess I'm learning it's easy to fall between the cracks."

Day 5

I wake at five, long before John. He is sleeping next to me as I sit and write these words by the dawn filtering through the broken blinds. Last night John, like the little boy who sometimes lied and made excuses, said, "Maybe I'll go back up to the barracks to sleep; you know, I need to do my writing for the day." But after he called his girlfriend Mollie he decided to stay with me.

I set him up with the phone in the motel bathroom, the cord just reached, so he could talk in private. He had a good one-hour talk. After that he wanted to stay with me, or rather agreed to. John had got what he wanted; rather, I guessed correctly at his actual agenda and provided the call. John is tender and passionate under a laid-back exterior, where he pretends to have no cares in the world. However, he does care about certain things, like getting his undisturbed evening call.

He is still stretched full length sleeping as I sit next to him writing this. It is a happy moment. We ate mangos I bought at a Mexican grocery on Fry Boulevard (the one and only main street in Sierra Vista, a couple of miles from John's base). They were excellent and reminded us of the mangos we ate in the Bahamas on our last vacation together before boot camp, the one where I lost his big fish for him.

The mangos brought back sweet memories as I sliced them into a couple of bowls I bought at the grocery store. I cut them into the bowls so John could eat with a fork and not get a drop of juice on his immaculate uniform. John's uniform is a sacred thing that needs to be kept perfect and pressed. John is a good Marine.

We ate the mangoes while a friendly, thick-hipped Mexican maid cleaned the room around us. Her little girl waited and watched from the door. We offered her mango, but she shook her head NO, making her little glossy black pigtails bounce. With John sitting across from me, the mangoes became a feast.

Day 6

John is a serious "squared-away" Marine. He does not like Marines with a "lack of bearing." John says of one of the female Marines I met that, "She's nice and always smiling but that's her problem. Marines with bearing aren't always smiling. They have to have an edge and can be serious." There is another female Marine John respects and pays his highest compliment to: "She's a good Marine."

To be a Marine's parent in peacetime is less about suffering than about disorientation. It is strange to be the parent of a Marine when most young people wouldn't be caught dead in the military. We keep our military on shabby bases in shabby towns surrounded by cheap motels like this one. When I see young Marines trying to get home for a holiday, they are the ones standing in line for the standby pass. They are the ones who can't afford to eat in the airport. I never used to notice them. I do now. They ride the bus while I catch the cab. When need arises the old-fashioned view prevails. Honor, courage, commitment are called upon to save the day; then, once saved, the cynics take over again and we send our defenders back to nowhere on the last flight, the cheap flight, and they feel lucky if someone gives them an extra bag of pretzels because they couldn't afford a burger in the airport.

John's boredom and loneliness is big enough that it obliterates the natural beauty of the landscape that surrounds him. He hates the hills and lovely desert with a vengeance. His loneliness for Mollie, combined with frustration as he waits for his security clearance, is driving him slightly mad. I ask John if he can study.

"How about enrolling in a local community college and taking a course?" I ask.

"No," said John, "I'm not allowed, not till I get my clearance and code school is done. We're not allowed to take college courses until then. You can't enroll in a civilian school while you are still in military school for your MOS, only once you're in the fleet. Then you can take night courses."

Day 7

I have followed John to his base because I refuse to have a son slip off into some world of which I know nothing. I will not lose John. Maybe I'm a Jewish mother! I will not grow distant from him. Genie visited John here; now it's my turn. While I am with John, the parents of another Marine visit. I do not meet them but I know them anyway. They have made a pilgrimage from Nebraska to the Mexican border to be whole again for a moment.

John describes many Marines' weekends. They drink Friday and Saturday, then spend Sunday talking about how drunk they were on Friday and Saturday. He hands me this poem he wrote before he was taken off PT.

The poem makes reference to the fact that any repetitive beeping noises, like his alarm clock, make John hear "code."

> it's 0430, I'm pissing in the general direction of the toilet, trying to remember
> what part of my identical week I am about to begin.
> I know it's a weekday, my alarm woke me pounding: "TANGO, TANGO, TANGO."
> I'll be in pain presently, running or crunching, it doesn't matter, PT always hurts.
> now I see.
> I can tell it's Monday,
> there are little pieces of Tawata and Carver's weekend
> all over the rim of the toilet.
> one of them ate steak, smells like Daisy Mae's.
> Heinz 57, protein and stomach acid, Bacardi 151.
> this morning is cold, within the space of ten minutes, hot.
> then I will know whose weekend rests on the rim of the toilet.
> because I will smell them sweating out their alcohol, I can always smell what
> someone has been drinking, rising from their green on green bodies.
> Caldwell drinks beer, everyone else changes their perfume Monday to Monday,
> but I will know whose face rested on the porcelain this weekend,
> and I will make them clean it.

Day 8

On Sunday as I sit at a picnic table in the "smoke pit" (the open hut where Marines are allowed to light up behind the barracks) I overhear this exchange about that weekend's hard drinking:

"I fell and chipped my tooth, I guess, but I don't remember it," said a male Marine.

"Awesome!" answered another male Marine.

A female Marine: "I noticed a rip in my jeans. None of you told me!"

"Were you wearing underwear?" asked a male Marine.

"I don't fucking remember!" answered the female as all the Marines laughed. At last I understand the "smoke-pit poem" John e-mailed me a few weeks ago.

the tree in the smoke-pit must have experience beyond my years,
it is privy to every secret of military life.
love, hate, violence, hazing, kisses, cheating spouses, queers.
everything comes to it.
the branches that face the smoke-pit are balding
each leaf picked, played with, and torn.
by Marines constantly moving through
from Texas, Michigan, Hawaii.
pausing just long enough to eat a few meals, sleep
a few nights, drink a few beers, fuck a few
girls, get what they came for, and blow away.
some to die, some to reenlist, some to just move.
but the tree stays, and we come to it telling our bullshit stories,
    cheating on our wives,
and drinking our beers.

John tells me the dirty jokes he hears. Some are truly disgusting, others silly and childish. I listen and laugh at them all without comment on how gross they are. I don't want him to feel any disapproval from me for his world in which he must survive for four more years. If he had not changed MOS it would be only three. I never bring this up.

The hardest thing for me to see in Ft. Huachuca is the narrowing of John's world. On the Friday evening of my visit John went back to the barracks early to help put his drunken Marine brothers to bed. He feels responsibility for them. When I see him do this, I know John is still the kid who once talked of becoming a priest. He is bigger than me in the heart department. I have slipped into the "adult" world of self-protection and selfish preoccupations. "What happens if some Marine you're helping falls? Will you get sued?" I ask, only half joking. John just laughs at me uproariously. John is still selfless and young. He wants to "be there" for his buddies, worries that they will have no one to help them to bed when they are drunk.

I wonder: How much is real in John's Marine "bearing" and how much is playacting? I don't know but I suspect some of both.

John hangs out with Marines very different from him and, as I can see when I visit, he is one of them and deeply imbedded in the camaraderie of the barracks and the fond memories of his platoon during his Parris Island boot camp days. He is a Marine all right—even though he hates this place—as the poem he gave me today so richly illustrates.

Basha's Mercado, Mexican groceries on the right
Subway fading in the rearview along with Budget Inn
Wal-Mart in my future,
last before the long road to Bisbee
there are only so many places to go before you run out
and then you might as well stay in your room
having seen all there is to see
south are mountains, east and west desert, north is Fry
the only place anyone seems to go.
Steaks in the old whorehouse where the waitresses know us now,
get us anything because we help them toss out drunk ex-boyfriends
who get rowdy when the girls try to convince us to take them out
    after work,
getting us free drinks and meat.
Tate so drunk he can't even drink more without help
Wendy brings another pitcher, and some shots of Jack for me and
    Todd, just a few more on the house
because Bigos took the bartender's fat daughter to the ball, our birthday.
Where once a year rank can be dropped and we can all just be,
roles and parts aside knowing that every man in the room would risk
    his life with
you in the most trivial of fights, simply because you would do the
    same for them.
And we are in Arizona, living just south of Fry waiting for honor
to be handed to us that takes us beyond this ridiculous place
where the only thing to do is head once more down Fry Blvd.

Day 9
John walks around the barracks jabbering in his imitation Scottish accent, following other Marines, sniffing, and telling them in a thick Scottish brogue

that they "smell strangely of urine," much to the amusement of the Marines who have taken to imitating John and doing their own versions of his demented Scottish, Mike Myers, *So I Married An Ax Murderer* routine.

Day 10

The mountains and desert around Old Bisbee are lovely. We went for a Sunday drive in my rented car. John sat up front. His weight-lifting buddy Tate sat in the backseat. John had to pretend the pristine desert, the newly blooming cactus flowers, the pale sky, and soft sandy colors were all awful. Nevertheless, I caught him gazing out the window, rapt, as we made our way up a bright sunny road into the red rocks of the mountains.

On the way to Old Bisbee, John and Tate talked about how they resented the National Rifle Association because the NRA "copied" the well-known Marine sticker, a gold and red circle with the eagle, globe, and anchor. The NRA gold and red circle with their own eagle and NRA logo is too much "like our Marines sticker," as far as Tate is concerned. (We'd just seen one on a truck ahead of us.) Then John said that both he and Tate didn't like the NRA anyway because they "allow assholes like David Duke to be members."

David Duke, as John reminded me, in a tone so full of loathing it was as if he was talking about some child molester, "was a KKK member!"

"The KKK," Tate added, "is big where Price grew up in Texas."

"Fuck David Duke!" said John.

Tate nodded in agreement.

"The KKK guys dragged some guy behind their pickup truck till he was dead in the town where Price is from," said Tate.

Price is a big black Marine John and everyone else in Ft. Huachuca like. In boot camp his good friend Reyes was a Hispanic. In Ft. Huachuca his good friend Tate is white. His other good friends are Tawata, an Okinawan from Hawaii, and Ludikowski "Ski," a white from upstate New York.

Price, the "giant black guy," is from Texas. Price told John that one of his earliest childhood memories was being taken to the barber and hearing the white barber drawl to Price's mother, "I never cut no nigger's hair before."

I ask John and Tate about Price. Price grew up on a farm with three hundred head of cattle. His family was "quite well off for the area they were in." Price's parents are still married. He was a weight lifter and football player in high school and college. Price completed two years of college studying black history. He lived in "one of the most racist areas of the country," says Tate. Price dropped out of college and figured he might as well "go all the way" and signed on for the tough Marine training. Price has arms that seem to burst from his rolled cammie sleeves.

The Marines' cammie sleeves are worn rolled up into a wide cuff over midbicep. They are worn in a way that shows off the muscular strength of the Marines. The cuffs are so tight the Marines need help from other Marines to get their blouses off, the stronger the Marine the tighter the cuff. The really big Marines, like Price, the ones with arms like hams, almost split their cuffs when they flex. John tells me that this is "awesome," that "Price is a good guy." Those who split their cuffs or are said to have done so are "adjudged gods."

The Marines's elite bearing pays off in other ways besides split cuffs, pride, and warrior motivation. John takes great pleasure in the fact that the Air Force women like the Marines better than their "pathetic Air Force men."

"See how we get all the warm smiles and how the Air Force guys hate us, won't even look over at us?" said John as we walked past a group of Air Force women and men outside his barracks. "The Air Force guys hate us!" laughed John as a high-decibel giggly female chorus of "Hi, Schaeffer!" followed John across the lot.

I turned and glanced at the pretty Air Force girls standing in a knot with their downcast Air Force men, sullen at their mere mortality. John didn't turn to look.

Day 11

For the last three days I sat in the TV room with John and the other Marines, from eight A.M. to four P.M., watching the same movies and hearing the same desultory gossip and jokes. By midday I am going mad. John has had to do this for over six months, and there is no end in sight. The security clearance people have not even started to do the requisite interviews with friends and family! Have they lost his goddamned paperwork? I hear that is what happened to Ski, Roth and Tawata. Tawata was stuck over a year before they told him they'd "misplaced the paperwork" and would have to start the whole process again! I wonder if this is how things would go down if the son or daughter of the typical Fortune 500 board member or any of the other children of our political, business, or academic elite were out here with John and company? I had pictured John getting shot at but not this mind-frying nothingness.

Tonight over dinner John relates how an Army officer returned his salute while holding a plastic water bottle in his right hand and lifting it to his face *while saluting with that same hand!* "It was the most disgusting thing I've seen yet!" said John and he meant it. "The Army is *truly* disgusting!"

Day 12

I sat with the Marines in their TV room all day again. There is a sweetness to these boys and girls, these half-grown, anxious children putting on a brave face. One, at nineteen, is an expectant father. When a female Marine walked in, he joked, "We can see your baby!" Later John told me she is pregnant and will marry the father, also a Marine, next month. He is stationed in Pensacola. (Lucky him, he must have gotten his clearance!)

The male Marines look out for this little pregnant Marine. She is a slender wisp of a child-woman with dark black hair and fair skin and a soft Texas accent. I notice her thin, very feminine wrist bones and can hardly imagine her surviving the pugil-stick training I know she must have undergone to graduate from PI.

The big male Marines treat her like their little sister. The little pregnant Marine seems happy and at ease with them and they are as solicitous as any big brothers. I even hear them offer morning sickness advice, "My mom used to eat crackers when she was pregnant with my little brother . . ." coming from a huge black Marine from New York. I hear friendly advice from several of the giants lounging away the hours in the TV room. One tall blond male from California scolds the Marine mother-to-be for drinking a Pepsi and goes to get her milk. "How many times I gotta tell ya the baby needs vitamin A and D?"

If a Marine gets pregnant she has a good chance of getting out of the Corps if she wants to. (There are no such "special circumstances" for male Marines.) John tells me that the little Texan female intends on staying in, as does her Marine fiancé. They hope to be posted together in the fleet when they finish training. They will probably be on food stamps once the baby comes and they marry.

I wish the Marine and her baby well and offer up a silent prayer for them whenever I see her slight figure hovering in the TV room or hall. I think of Genie, of her slender wrists, and of how I got her pregnant when I was seventeen. I think of all the help we got from my very kind and forgiving parents and Genie's ever so gentle mother and father. I think of living as a young bewildered father near my compassionate older sisters Prisca, Susan, and Debby, and the help they were to Genie and me in the early years of being child-parents. I think about the fact Marines are moved constantly and how shockingly low their pay is and how family visits are rare and expensive. I wonder mightily about how this little girl-woman and her baby girl will do. I know that the military is the last place on earth I'd want my daughter even though I admire the women who join. I wonder about the wisdom of mixing sexual electricity and military life.

The young Marines maintain Marine "bearing" and stern faces. Once they get used to having me hanging around the barracks, these tough faces relent and melt a little. I notice John is not embarrassed to say, "I love you, Dad" when I leave in the evening to go back to my motel. He says this and gives me a hug whether the other Marines are around or not.

I find myself washing the dust off my boots after a walk in the desert. I also take my three pairs of pants to the cleaners, even though they are not really dirty, only wrinkled. I don't want to wear wrinkled clothes when I'm with Marines.

Day 13

I witness a wedding. A tall gangling young Texan Marine is to be married by a judge. There need to be two witnesses. The groom brings a Marine friend, and I volunteer to be the other witness. The young Marine and his bride, both nineteen, take their vows in the courthouse. (She is not a Marine.) They are serious and sweet. There is no family there. I take the only pictures and run them over to a CVS to get them developed. An hour later I give the bride and groom a couple of framed photographs and a small album with about ten pictures in it of their wedding.

After delivering the photographs to the restaurant where the bride and groom are having their "reception" (dinner alone at a fast-food joint), I drive back to the barracks and say good-bye to John. As I leave I watch three

Marines, two males and one female, do a color guard. Their job is to strike the colors at sunset.

I sit in my car. The interior is still hot from baking in the Arizona sun all day. I roll down all the windows and watch as the color guard form up by the door to the barracks then march to the flagpoles where the Marine flag, Navy flag, and American flag are snapping in the hot evening breeze.

There is no officer present, just me in a parked car watching unseen from a distance and two Marines who happen to be passing on the path as the color guard forms up. The two Marines on the path are both at liberty (off duty) and in civilian clothes. Nevertheless they stop walking and stand respectfully at attention as the small ceremony unfolds.

The three Marines of the color guard lower and carefully fold the flags. All their movements are crisp and reverential. The colors are handled with care and each salute is precise. The flag is held and folded with such gentle tenderness that it might be a living thing, perhaps an injured child.

The color guard duty roster rotates to every one of the Marines in the barracks at different times, so I know that my son has done this many times. These three young Marines could be any of the Marines in the barracks. I recognize one of them, Trevor. She is a pretty female Marine. She has been calling me "Dad" during my visit. Trevor is petite, smiling, and kind ("nice but not a good Marine, too damned cheerful and no edge" according to John). Tonight she has all the "bearing" and serious "edge" anyone could want.

I watch Trevor's solemn face as she marches, salutes the colors then receives the carefully folded flag. Moments later she carries it the few steps back to the barracks, hands held, one over, one under, in an exact ritual. I watch and think of the fact that as the sun sets in time zone after time zone this simple scene will be repeated all over the world in far-flung outposts of American power where my Marines are performing this beautiful set-piece of patriotic liturgy.

I have already said my good-bye to John and will leave at four A.M. tomorrow morning to drive to Phoenix and catch my plane. As I start the engine and drive away I glance in the rearview mirror at the hills that lead to Mexico, South America, and the world beyond. My last sight of the barracks is of the darkened building with the color guard lowering the American flag, saluting it by the fading light.

A Year Later . . .

O n January 20, 2001, we got a call in the morning from John. He had smashed up his foot, *again!* This time the damage was not done in training but in a stupid accident. Tate and John were in the weight room working out. Tate accidentally dropped a seventy-pound weight on John's foot. The weight hit a bull's eye *right on the scar of the first operation* and shattered the bones and bent the titanium two-inch screw that had been used to fuse the joint. The day before John called, during his second surgery in a year, the doctor had more or less dissected John's foot. My son might or might not be able to stay in the Corps.

"The doctor got the bent screw out and put in another one," said John.

"Will you be able to stay in the Corps?" I asked.

"He said we'll have to wait and see. Then he asked me to level with him and say if I wanted to get out or not. He said if I did, no problem, since the foot is a mess and he can arrange for me to be med-boarded out."

"What did you tell him?" I asked.

"That I'd like to try and stay in the Corps if at all possible."

"What did he say?"

" 'You Marines are nuts!' " John laughed groggily.

John had just been given the opportunity to get out of the Corps on a medical discharge. He had plenty of cause to be frustrated as "four months" of training had turned into a year of more or less of solid bullshit in Ft. Huachuca. Nevertheless, John turned down the chance to get out, to see Mollie, to reenter civilian life and take the safe easy path by going to college.

The waiting, the dumb injury, and the frustrations of the last year had been a far greater test of John's character than boot camp. He wasn't happy at Ft. Huachuca but he was hanging tough and never had a bad word to say about the Corps. John believed in and loved the Corps and he wasn't going to let his brother Marines down. His DIs would have been proud of him. I certainly was.

What amazed me was John and the other Marines' capacity to remain loyal to the Corps and its glorious tradition, and to each other. They seemed to see the Corps they belonged to as something separate from our country's political leadership, let alone the civilian pencil pushers in Washington who—when it came to Marines in Intel—were taking so insanely long to process their paperwork.

At last on April 20, 2001, after waiting for over a year, John finally got his provisional clearance. He called right away, overjoyed.

Two days later, after undergoing three months of slow painful recovery of his crushed foot, John started back into his training at AMS. The bones had knit around the new pin. His foot still hurt, but John was keeping his mouth shut about it and was put back on PT. At last he sounded like himself again. Back in school, John was flying high and doing well passing each phase's requirements in record time.

As he neared completion of his time in Ft. Huachuca, John was promoted to corporal, his first merit-based promotion. (The others: from private to private first class to lance corporal came automatically with time in the service. John was now an NCO—a noncommissioned officer.)

A month after he got his clearance, he took the final four-hour exam, scored 99 percent, and graduated top of his class. The staff sergeant instructor told my son he was one of the best students he had ever taught. He gave John his sergeant's chevrons and told John to keep them until he made sergeant himself.

John was also called before a board of officers along with several others and given a "meritorious mast" for the excellence of his exam score and his "general bearing as a Marine." (A meritorious mast is a commendation that is a mark of pride throughout the Corps.)

The day he got his meritorious mast, John called to say that he was on his way home for a week of leave. Then, God willing, it was off to Pensacola, training in signals intercept—at last something more interesting and relevant than Morse code!—and on to points unknown in the fleet. (Just how far-flung John's eventual posting might be was made stomach-churningly clear to Genie and me by the fact that one of his MOS classmates from Ft. Huachuca was the lone Marine onboard the Navy surveillance plane impounded by the Chinese after it was struck by a Chinese fighter and forced to land in China.)

I was hard at work polishing the chapters of this book so that John and I could go over the manuscript while he was home for the all-too-brief week of leave. I warned him we'd be working at least eight to ten hours a day.

"No problem," said John. "Mollie understands these things."

"Not like some people we could mention," I said.

"Are you going to start in again?" John laughed.

"Hey, I forgot to ask, what do you think of George W?"

"He's the commander in chief."

"Yeah but what do you *think* of him?"

"Dad, Marines respect the commander. We don't get into this stuff."

"Off the record."

"I'm a Marine and he's the commander in chief."

Pensacola Florida, July 27, 2001

E-mail to Dad from John

Dear Dad,

I left Arizona (eighteen months and one day after I arrived!) for Pensacola Florida. I'm here now and all is well. I started my new Intel classes and am also working on my close combat skills with an awesome instructor from recon. He kicks the crap out of us and is a terrific teacher and great Marine.

I am at last on the road to the fleet! I look forward to it every day. In the long term I'm not sure what I want to do but I love the life in the Corps. On the other hand if I ever have a family I want to be with them, too many divorces in the Corps, rough life for the families. So I just can't say right now what my plans are.

Love,

John

John was soon first in his Signals Intel class at his new base, a position he maintained until graduation. He was also made a squad leader and nominated by his platoon to represent them as "Marine of the Quarter" as their most outstanding and "squared-away" Marine. I was so proud of John and not a little amazed. My son was excelling at studies involving math. That's all he could tell me about his classified training in signals intercept. "It's math, Dad! Math!" he groaned. John was getting one hundred on his tests. John hates math! Was *this* the boy who never did his homework in high school if he could help it?

He sounded so vibrant (though tired) when we talked on the phone. I was grateful to the Marines. I was watching my son grow and mature by leaps and bounds. I could only envy this great and life-shaping experience. At twenty John was brother to a larger cross section of humanity, from incredibly diverse economic, religious, and racial backgrounds than I had ever met, let alone lived, sweated, and worked with. He was brother to ex-gang members from South Central LA, to the sons of coal miners from West Virginia and the daughters of crack addicts in New York City. Sons of African American farmers from the Mississippi delta were officers in the chain of command. He numbered first-generation Latino immigrants, as well as many middle-class and lower-middle-class young men and women, from just about every ethnic background and town in America as his friends. Many who were serving with my son were carrying on proud family traditions of service in the USMC.

One Marine told John "Before I was a Marine if I had ever seen you on my block I would've probably killed you just because you were standing there." This was a serious statement from one of John's good friends, an African American ex-gang member from Detroit who, as John said, "Would die for me now, just like I'd die for him."

I was packing for my flight to Florida to visit my boy and making a list of the food and other treats. I planned to be there to spend a week reviewing our book with him one last time. On our final day together, we were going to celebrate his twenty-first birthday. I owed my son a drink!

We'd picked our peaches a week early so that Genie could make a cobbler for me to take to John, along with the turkey I roasted that was cooling in the refrigerator with mounds of extra stuffing, his favorite holiday treat. My biggest worry was whether or not I would have trouble checking the cooler full of food. It was September 10.

The next day all flights were canceled and civil air traffic over the United States was shut down for the first time in history. The cooler of food sat forgotten. I was so scared for my boy. I longed to hold on to him for dear life any way I could. In the grip of that fearful moment, with all the talk of war ringing in my ears, suddenly every word of our book seemed to read like an obituary for my son, for carefree days together, for a childhood ended. I could picture nothing but my worst fears.

As to how John was feeling, I learned when I called him the day after the attack. (I tried again and again on September 11 and couldn't get through.) He sounded so calm and confident.

"I'm still going to try and come down, John."

"I don't want you flying even if they let you, Dad. Not till we know what's happening."

"I'm coming down no matter what. I'm rebooking for the fourteenth and will be there for your birthday." I had to wait a moment before I could continue to speak. "I love you. John I'm proud of you."

"Hey Dad, this is worse for you than for me."

"How's that?"

"All you have to do with yourself is worry but we have a job to do." John paused. "Dad?"

"Yes?"

"I love you."

After I hung up I stared at the TV. There were firemen, cops and military personnel struggling to find survivors and thousands of our war dead. I felt deeply frustrated at being able to do nothing. At least I knew that I could look the men and women in uniform in the eye. My son was one of them. He is the best I have to offer. He is my heart.

Postscript

the Marines are a religion,
they worship many gods.
they have a hymn, "from the halls of Montezuma,
to the shores of Tripoli."
they have short maxims like,
"pain is good,
extreme pain is extremely good."
they are a mystery religion.
exclusive and closed and semper fidelis.

As for life in the Corps, it goes on.

Progress on this book was slow, at least for me. It was very hard to wake up at 0445 or earlier every day for PT, put in a full day (or in Ft. Huachuca an empty depressing day) and then, that night, try to find the energy or the motivation to write more than two coherent sentences. For me the reward of writing this book was that through the process of working on it together Dad and I left a lot of baggage behind. I'm stubborn and Dad is intense. There was quite a bit of static building up over the last year I was home that all came to a head during the "Last Summer."

Writing our book together was the end of the process of my moving out. When did we go from a father trying to force his son to do what he wanted and a son stubbornly resisting to friends working together? The fact is, somewhere during the process of writing, we got to a new place. I'm not sure when the moment came but now, when we talk on the phone, or sit down over a drink in some dive down the street from whatever base I'm on, we are two men comparing notes on work and shooting the breeze.